YOUR
Health

Orlando • Austin • Chicago • New York • Toronto • London • San Diego

Visit *The Learning Site!*
www.harcourtschool.com

CONSULTING AUTHORS

Charlie Gibbons, Ed.D.
Associate Professor
Alabama State University
Health, Physical Education and Dance Department
Montgomery, Alabama; and
School Age Coordinator
Maxwell Air Force Base, Alabama

Jan Marie Ozias, Ph.D., R.N.
Director, Texas Diabetes Council; and
Consultant, School Health Programs
Austin, Texas

Carl Anthony Stockton, Ph.D.
Professor of Health Education and Department Chair
Department of Health, Physical Education, and Recreation
The University of North Carolina at Wilmington
Wilmington, North Carolina

Printed in the United States of America

ISBN 0-15-334303-6

  4 5 6 7 8 9 10 032 10 09 08 07 06 05 04 03

Contents

Your Health Skills . . . . **viii**

Understanding Life Skills . . . . **viii**

Being a Wise Health Consumer . . . . **xiv**

The Amazing Human Body **1**

Sense Organs **2**

Skeletal System **4**

Muscular System **6**

Digestive System **8**

Circulatory System **10**

Respiratory System **12**

Nervous System **14**

Chapter **1** **Your Needs and Feelings** **16**

1 Learning About Yourself **18**

2 We All Have Needs **22**

3 We All Have Feelings **26**

Life Skills Manage Stress Every Day **30**

4 The Challenges of Friendship **32**

Life Skills Resolve Conflicts at School **38**

5 Working with Others **40**

Chapter Review **44**

Activities **46**

Chapter Test **47**

Emotional,
Intellectual,
and Social
Health

Chapter 2 — Living and Growing 48

1 Families Meet Their Needs 50
2 Families Work Together 56
Life Skills Communicate with Your Family 62
3 You Are Growing Cell by Cell 64
4 Your Brain and Nervous System:
The Control Center for Growth 70
Chapter Review 74
Activities 76
Chapter Test 77

Family Life, Growth, and Development

Chapter 3 — Your Health and Fitness 78

1 Your Skin and Its Care 80
2 Your Teeth and Their Care 84
3 Your Vision and Hearing 90
4 Your Posture 94
5 Your Physical Fitness 98
Life Skills Setting Goals About Fitness 104
Chapter Review 106
Activities 108
Chapter Test 109

Physical Health and Physical Fitness

Chapter 4 — Food and Your Health 110

1 Nutrients and Your Digestive System 112
2 Food and the Nutrients It Contains 118
3 Using the Food Guide Pyramid 122
Life Skills Make Decisions About Breakfast 126
4 Understanding a Food Label 128

Nutrition

5 Preparing Foods Safely **132**

Chapter Review **136**

Activities **138**

Chapter Test **139**

Chapter 5 Guarding Against Disease . . 140

Disease Prevention and Control

1 Why People Become Ill **142**

2 Infectious Diseases **146**

3 Fighting Infectious Diseases **150**

4 Noninfectious Diseases **156**

5 Staying Well **162**

Life Skills Manage Stress at the Doctor's Office . **166**

Chapter Review **168**

Activities **170**

Chapter Test **171**

Chapter 6 Medicines, Drugs, and Your Health 172

Drug Use Prevention

1 Medicines Affect the Body **174**

2 Common Substances That Can Be Harmful **180**

3 Marijuana and Cocaine **184**

4 Refusing to Use Drugs **190**

Life Skills Refuse OTC Medicines **194**

5 How Drug Users Can Get Help **196**

Chapter Review **200**

Activities **202**

Chapter Test **203**

Chapter 7

Harmful Effects of Tobacco and Alcohol 204

Drug Use Prevention

1 How Tobacco Harms Body Systems **206**

2 How Alcohol Harms Body Systems **212**

3 Saying *No* to Alcohol and Tobacco **218**

Life Skills Refuse to Use Alcohol and Tobacco .. **222**

4 How Alcoholics and Tobacco Users Get Help ... **224**

Chapter Review **228**

Activities **230**

Chapter Test **231**

Chapter 8

Staying Safe 232

Injury Prevention

1 Responding to Emergencies and Giving First Aid **234**

2 Staying Safe at Home and While Camping **238**

3 Staying Safe Outdoors **244**

Life Skills Make Decisions About Staying Safe .. **248**

4 Staying Safe on the Road **250**

5 Staying Safe Near Water **254**

6 Staying Safe in a Conflict **258**

Life Skills Resolve Conflicts with Friends **262**

Chapter Review **264**

Activities **266**

Chapter Test **267**

Chapter 9 — Living in a Healthful Community 268

Community and Environmental Health

1 Enjoying a Healthful Environment 270
2 Keeping the Community Clean and Safe 274
3 Our Natural Resources 278
4 Preventing Air, Water, and Land Pollution 282
5 Ways to Practice Conservation 288
Life Skills Set Goals to Conserve Resources 292
Chapter Review 294
Activities 296
Chapter Test 297

Health Handbook 298

Good Nutrition 300
Preparing Foods Safely 306
Being Physically Active 308
Being Safe 316
First Aid 328
Alcohol, Tobacco, and Other Drugs 332

Glossary 334
Index 347

Understanding Life Skills

Having good health isn't just knowing the facts. It's also thinking critically about those facts and knowing how to use them every day. The Life Skills in *Your Health* can help you do just that.

Setting Goals for Self Improvement

In soccer or ice hockey, scoring a goal is something that a team wants to do to win the game. In life, you set goals for things you want to do to improve yourself. Planning and checking your progress makes it easier to reach your goals. You feel better about yourself because you know you are getting closer to your goals.

▼ Lee Ann is falling behind in social studies. How can she set a goal to improve her schoolwork?

Steps for Setting Goals

1. Set a goal.
2. List and plan steps to meet that goal.
3. Check your progress toward the goal.
4. Evaluate the goal.

🍎 Making Decisions

Every day you make decisions, or choices, about what to do. Some decisions, such as what color socks to wear, don't affect your health. Other decisions, such as what to eat for a snack or what to do before you exercise, can affect your health. Decisions that affect your health are important. For important decisions, you should think carefully about all the choices and the possible results, then decide.

Imagine the results of your choices.

▶ Victor has an important soccer game this morning. He's trying to decide what to eat for breakfast. How can he make the best decision?

Steps for Making Decisions

1. Find out about the choices you could make.

2. Imagine the possible result of each choice.

3. Make what seems to be the best choice.

4. Think about the result of your choice.

Managing Stress

"I'm so stressed!" Maybe you or a parent said that today. Stress is tension in your body or your mind. Maybe you feel stress because of a class report, a quiz, or a doctor's appointment. Some stress is a normal part of life. You even need a little stress to stay healthy. But, it's important not to let stress harm your health.

◀ Louisa has to give a short oral report for her science group. She is worried and feels nervous and scared. How can she manage her stress to get through the report?

Steps for Managing Stress

1. Know what stress feels like and what causes it.

2. When you feel stress, think about ways to handle it.

3. Focus on one step at a time.

4. Learn ways to reduce and release tension.

🍎 Refusing

Sometimes people can try to make you do things you really don't want to do. Knowing how to refuse, or say no, to things that are unsafe or risky can keep you healthy. This is also an important reason for learning more about your health. Knowing how a bad choice—such as using alcohol, tobacco, or other drugs—will affect you makes it easier to say no firmly.

▶ **Paulo's friends urge him to come swimming with them in a pool that is closed for the day. It's unsafe and against Paulo's family rules. How can Paulo refuse?**

How to Refuse

1. Say **no** and say why not.
2. State your reasons for saying **no**.
3. Suggest something else to do.
4. Repeat **no**; walk away.

Communicating

Communicating is another word for "sharing information." You have ideas, needs, and feelings. To meet your needs, you often need to communicate with other people. You also need to listen to people and understand their needs and feelings. Communicating is vital to your health, but it is also important in many other parts of your life.

▼ Padma wants to have time to herself to use the family's computer. It's hard to get time without being interrupted. How can she communicate her needs to her family?

How to Communicate

1. Understand your audience.
2. Give a clear message.
3. Listen.
4. Gather feedback.

Resolving Conflicts

Conflict, or disagreement, is a normal part of life. Disagreeing with a classmate about how to finish a project is a conflict. Bigger conflicts may lead to bad feelings or even violence. A fight or an argument is a poor way to deal with a conflict. If you communicate well, you often can find a peaceful way to resolve, or end, a conflict. You may even find that communicating well leads to a solution that is better for everyone.

▼ Jean lost her pencil. She finds a pencil on the floor that she thinks is hers. Amal says that it is really his pencil. How can they resolve this conflict?

Steps for Resolving Conflicts

1. Use I-messages to tell how you feel.

2. Listen to each other.

3. Think of the other person's point of view.

4. Decide what to do and do it.

Being a Wise Health Consumer

Being a wise consumer means making good buying decisions. As you get older, you will have more responsibility for buying health products and services. You need to learn how advertisements can mislead you. You also need to learn how to get valid, or correct, health information.

Making Buying Decisions

Advertising can help you make buying decisions. However, advertisements shouldn't be the only information you use. Using product information wisely helps you to get the most value for your money.

▲ **Which of these sunscreen products would you choose to buy? Why?**

Steps for Making Buying Decisions

1. Decide whether the item is something you need, want, or don't really need at all.

2. Compare several brands of the same item.

3. Choose the least expensive item that meets your needs.

4. Think about the result of your purchase decision.

Analyzing Advertising and Media Messages

Advertising is everywhere, even places you may not notice. Ads can give you good information about a product. They also can mislead you. Be aware of these tricks to get you to buy:

PUT DOWN

TRICK The ad says another product is bad.

TIP Maybe the other brand isn't that bad. Compare the products for yourself.

IDEAL PEOPLE

TRICK Everyone in the ad looks pretty and happy.

TIP The product doesn't make people pretty or happy. Find out what it really does.

BE COOL

TRICK People who use the product become more popular.

TIP A product can't make someone more popular.

JOIN THE CROWD

TRICK It seems like everyone is using this product and you're left out.

TIP Most people probably aren't using the product. It's wise to buy only things that you need.

STAR POWER

TRICK Your favorite sports or music star tells you to buy a product.

TIP The star can't know that the product is right for you. Find out if it really meets your needs.

How to Analyze Advertising and Media Messages

1. Find out who made the message and why.

2. Watch for tricks to make you notice or agree with the message.

3. Notice the values and points of view shown.

4. Learn whether anything is left out.

Accessing Valid Health Information

It's important to know the facts about your health. However, not everything you read or see is the truth. You should make sure health information is reliable. The best source of health information is health professionals, such as nurses, doctors, and pharmacists. For other sources, especially the Internet, you should think about the source of the information. Also, check to see if other sources agree.

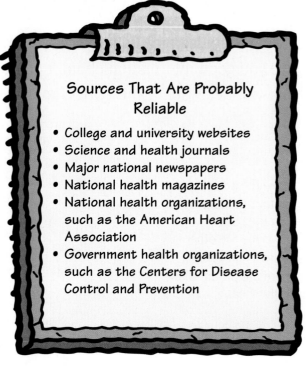

Sources That Are Probably Reliable

- College and university websites
- Science and health journals
- Major national newspapers
- National health magazines
- National health organizations, such as the American Heart Association
- Government health organizations, such as the Centers for Disease Control and Prevention

Access Valid Health Information

1. Find out who is responsible for the information. Notice whether they are selling something.

2. Decide if the information is reasonable.

3. Check the information against other reliable sources. Keep a questioning attitude.

4. Discuss the information with a trusted adult or a health professional such as a nurse, doctor, or pharmacist.

You will learn and practice these important skills as you use *Your Health*.

The Amazing Human Body

Sense Organs **2**
Your sense organs let you see, hear, smell, taste, and touch
everything in the world around you.

Skeletal System **4**
Your skeletal system holds your body up and allows you to move
in many directions.

Muscular System **6**
Your muscular system works with your skeletal system to allow
your body to move and function.

Digestive System **8**
Your digestive system turns the food you eat into the energy your
body needs to work and grow.

Circulatory System **10**
Your circulatory system delivers necessary substances all over your
body and carries away waste products.

Respiratory System **12**
Your respiratory system takes in the oxygen you need to
survive and releases carbon dioxide.

Nervous System **14**
Your nervous system is the control center of your body. It is
responsible for everything your body does or feels.

*Staying active, eating
right, and getting enough
rest are the first steps
to a healthful life.*

Eyes

Light passes through the clear front (cornea) of the eye. A lens focuses light on the retina at the back of the eye. People who need glasses have eyes that focus light slightly behind or slightly in front of the retina.

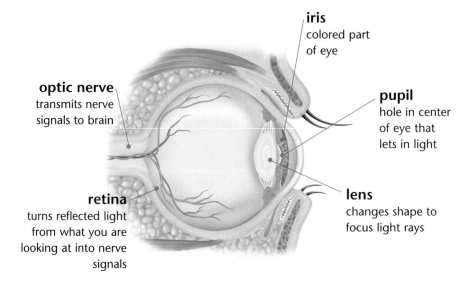

optic nerve
transmits nerve signals to brain

iris
colored part of eye

pupil
hole in center of eye that lets in light

lens
changes shape to focus light rays

retina
turns reflected light from what you are looking at into nerve signals

Ears

Sounds make the eardrum move back and forth. The small bones in the middle ear send waves to the fluid in the inner ear. Hairs in the inner ear then move, passing signals to a nerve. Your brain reads the signals, and you hear the sound.

Outer Ear | Middle Ear | Inner Ear

eardrum
moves back and forth when hit by sound waves

ear canal
connects outer ear to middle ear

Caring for Your Eyes and Ears

- Wear safety glasses when participating in activities where you can get hit or where a foreign object can hit an eye, such as sports and mowing grass.

- Avoid listening to very loud sounds for long periods of time. Loud sounds destroy the delicate hairs in the inner ear. You can lose your hearing little by little.

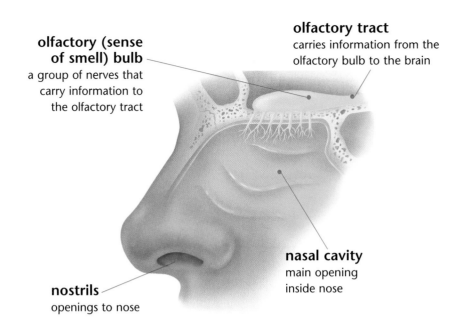

olfactory (sense of smell) bulb
a group of nerves that carry information to the olfactory tract

olfactory tract
carries information from the olfactory bulb to the brain

nasal cavity
main opening inside nose

nostrils
openings to nose

Nose

The inside of your nose is lined with moist surfaces that are coated with mucus. When these surfaces are irritated, they swell and make more mucus. This extra mucus causes a runny nose. Pollen or cold germs can cause this to happen.

Tongue

Germs live on your tongue and in other parts of your mouth. Germs can harm your teeth and give you bad breath.

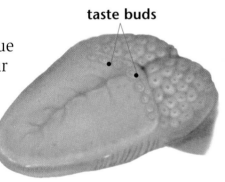

taste buds

Skin

Your skin protects your insides from the outside world. Your skin has many touch-sensitive nerves. Because your skin can feel temperature, pain, and pressure, you can avoid cuts, burns, and scrapes.

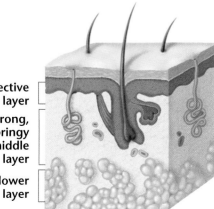

protective outer layer

strong, springy middle layer

fatty lower layer

Caring for Your Skin, Tongue, and Nose

- If you have a cold or allergies, don't blow your nose hard. Blowing your nose hard can force germs into your throat and ears.

- When you brush your teeth, brush your tongue too.

- Always wear sunscreen when you are in the sun.

Skeletal System

Each of your bones has a particular shape and size that allow it to do a certain job. You have bones that are tiny, long, wide, flat, and even curved. The job of some bones is to protect your body parts.

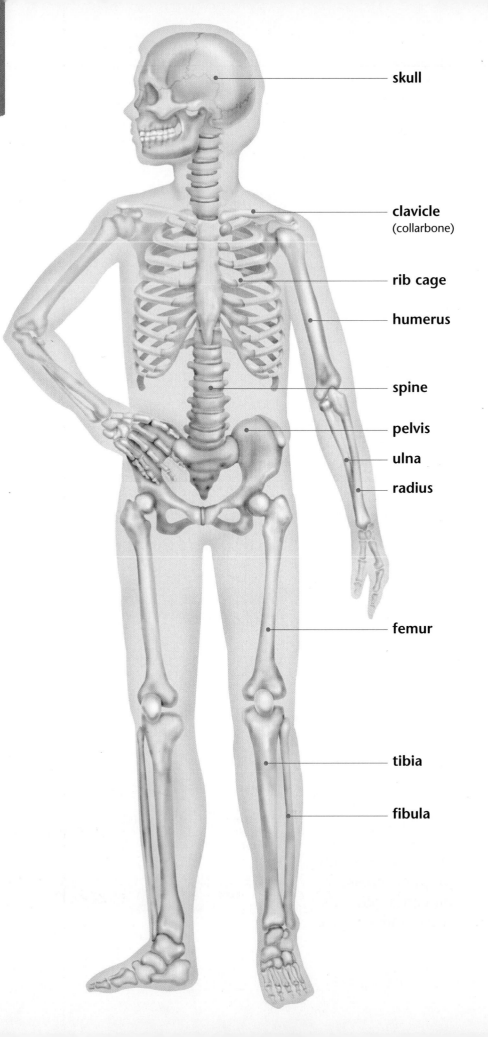

- skull
- clavicle (collarbone)
- rib cage
- humerus
- spine
- pelvis
- ulna
- radius
- femur
- tibia
- fibula

Skull, Spine, and Pelvis

Skull The bones in your head are called your skull. Some of the bones in your skull protect your brain. The bones in your face are part of your skull too.

Spine Your spine, or backbone, is made up of small bones called vertebrae that protect your spinal cord. Each vertebra has a hole in it, like a dough-nut. These bones fit together, one on top of the other, and the holes line up to form a tunnel. Cartilage disks sit like cushions between the vertebrae. Your spinal cord runs from your brain down your back inside this tunnel.

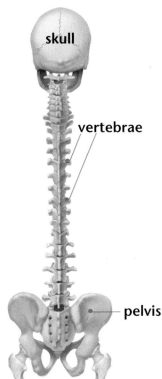

skull

vertebrae

pelvis

Pelvis Your spine con-nects to your hipbone, or pelvis. Your pelvis connects to your thighs. Your flexible spine, pelvis, and legs are what let you stand up straight, twist, turn, bend, and walk.

Caring for Your Skeletal System

- Calcium helps bones grow and makes them strong. Dairy products like milk, cheese, and yogurt contain calcium. Have two to three servings of dairy products every day. If you can't eat dairy products, dark green, leafy vegetables such as broccoli and collard greens or canned salmon with bones are also sources of calcium.

- Sit up straight with good posture. Sitting slumped over all the time can hurt muscles around your spine.

Activities

1. **Make a stack of Life Savers® and run a string down through it. This is how your spinal cord runs through your spine.**

2. **Stand facing a wall. Without moving your feet, how far can you twist your body? How far can you see behind you?**

3. **Find the bony part of your hipbone that sticks out near your waist. Pick up one leg. Where does the thigh bone connect to your pelvis? How far is it from the bony part?**

5

Muscular System

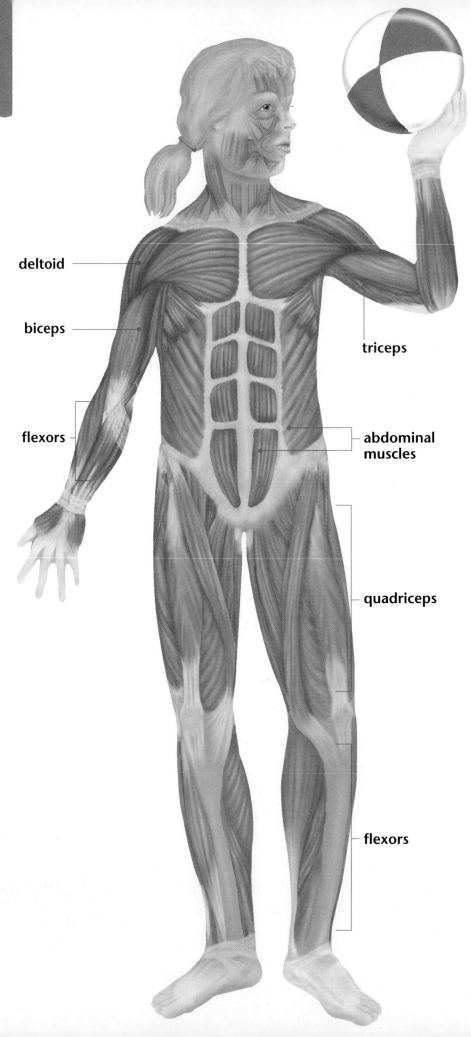

Like your bones, each muscle in your body does a certain job. Muscles in your thumb help you hold things. Muscles in your neck help you turn your head. Your heart muscle pumps blood through your body. Small muscles control your eyes.

deltoid

biceps

flexors

triceps

abdominal muscles

quadriceps

flexors

Voluntary and Involuntary Muscles

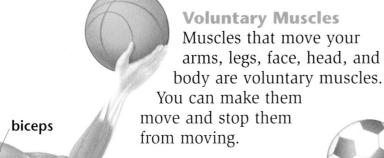

Voluntary Muscles
Muscles that move your arms, legs, face, head, and body are voluntary muscles. You can make them move and stop them from moving.

biceps

triceps

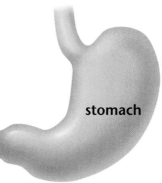

hamstring

gastrocnemius

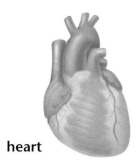

Involuntary Muscles Other muscles are responsible for movements you can't see or control. These involuntary muscles include your heart, your stomach, and muscles in your eyelids. They work automatically when they need to.

heart

eyelid

stomach

Caring for Your Muscular System

- Exercise makes your muscles stronger and larger.

- Warming up by moving all your big muscles for five to ten minutes before you exercise helps prevent injury or pain.

Activities

1. Look into a mirror and cover one eye. Watch the pupil in the other eye. How does it change? Did you change it?

2. Try not to blink for as long as you can. What happens?

3. Without taking off your shoes, try moving each of your toes one at a time. Can you move each of them separately?

Digestive System

Food is broken down and pushed through your body by your digestive system. Your digestive system is a series of connected parts that starts with your mouth and ends with your large intestine. Each part helps your body get different nutrients from the food you eat.

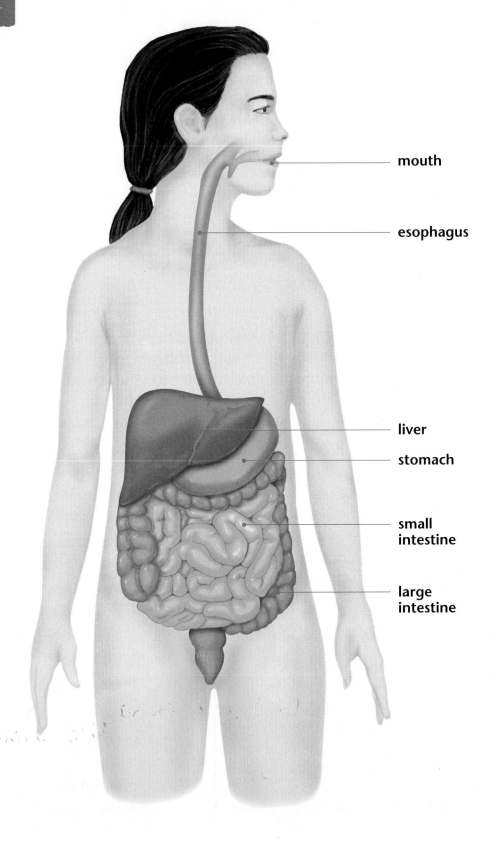

mouth

esophagus

liver

stomach

small intestine

large intestine

Small and Large Intestines

Small Intestine When food leaves your stomach and goes to your small intestine, it is a thick liquid. The walls of the small intestine are lined with many small, finger-shaped bumps. Tiny blood vessels in the bumps absorb nutrients from the liquid.

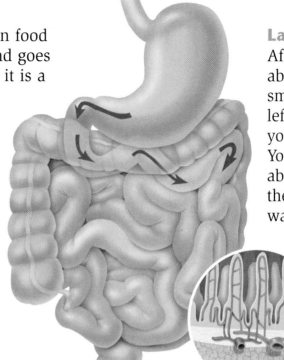

Large Intestine After nutrients are absorbed in your small intestine, the leftover liquid goes to your large intestine. Your large intestine absorbs water from the liquid. The solid waste leaves your large intestine when you go to the bathroom.

Caring for Your Digestive System

- Fiber helps your digestive system work better. Eat foods with fiber, such as fresh vegetables, beans, lentils, fruits, cereals, and breads, every day.

- Eat a balanced diet so that your body gets all the nutrients it needs.

Activities

1. Find the small and large intestines on the diagram of the digestive system. About how far is it from your belly button to where the small intestine starts?

2. On the diagram of the digestive system, trace the path that food takes through your body.

3. Draw a long line on a sheet of notebook paper. Fold the paper like an accordion. The line is like the path of food over the bumps in the small intestine.

Circulatory System

Food and oxygen are carried by your blood through your circulatory system to every cell in your body. Blood moves nutrients throughout your body, fights infection, and helps control your body temperature. Your blood is mostly made up of a watery liquid called plasma. It also contains three kinds of cells.

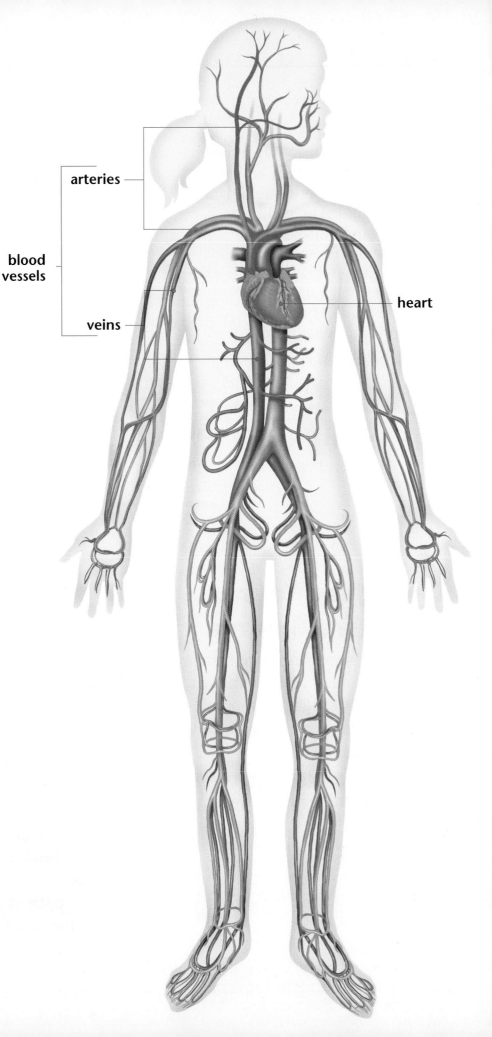

arteries

blood vessels

veins

heart

Blood Cells

Red Blood Cells Red blood cells carry oxygen from your lungs to the rest of your body. They also carry carbon dioxide from your body back to your lungs, so you can breathe it out.

Platelets

Platelets help clot your blood, which stops bleeding. Platelets clump together as soon as you get a cut. The sticky clump traps red blood cells and forms a blood clot. The blood clot hardens to make a scab and seals the cut.

White Blood Cells

When you are ill, your white blood cells come to the rescue. Some types of white blood cells identify what is making you ill. Some organize an attack. Others kill the invading germs or infected cells.

Caring for Your Circulatory System

- Never touch another person's blood.
- Don't pick scabs. If you pick a scab, you might make it bleed and the clotting process must begin again.

Activities

1. **On the diagram of the circulatory system, trace the path of blood from the heart to the knee.**

2. **Red blood cells are medium-size and are the most common cells in your blood. White blood cells are larger and are the least common. Platelets are the smallest blood cells. Draw a picture of what a drop of blood might look like under a microscope.**

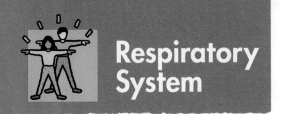

Respiratory System

Your body uses its respiratory system to get oxygen from the air. Your respiratory system is made up of your nose and mouth, your trachea, your two lungs, and your diaphragm.

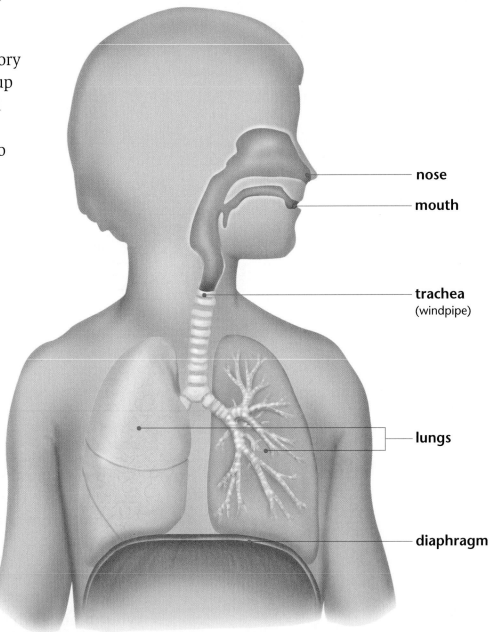

nose

mouth

trachea
(windpipe)

lungs

diaphragm

Functions of the Lungs

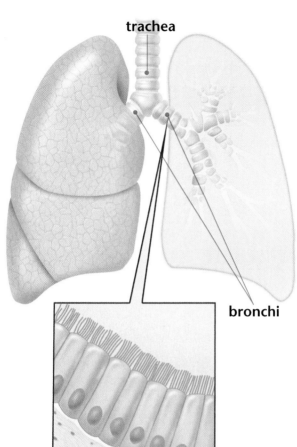

trachea

bronchi

Breathing When you inhale, or breathe in, air enters your mouth and nose and goes into your trachea. Your nose helps warm the air and add moisture to it. Your trachea connects your nose and mouth to your lungs. Your trachea divides into two smaller tubes that go to your lungs.

Filtering The two smaller tubes are called bronchi. Your trachea and bronchi are lined with many small hairs and coated with mucus. The mucus traps germs and small bits of dust and dirt. The small hairs constantly sweep the mucus up and out. This keeps dirt and germs out of your lungs.

Caring for Your Respiratory System

- Avoid smoke and other air pollution. They can paralyze the tiny hairs and cause you to become ill.
- Get plenty of exercise to keep your heart and lungs strong.

 **Activities**

1. Take several breaths through your nose. Notice how the inside of your nose feels when you breathe in. Moisten a paper towel and take several breaths through the towel. Does your nose feel different?

2. Take a deep breath and hold it. Have someone measure your chest with a tape measure. Breathe the air out, and have someone measure your chest again. Is your chest bigger when you breathe in or when you breathe out?

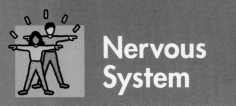

Nervous System

Your nerves send information to your brain from various parts of your body and from the outside world. Your brain analyzes the information and sends instructions through your nerves back to your body parts.

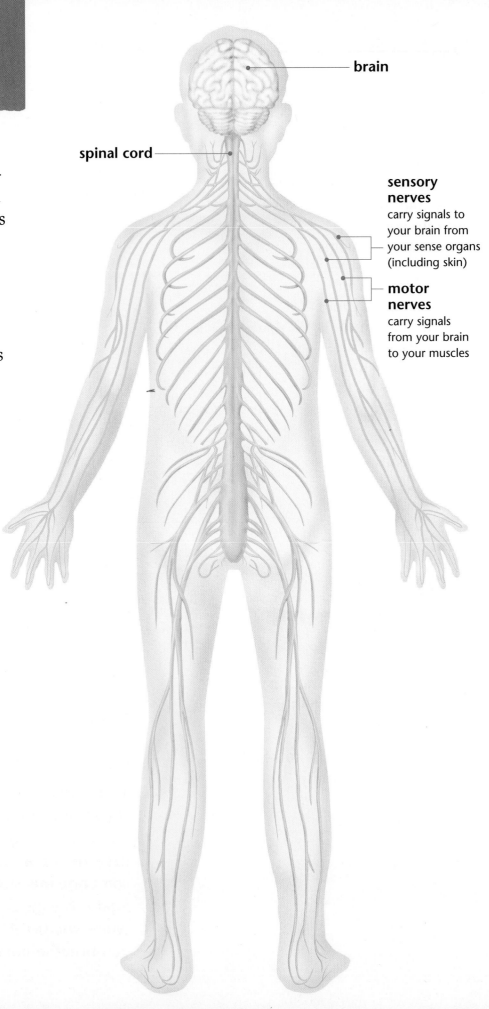

brain

spinal cord

sensory nerves
carry signals to your brain from your sense organs (including skin)

motor nerves
carry signals from your brain to your muscles

Messages to and from the Brain

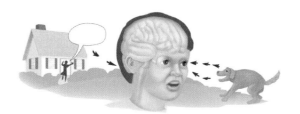

Incoming Messages Your sensory nerves send signals to your brain from your sense organs. Every minute your brain receives millions of these signals. Your brain has to decide how to deal with each of these pieces of information. For example, your brain might decide to deal with a barking dog nearby before it deals with a person calling to you from a distance.

Outgoing Messages Every minute, millions of nerve signals also leave your brain. Your motor nerves carry these messages. Your motor nerves connect to your muscles and tell them what to do. When you ride your bike, your brain helps you maintain balance and sends instructions to all the muscles you use to ride a bike.

Caring for Your Nervous System

- Eat a healthful, balanced diet. Your brain needs energy and nutrients to work well.

- Always wear a helmet when you ride your bike, skate, or use a skateboard.

Activities

1. Balance on one foot for as long as you can. Close your eyes and try again. Was it easier or harder the second time?

2. Pick up five pennies. Try it again wearing a glove. Why was it harder?

3. Hold a ruler at one end and dangle it just above a partner's open index finger and thumb. Drop the ruler through the gap. Where on the ruler does your partner grab? Try it several times, and then switch roles.

Your Needs and Feelings

CONFLICT RESOLUTION SKIT

With a Partner Friends sometimes have disagreements. As you work through this chapter, use what you learn about resolving conflicts to write and perform a skit showing an imaginary disagreement between friends. Be sure to include all the feelings involved and the steps needed to resolve the conflict.

For other activities, visit the Harcourt Learning Site. www.harcourtschool.com

Learning About Yourself

You are a very special person. In the whole world there is no one quite like you. Your traits make you special. **Traits** are special qualities that make up a large part of who you are. People often describe other people in terms of their traits. They might say you are friendly or quiet and shy.

Knowing as much as you can about yourself gives you a picture of yourself. The general picture you have of yourself is called your **self-concept**. If the picture is a positive one, you have **self-respect**—a satisfied, confident feeling about yourself.

What are different kinds of traits?

You have physical, mental, emotional, and social traits. Physical traits include your height, the length of your fingers, and the color of your hair. How well you see and hear are other physical traits.

▶ What physical traits do these family members share?

18

Your mental and emotional traits affect how you think, learn, and act. These might include your good memory, short temper, or kind heart. Perhaps you have a **talent**, or natural ability, for playing the violin or for painting. You can't see these qualities as easily as you can see your physical traits, but they are still an important part of what makes you a special person.

Your social traits also shape who you are. You may be comfortable when you speak in front of your class, or you may tend to be the leader of a group. Perhaps you are a person who likes to spend time alone. Or maybe you're shy around adults. Can you think of other social traits that you have?

Your physical, mental, emotional, and social traits are all part of what makes you special. You don't have to like everything about yourself, but your **attitude**—the way you look at things—is very important. If you have a positive attitude about yourself, you can respect yourself. A positive attitude also helps you respect others.

JOURNAL

Make a list of 20 words that describe who you are. Make at least ten of the words things that you like about yourself. Underline three words that describe things you would like to change. Remember, your journal is private and need not be shared with others.

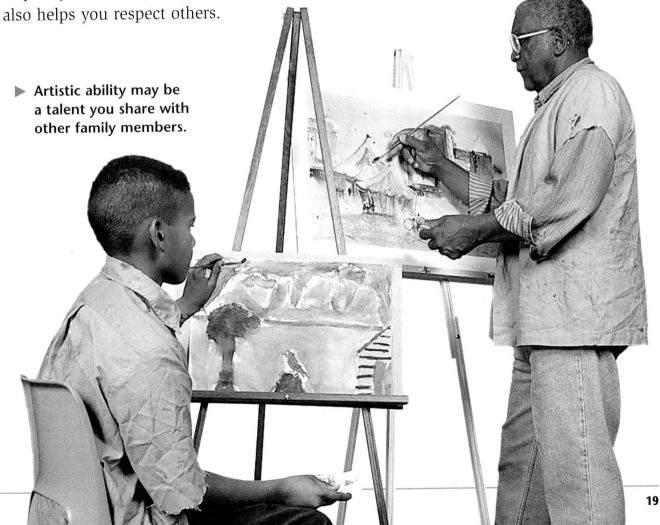

▶ Artistic ability may be a talent you share with other family members.

What makes you special?

All of your physical, mental, emotional, and social traits make you special. Your interests, your ideas, and all of your strengths and weaknesses are part of what makes you different from anyone else.

Some of your traits are influenced by your **environment**—where you live and all the things around you. If you live on a farm, you may find it easy to spend time alone, because you may not have friends nearby. If you belong to a musical family, you may play an instrument. Your traits are not right or wrong. They are simply part of who you are.

You have some traits that you cannot change. You can't change physical traits such as your height. But you *can* change mental, emotional, and social traits that you don't like about yourself. You can learn to play an instrument even if your family isn't musical. You can learn to control your temper. With practice, you can become more comfortable speaking in front of a group.

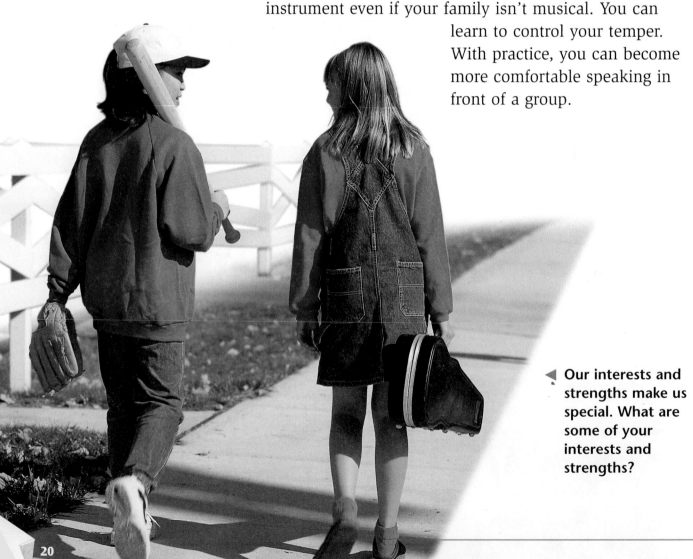

◀ **Our interests and strengths make us special. What are some of your interests and strengths?**

How do groups affect you?

There are many kinds of groups. There are clubs, church groups, music or dance groups, youth groups, and sports teams. Your family is a group, and so is your class. Together, you and your friends make up a group. Part of getting to know yourself is learning how you feel and act when you are in a group.

You can have different roles in different groups. You may be captain of your soccer team and a singer in the school chorus. You may be the computer expert in your social studies club and a beginner in your Saturday art class. Your roles in different groups can and do change over time.

Members of a certain group often share interests or goals. A **goal** is something you are willing to work for. The goal of your art class may be to finish a mural before the fall art show.

When you are involved in group activities, think about what the group is doing. Ask yourself these questions.

- Is this something I want to do?
- Will I feel good about myself after I do it?
- Is it safe?
- Would my parents approve?
- What could I do instead?

▲ You can have different roles in different groups.

LESSON CHECKUP

Check Your Facts

1. Name the four kinds of traits that make you special.

2. What are some traits that family members may share?

3. CRITICAL THINKING Suppose you are playing during recess and a friend suggests that you go down the slide head-first. You know that this is against school rules. List the things you should ask yourself before you decide what to do.

4. CRITICAL THINKING How can goals improve self-concept?

Set Health Goals

5. Sometimes it is hard to remember the good points about yourself. Think back over the past week. List a good thing you did each day.

We All Have Needs

Each of us is different, and yet we are all the same—we all have needs. A need is something we must have in order to be healthy. The physical, mental, emotional, and social needs that we all share are called **basic needs**.

What physical needs do people have?

People all over the world have the same physical needs. Physical needs are related to the body. To keep our bodies healthy, we all need food and water. We also need clean air to breathe. Finally, we need shelter—a place to live.

When you were a baby, you depended on adults for your physical needs. You could not have lived without people to care for you. Adults fed you, wrapped you in a warm blanket, and kept you safe. Now that you are getting older, you are beginning to meet some of your own physical needs. When you make yourself a snack, for example, you are meeting your need for food. When you are grown up, you will be responsible for meeting all of your own physical needs.

Each of us, no matter what our age, needs food, water, air, and shelter. If these physical needs are not met, we can become ill or die.

What emotional, mental, and social needs do people have?

Physical needs are just one part of our basic needs. People also have emotional, mental, and social needs.

Emotional needs are related to your feelings. In general, people share emotional needs for love, for security, and for a place to belong. You need to be able to talk to others about your feelings. You also need to trust others and feel that they trust you. Your family probably fills most of your emotional needs, but your friends and other people also help meet these needs.

Mental needs include thinking, learning, and using your mind. You need to know math so you can use your money wisely. You need to be able to read so you can follow the directions so you can put a model airplane together. You may take music lessons, practice martial arts, or go to dance class. All of these activities take a lot of concentration and help you satisfy your need to think and learn.

SCIENCE CONNECTION

What Plants Need

On Your Own Plants have needs just like you. Use three plants of the same type and size. Put each plant in a different environment in your home. Compare their growth after a month.

○ ○ ○

Activity **Identify Needs** Study this picture. List the physical needs being met. Then write a paragraph describing any emotional and mental needs that you think are being met.

▲ Having fun together is a good way for families to meet their emotional needs.

Think of two emotional or social needs you have that seem to be different from those of your friends or family members. In your Health Journal, make a plan to help you meet those needs. Remember, your journal can be kept private.

Social needs involve other people. The need to be part of a group and the need to be alone are social needs. When you join a club or choose to spend time alone, you are taking care of your social needs. Getting along with family members and friends is another way of meeting your social needs.

Sometimes the needs you have may be different from those of your friends or family. That is to be expected, because there is no one else exactly like you! You may be the only member of your family who needs a quiet place to read. You may need more **privacy** (PRY•vuh•see), or time by yourself, than your friends do.

Right now, your family has a large part in meeting most of your emotional, mental, and social needs. As you get older, you will be responsible for meeting more of your own needs. The choices you make and the goals you set can help you meet many of your needs.

You can start meeting some of your needs now by setting a goal for yourself. For example, Bill never had time to eat breakfast before he left for school. It seemed as if he was always running out the door at the last minute. Bill decided to set a goal to eat breakfast every day. Look at the chart on this page to see how he planned to reach his goal. How could you make a similar plan to reach a goal of your own?

My Goal: Having Time to Eat Breakfast

1. **The night before, lay out clothes for tomorrow and pack my backpack.**
2. **Set alarm.**
3. **Get up when alarm rings!**
4. **Get dressed for school.**
5. **Eat breakfast.**
6. **Clean up kitchen.**
7. **Brush my teeth.**
8. **Add star to the chart on the refrigerator, and leave for school on time.**

LESSON CHECKUP

Check Your Facts

❶ What basic needs do all people have?

❷ List two physical needs you can meet by yourself.

❸ Name two needs, one mental and one social. How do people meet these needs?

❹ CRITICAL THINKING How do goals help you meet your needs?

Set Health Goals

❺ Suppose you want to set a goal to read fifteen minutes every day. Make a plan in the form of a chart like the one above to help you reach your goal.

3

We All Have Feelings

MAIN IDEA It is important to express your feelings in ways that make you feel confident and safe.

WHY LEARN THIS? Part of growing up is learning how to express your feelings in ways that make you feel in control.

VOCABULARY
• stress
• body language
• self-control

Everyone has feelings and emotions. We have many feelings—joy, sadness, and anger, for example—in common with other people. But the reasons we have a certain feeling may be different for each of us. What makes you feel sad may not affect your friend in the same way. What makes you happy may be different from what makes your parents happy.

Understanding as much as you can about what you feel and why you feel it is an important part of growing up. Expressing your feelings in a safe and respectful way can help you feel in control of yourself.

Why do people have feelings?

Just as a detective looks for clues to solve a case, your feelings can give you clues about yourself. Your feelings can help you know when something is right or wrong for you. If you feel happy, you know that something you are doing or thinking makes you feel good. For example, sometimes cleaning your room is something you do not want to do. But the good feeling you have inside afterward tells you it was the right thing to do.

Unpleasant feelings can be a warning signal. When you are angry or when you are scared, your feelings are telling you that something is not right. It is important to listen to those feelings. You should try to understand what you are feeling and why. If you can find a safe way to express that feeling then you'll probably feel better.

Feelings are not good or bad, but some just *feel* better than others. Unpleasant feelings can make your body tense and upset. For example, when you feel **stress** —tension in your body and your mind—it can show in your face and in your words. It can also show in your **body language**, body movements that go with your words, like a nod. Feelings of stress can cause you to have butterflies in your stomach. You may get a headache or stomachache. Knowing what you are feeling and naming it can help you choose how to act.

Myth and fact

Myth: Any stress is bad.

Fact: People need a certain amount of stress in their lives to perform at their best. This positive stress is called *eustress*. Too much stress, however, can have negative effects. Negative stress is called *distress*.

• • • • • • •

Activity **Identify Feelings**
Write down what you think each of these people is feeling, and why.

How do feelings affect your actions?

Part of growing up is learning to express your feelings in ways that make you feel safe and confident. When you can restrain your emotions or desires, you have **self-control**. Like any other new skill, self-control takes a lot of practice. It's also helpful to know as much as you can about yourself and your feelings.

For example, imagine that you are being teased at school. You want the person who is teasing you to stop. As the person keeps teasing you, you begin to feel upset. You feel a lot of stress. Your stomach hurts, your body is stiff, and your face is tense. Your teeth are tightly clenched, and your hands are shaking. Suddenly, you blow up in anger at the person.

You are out of control, and it's not a comfortable feeling. You *can* learn to control your anger. If you face your anger in the beginning, you can *choose* how to respond.

JOuRNaL

Write about a time you felt very angry.
• How did your body feel?
• What did you do?
• Look at the anger management steps on page 29. How would you use these steps to handle a similar situation? Remember, your journal can be kept private.

Cool off!

▶ Joe knows he must control his anger at Fred. After he counts to ten, he will tell Fred what's bothering him.

Imagine that as soon as you *start* to feel angry with the person who is teasing you, you stop what you are doing or saying. You allow yourself to cool down by counting to ten or taking three long, slow breaths. You think about what is really happening. Now you are ready to take action. You can either walk away or express your feelings. If you walk away, you can talk to the person about your feelings once you are in control again. If you choose to express your feelings, use I-messages that focus on telling the person how you feel about what they are doing. For example say, "I don't like it when you tease me. It makes me angry. Please stop."

These steps can help you manage your anger and practice self-control. You can use these steps to learn to identify other feelings and make good choices about how to express them. Learning self-control in expressing feelings is an important part of growing up and being responsible for yourself.

LESSON CHECKUP

Check Your Facts

1. How can stress show in your body?
2. What can happen if you don't control yourself when you begin to get angry?
3. CRITICAL THINKING Why do you think it is important to name what you are feeling?
4. What are the five steps for anger management?

Set Health Goals

5. Imagine that you are angry at your brother because he borrowed your backpack without asking. Use the steps for anger management to show how you will handle the situation.

MANAGE STRESS
Every Day

Everyone faces stress at times. Use the following steps to help you learn how to handle stressful situations in a healthful way.

Learn This Skill

Dolores's softball team has made it to the play-offs. Dolores is up at bat in the bottom of the seventh inning. There are two outs, and the game is tied. How can she handle the stress she feels in this situation?

1. Know what stress feels like and what causes it.

2. When you feel stress, think about ways to handle it.

Dolores has butterflies in her stomach, and her teeth are tightly clenched. She's feeling stress because of the big game.

Dolores thinks about her last time at bat. She waited for the right pitch—just as her coach had suggested—and hit a double to left field.

3. Learn to release tension.

Dolores takes a deep breath. She glances at her coach for support.

4. Focus on one step at a time.

WINNER
GO TEAM!

Dolores decides not to swing at the first pitch. It's low and outside.

Practice This Skill

Use this summary as you solve the problems below.

Ways to Manage Stress

1. Know what stress feels like and what causes it.

2. When you feel stress, think about ways to handle it.

3. Learn to release tension.

4. Focus on one step at a time.

A. Janie is worried about giving her oral report. How can she manage her stress so she does her best?

B. Paul has to sing a solo in one part of a musical. How can Paul manage his stress so he performs his solo well?

The Challenges of Friendship

MAIN IDEA
Learning how to solve problems with friends is an important skill.

WHY LEARN THIS? You can use the ideas in this lesson to help you be a good friend.

VOCABULARY
- conflict
- conflict resolution
- negotiate
- compromise

Can you remember a time when you and your friends were sure you would be friends forever, but something happened and suddenly you weren't speaking to each other? It might help to know that all friendships have problems, especially friendships among people your age. You and your friends are changing. You are learning more about who you are and what you like and dislike. It's all right if you and your friends sometimes disagree.

There are many important questions to ask about friendship. How do you choose and keep your friends? What qualities do you like in a friend? Do you have different kinds of friends in different places? How do you and your friends solve disagreements?

Friendships can be very challenging. And like other skills, the art of making and keeping friends improves with practice.

◀ What goal do you think these friends have in common? How can working together strengthen their friendship?

Why are friendships valuable?

What is it about having friends that makes all the problems worth it? For one thing, friends satisfy our need to belong to a group. We all need to feel cared for, and it is usually our friends, along with our families, who encourage us and help us feel good about ourselves.

You may meet new friends through shared interests. You and your friends may be members of the same sports team or scout troop. Being involved in the same activity is a good basis for friendship because your shared interest can help you stay together even when you have problems. You may become friends with other boys and girls in your class after working together on a school project. Working with other people helps you get to know each other better. You may learn that you share other interests, too. You may also meet a friend because you have the same goal.

What qualities do you like in a friend? What kind of friend are you? Do you and your friends like having different opinions and ideas at times? Do you and your friends forgive each other easily? Can you be silly as well as serious with your friends?

You can have different friends in different places. You may have friends that you see only in school, another group of friends that you play ball with on Saturdays, and one or two best friends. With different groups of friends you can express different parts of yourself. Your friends in music class may know you as the serious piano player, but your juggling partners may know you as the funniest person in the group.

Did you know?

You may find it hard to imagine now, but many people remain friends for their entire lives. For example, two women who live in New Jersey were friends for eighty years.

▶ **Sometimes friends have to be very patient with each other.**

How do friends solve problems?

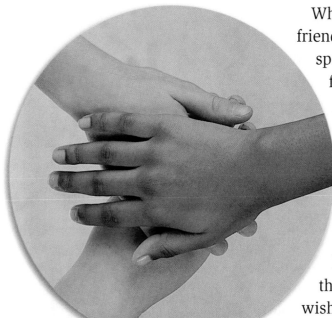

▲ Reaching agreement is one way to solve a problem.

What causes problems between you and your friends? Do you feel jealous when your friend spends time with someone else? Does your friend get mad when you disagree with him or her? Do you feel bad when your friend says something untrue about you to another friend? Does your friend get mad at you when you won't let her or him borrow your new bike?

No matter how strong your friendships are, sometimes you and your friends will have conflicts. A **conflict** is a disagreement that occurs when people have different needs or wishes. Even you and your best friend may have conflicts at times. Although it is normal to disagree, you can learn how to solve the problems you and your friends may have. This is called **conflict resolution** (KAHN•flikt reh•zuh•LOO•shuhn). The skills you use to solve your problems now also can help you solve problems when you're an adult.

One way to solve problems is to make agreements ahead of time about how you and your friends will deal with problems. One group of friends came up with the friendship rules shown in the chart below. What rules would you change or add?

CONNECTION

Getting Attention
If you have a very young brother or sister at home, you know how they get attention. They cry, scream, or otherwise demand it. As young children grow up, they learn better, more acceptable ways to get attention at home and at school. Write a paragraph explaining the acceptable ways you use. Share it with a classmate.

OUR FRIENDSHIP RULES
• Don't talk behind each other's back.
• Tell the truth.
• Set up a time to talk about problems.
• Listen carefully to each other.
• Avoid hurtful comments and put-downs.
• Don't fight.

You and your friends can agree to negotiate when there are problems. When people **negotiate** (nih•GOH•shee•ayt) they work together to resolve their conflict. Negotiation often results in a **compromise** (KAHM•pruh•myz), or a solution that considers everyone's feelings and ideas. Suppose you and a friend argue over which game to play at recess. You negotiate and reach a compromise. You and your friend agree to play one of the games this recess and the other game next recess.

What else can you do when you and a friend disagree?

- **Ignore it!** Ignoring something small is an easy way to avoid a problem.
- **Laugh.** It is hard to stay angry when you and a friend are laughing together.
- **Take a break.** Everyone needs time away from friends now and then. Taking a break may give both of you a chance to make new friends. Then later maybe all of you can be friends!
- **Say you're sorry.** Sometimes you do or say something that makes a friend feel bad. You can talk to your friend, write a note, or do something to let him or her know that you're sorry. If your friend does something that makes you feel bad and later apologizes to you, forgive him or her. Forgiveness is an important quality in a friend.

LIFE SKILLS
FOCUS

Communicate
Olivia and her friend Luis wanted to play together after school. Olivia wanted to play at her house. Luis wanted to show Olivia a new game at his house. What friendship rules could Olivia use to let Luis know how she feels? Use the steps for communicating shown on page *xii*.

▼ The members of these two baseball teams are having a disagreement. Jorge is telling everyone to listen carefully to both sides. What else can they do to resolve this conflict?

Learning to solve problems you have with friends makes you feel good about yourself. It increases your self-respect to know that you are growing up and can accept responsibility for yourself and your actions.

Who can help when friendships don't work?

You and your friends may be able to take care of most disagreements by yourselves. Still, there may be times when you need help solving a problem.

A friend may ask you to do something that doesn't feel right to you. Remember that a true friend will not want you to do something that goes against your values or family rules. It's important to stand up for what you believe in, even if it means that you lose a friend or are not popular. If you've said *no* to a friend because something didn't feel right to you, you should be very proud of yourself. It means you are taking responsibility for yourself.

It doesn't feel good when your friends are angry with you. Have your friends ever been mad at you because you did not go along with something they wanted you to do? It can be hard to tell your friends that you don't agree with them. But there's nothing wrong with having an opinion different from that of your friends.

If a problem with a friend has lasted for a long time, or if you have been unable to talk to your friend about the problem, you may want to ask an adult to help you. A parent or other family member, a teacher, a school counselor, or another trusted adult may be able to advise you. An adult can help you reach a solution that both you and your friend can agree on.

School Counselor

What They Do

School counselors help students with many different problems. They are part of the team that helps students stay safe at school.

School counselors are good listeners. If you have a problem at school or at home, you can go to your school counselor for help. Counselors help students solve their own disagreements. They can bring students together and help them negotiate a compromise to a problem.

Education and Training

In most states, school counselors must have a four-year college degree plus one or two years of training in counseling. Many states also require a teaching certificate or teaching experience. Some counselors are psychologists who have an advanced college degree.

LESSON CHECKUP

Check Your Facts

❶ Why is it possible to have different kinds of friends in different places?

❷ What are four rules that you and your friends can use to deal with problems?

❸ CRITICAL THINKING Why is it important to stand up for what you believe, even if you lose a friend?

❹ List four things you can do when you and a friend disagree.

Use Life Skills

❺ RESOLVE CONFLICTS Suppose you and a friend have a conflict over which movie to watch. What information in this lesson would help you the most? Write a plan telling how you would resolve this conflict.

RESOLVE CONFLICTS
at School

Isabel and Andy are having a disagreement. How can they work together to resolve it?

Learn This Skill

Isabel notices that Andy is writing with a brand new blue pencil. It looks exactly like the pencil she lost yesterday. Isabel is sure it's her pencil, and she wants it back. She reaches over and takes it away from Andy. Andy grabs it back. Isabel is about to take it away again. But then she thinks of several other ways to resolve the conflict.

1. Use humor.

2. Take a break. Solve the problem after everyone cools down.

Humor works well if the situation isn't too serious.

Sometimes the best thing to do is to take a break. This allows everyone to cool down and think things over.

3. Ask for a mediator.

Maybe we need to ask our teacher to help.

Sometimes the best way to resolve a conflict is to ask for a mediator. A mediator is someone who listens to both sides of a problem and helps find a fair solution.

4. Choose the best way.

Isabel decides to take a break. She knows that a pencil isn't worth fighting over. She also knows that both she and Andy will cool down if they have time to think about things.

Practice This Skill

Use this summary as you solve the problems below.

> ### Ways to Resolve a Conflict
>
> 1. Use humor.
> 2. Take a break. Solve the problem after everyone cools down.
> 3. Ask for a mediator.
> 4. Choose the best way.

A. Marcia is playing a computer game. Her brother announces that he needs the computer to do homework. Marcia wants to keep playing. How could Marcia resolve this conflict?

B. Troy's sister is tracking mud all over the floor he has just finished sweeping. When Troy asks her to clean up the mess, she tells him that sweeping the floor is his job. How could Troy resolve this conflict?

MAIN IDEA
Learning how to work peacefully and respectfully with all people is important.

WHY LEARN THIS? Finding ways to respect differences and looking for things you have in common with others helps you get along.

VOCABULARY
• disability
• compassion
• role model

► How is this girl showing compassion?

Working with Others

How do you deal with differences?

Imagine going to a school where no one makes fun of anyone else. When you get new glasses for the first time, your classmates are excited for you. If a friend has a new haircut, no one teases him because he looks different from the way he did the day before. If a new student enters your class, she is welcomed by other students. If a student with a **disability** (dih•suh•BIH•luh•tee)—a physical or mental impairment—is in your class, you and your friends make sure to get to know him or her. You understand that just because someone has a disability doesn't mean you can't have many interests in common.

Did you know that you can create an environment like that? You can practice meeting new people with an open mind, with respect, and with compassion. If you have **compassion** (kuhm•PA•shuhn), you are sensitive to the needs and feelings of others. You can understand how someone feels even if you don't know the person. You can help someone who is having a bad day because you can imagine how you would feel in a similar situation.

◄ Learning sign language lets you communicate with someone who is hearing impaired.

Are you sometimes nervous when you first meet someone who is different from you in some way? Perhaps the person is much older or comes from a different country. It's fine to be a little nervous at first. Many people are shy in new situations. Remember that the more you get to know someone, the more at ease you will feel.

At times it takes patience to get to know someone. If a classmate has a speech impairment such as stuttering, talking together easily may take a little time and effort for both of you. If a student from another country joins your class and speaks a different language, try to learn some words in that language. Getting to know people who differ from you in some way can make your life more interesting and exciting! And, as you learn new things from someone different from you, you may also find that the two of you have many interests in common.

You do not have to be friends with everyone you meet. Sometimes you may meet someone whose values and opinions are very different from yours. Even though you don't agree with someone, you can still get along with that person and respect his or her right to think differently from you.

SOCIAL STUDIES CONNECTION

Practice Sign Language

With a Group Use the library to find a copy of the American Sign Language Alphabet. Learn to make the letters that spell your name. Practice signing your name with classmates.

● ●●

How can you make a difference?

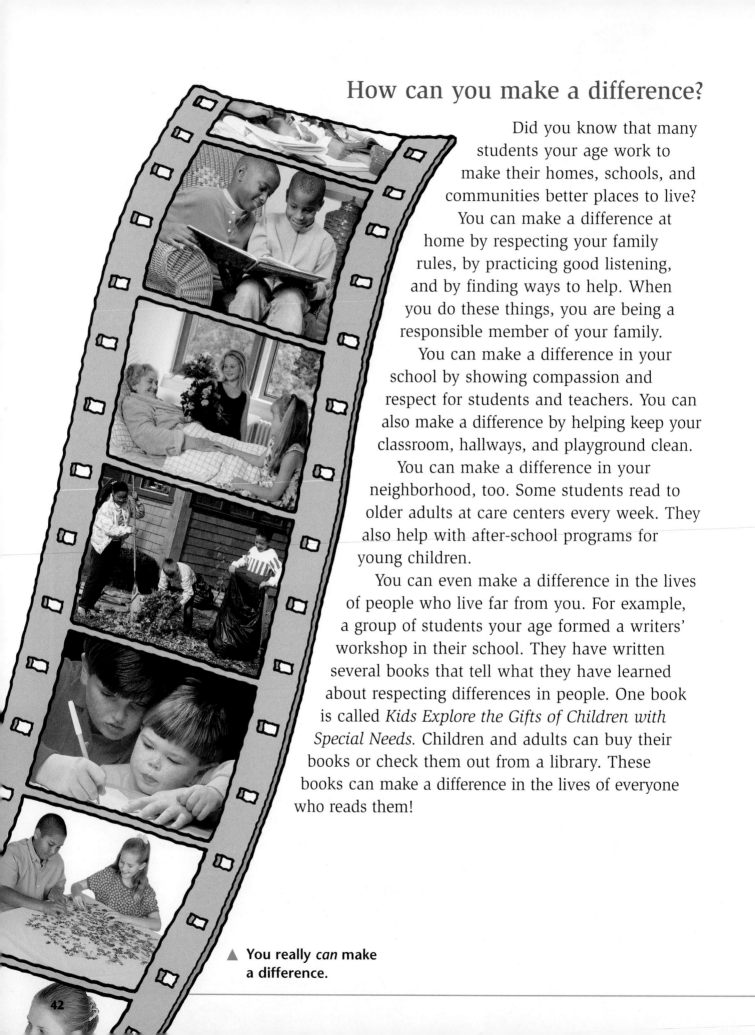

Did you know that many students your age work to make their homes, schools, and communities better places to live? You can make a difference at home by respecting your family rules, by practicing good listening, and by finding ways to help. When you do these things, you are being a responsible member of your family.

You can make a difference in your school by showing compassion and respect for students and teachers. You can also make a difference by helping keep your classroom, hallways, and playground clean.

You can make a difference in your neighborhood, too. Some students read to older adults at care centers every week. They also help with after-school programs for young children.

You can even make a difference in the lives of people who live far from you. For example, a group of students your age formed a writers' workshop in their school. They have written several books that tell what they have learned about respecting differences in people. One book is called *Kids Explore the Gifts of Children with Special Needs*. Children and adults can buy their books or check them out from a library. These books can make a difference in the lives of everyone who reads them!

▲ **You really *can* make a difference.**

When you find ways to show respect and compassion for other people at home, at school, and in your community, you are making a difference. You are also being a good role model for people both older and younger than you. A **role model** is someone who sets a good example. If other people see you as a role model in your school and community, they may try to make a difference, too.

Each of your good deeds is like a pebble dropped into a lake. The ripples of your effect on people can be wide and far-reaching. You do not have to be an adult to make a difference in the world.

CONSUMER FOCUS

Analyze Advertising and Media Messages
Watch a television show that has a character in grade-school or middle-school. Take notes about what he or she says and does. Is the character a good role model? What else is the show telling you? Use the steps for analyzing advertising and media messages on page xv.

◀ Helping a neighbor is one way to make a positive difference.

LESSON CHECKUP

Check Your Facts

1. CRITICAL THINKING Someone has said that the more you learn, the less you fear. What does this have to do with respecting differences?

2. How can getting to know someone who is different from you make both of your lives more interesting and exciting?

3. Why do you think you are often less nervous and afraid after you get to know someone a little better?

4. What are some new ways you can think of to make a difference in your home, school, and neighborhood?

Set Health Goals

5. Make a list of ways students can show compassion and respect for each other in school. Put a star by the ones you want to do.

Review

USE VOCABULARY

attitude (p. 19)
basic needs (p. 22)
body language (p. 27)
compassion (p. 40)
compromise (p. 35)

conflict (p. 34)
conflict resolution (p. 34)
disability (p. 40)
environment (p. 20)

goal (p. 21)
negotiate (p. 35)
privacy (p. 24)
role model (p. 43)
self-concept (p. 18)

self-control (p. 28)
self-respect (p. 18)
stress (p. 27)
talent (p. 19)
traits (p. 18)

Use the terms above to complete the sentences. Page numbers in ( ) tell you where to look in the chapter if you need help.

1. A _____ is a physical or mental impairment.

2. When people _____, they work together to resolve their conflict.

3. The physical, mental, emotional, and social needs that we all share are called _____.

4. Solving a disagreement between you and your friends is called _____.

5. Tension in your body and your mind is called _____.

6. If you have _____, you have a satisfied, confident feeling about yourself.

7. If you have _____, you are sensitive to the needs and feelings of others.

8. A _____ is a solution that considers the feelings and ideas of everyone involved.

9. A _____ sets a good example for others.

10. The general picture you have of yourself is called your _____.

11. A _____ is something you are willing to work for.

12. You have _____ when you can restrain your emotions or desires.

13. If you need time by yourself, you need _____.

14. _____ are special qualities that make up a large part of who you are.

15. Where you live is a part of your _____.

16. Your _____ is the way you look at things.

17. The body movements that go with your words are your _____.

18. A _____ is a natural ability.

19. A _____ is a disagreement that occurs when people have different needs or wishes.

Page numbers in ( ) tell you where to look in the chapter if you need help.

20. List the five questions you should ask yourself when you need to make up your mind in a group situation. (p. 21)

21. Write down five things you could do to satisfy your mental needs. (p. 23)

22. List the steps for anger management. (p. 29)

23. List three things you can do when you and a friend disagree. (p. 35)

24. List two things you could do to make a difference in your school. (p. 42)

THINK CRITICALLY

25. Describe a situation in which a person loses self-control. What steps would that person take to stay in control the next time?

26. Make your own list of friendship rules that you can use to solve problems with your friends.

27. Resolve Conflicts Suppose you and a friend have a disagreement over which sport to play after school. List two ways to come to an agreement.

28. Manage Stress Suppose you are under a lot of stress because you never have time to finish your homework. Set a goal to find the time you need. List the steps needed to reach your goal.

Promote Health **Home and Community**

1. Talk with your family about what you could do to make a difference in your neighborhood.
2. Make a poster that shows at least four different ways you can resolve a conflict with a friend.

Activities

Stress Reducers

With a Partner • Exercise is one way to help reduce stress. Make a list of other things you can do to help relieve your stress. You may want to ask your parents how they handle stress.

Overcoming Adversity

At Home • Many people live with traits that keep them from doing certain things. Thomas Edison was once a poor student. But he went on to invent many useful things, including the light bulb. Find out more about Thomas Edison. How did he learn to overcome a negative mental trait?

Community Involvement

With a Team • Think about something your community needs to make it a better place. For example, some elementary students in New York set up their own bookstore in a neighborhood that had no bookstores. Put together a poster that explains your idea. Include examples of how your idea would benefit your community.

Conflict Resolution

On Your Own • Ask your teacher or a librarian to recommend a story to read in which the main character resolves a conflict with another character. Identify choices the main character made to help resolve the conflict. Compare these choices with the ones discussed in Lesson 4.

Multiple Choice

Choose the letter of the correct answer.

1. You have physical, emotional, and social _____.
   a. emotions   b. personalities
   c. traits   d. talents

2. Food, water, air, and shelter are _____ needs.
   a. physical   b. mental
   c. emotional   d. social

3. People need a certain amount of _____ in their lives to perform their best.
   a. anger   b. stress
   c. self-control d. energy

4. Who can help you solve a problem between friends?
   a. a parent   b. a counselor
   c. a teacher   d. all of the above

5. If you are sensitive to the feelings of others, you have _____.
   a. pride   b. imagination
   c. compassion   d. self-control

Modified True or False

Write *true* or *false*. If a sentence is false, replace the underlined term to make the sentence true.

6. The general picture you have of yourself is called your <u>talent</u>.

7. Your height is a <u>mental</u> trait.

8. <u>Emotional</u> needs are related to your feelings.

9. <u>Physical</u> needs include thinking, learning, and using your mind.

10. Setting <u>goals</u> can help you meet many of your needs.

11. When you can restrain your emotions or desires, you have <u>self-respect</u>.

12. Negotiation sometimes results in a <u>compromise.</u>

13. A compromise between two friends considers <u>one person's</u> feelings.

14. Sign language helps you communicate with someone who is <u>seeing</u> impaired.

15. A role model is someone who sets a <u>bad</u> example for others.

Short Answer

Write a complete sentence to answer each question.

16. Describe how environment can influence your traits.

17. Name five roles you play in groups.

18. Imagine that you are angry at a friend for not returning a borrowed book. Use the steps for anger management to show how you will respond.

19. How can your feelings help you know when something is right for you?

20. Give three examples of how stress shows in your body.

21. Name two needs that friends satisfy.

22. Why is being involved in the same activity a good basis for friendship?

23. Describe a disagreement you could solve using conflict resolution.

Writing in Health

Write paragraphs to answer each item.

24. How can solving problems with a friend help you solve problems later in life?

25. Write about something positive you could do to make a difference in your school.

CHAPTER 2

Living and Growing

CHART FAMILY ACTIVITIES

The world is made up of families. Families live and work together. They also do many activities together. Look in magazines for pictures of families doing things together. Then make a chart showing the pictures you have found and list the activities families do together.

For other activities, visit the Harcourt Learning Site.
www.harcourtschool.com

Families Meet Their Needs

Like humans, some animals live in family groups. You may have seen families of birds building nests and raising young. Lion families teach their young how to survive. These families work together to meet their needs. Human families also work together to meet their needs.

What is a family?

You know that you are unlike any other person in the whole world. Your family is unique too. A person's basic needs are usually met within a family. Your family gives you food, a warm place to sleep, and clothes to wear. Family members support and take care of you. They try to make sure you are safe. When you are scared or hurt, family members try to help and protect you. Most parents try hard to make a safe and loving home for their children.

Although everyone begins life with two parents, children do not always grow up living in a **nuclear family** with a mother, father, and one or more children. Some children live with one parent in a **single-parent family**. This may be due to the death of a parent or because their parents are divorced.

▼ Families come in all sizes. Some children live with one parent. Others live with both parents.

50

Some children are members of a blended family. A **blended family** forms when two single parents marry. The children of both parents become part of the new family. The new parent is called a stepparent. Children of the stepparent are called stepbrothers or stepsisters.

Some children live with parents who adopted them, or they live in a foster family with adults who take care of them. When families adopt children or invite foster children to join them, those children become part of the family even though they are not related by birth.

Not all families look alike or do the same things. Families live in different kinds of homes and eat different kinds of food. Some families speak two languages. Other families go fishing together. Some work together on family farms or play music together. Some families have large groups of relatives who celebrate holidays together.

Your family may be different from the family that lives next door or down the street. Your family may like to do different things than your friends' families do. Whatever kind of family you have, the grown-ups in your family try to do their best to support and care for you.

▼ Sometimes families include grandparents.

 Activity **Think About Families** Look carefully at the pictures of the families here and on page 50. Which type of family is each family pictured an example of? Think about ways in which each family is different. Explain how each of these families is both alike and different.

► Sometimes families combine through remarriage and include stepchildren and stepparents.

What roles do people have in families?

ART CONNECTION

Your Gifts

On Your Own Make a poster showing what you give to members of your family. It might be your love of shooting baskets, your patience, your sense of humor, or your talent in art.

• • •

All family members are important, including you. Each family member has a different role. A parent's main role is to support and take care of the children. Your main role in the family now is to learn to be a responsible family member.

When you were a baby, your family did everything for you. Now that you are older, your family may count on you to help with chores. You also might be a brother or sister. If you have a younger sibling, you might help care for him or her. As you get older, you will become an even more responsible member of your family.

Each person's role in a family changes over time. How might a child's role in the family change after an older brother or sister leaves home? How does a parent's role change as children get older?

No matter how young or old each member of your family is or what role each person has, it's important to respect each family member. When you respect each member of your family, you value each person for who she or he is. You don't expect your three-year-old sister to act older than three, and you don't expect your grandmother to think the way you do. You can respect family members for being who they are at their ages. Of course, you want your family to respect you in the same way.

Think about your family. What is special about each person in it? What have you learned from each other? Maybe your grandmother taught you how to swim. Perhaps she showed you how to bake the world's best pies. You might have learned about patience from

▲ **How might things change in a family when a new baby arrives?**

Congratulations!

▲ **Why might this boy be both proud and sad at his older sister's graduation?**

Family Gifts

On Your Own Make a list of the special gifts you give to your family. Pick one gift per family member, and write a poem or story describing why you think the gift is special. Draw gift boxes around your poems or stories. Decorate the boxes, and give the gifts to family members.

○ ○ ○

building models with your older brother. Your mom might have taught you to write poetry and to ride a bike. You might have learned that being honest is important because your dad set a good example. And you might have learned that you are good with children because of all the time you've spent playing with your baby sister.

Everyone in your family, including you, will continue to change. Everyone in your family will get older. You will have new things to teach each other and to learn from each other. You and your family can practice loving, respecting, and supporting each other through all the changes, big and small, that you will experience together.

▶ **Some changes in families might make you feel sad. These changes may take time to get over.**

What is an extended family?

An **extended family** is made up of parents, children, and grandparents or other close relatives. You can share many special times with members of your extended family.

Sometimes you can learn from extended family members like aunts, uncles, cousins, or grandparents. Your parents may be busy, but your grandparents may always be ready to take time to listen as you talk about your day. If your grandparent is retired, you could spend the whole day learning how to build a birdhouse.

Grandparents often have interesting stories to tell. Ask your grandparents to tell you stories about their lives when they were your age. One story may lead to many more.

Your grandparents may also have passed down special **traditions**—customs you do over and over—that are now part of the way your family celebrates holidays or other special occasions. Shared traditions can bring members of a family together in special ways.

Grandparents also have talents and skills to teach other members of the family. You may have a grandparent who knows where to catch the biggest fish, where to buy the best doughnuts, how to draw the best pictures, and just what to do to make things better when you're feeling sad. You may have grandparents who run marathons, swim laps, or climb mountains, or you may have grandparents who are less active because they are not well.

"My family will love this house!"

◄ Grandparents often enjoy working on projects with their grandchildren.

◀ Grandparents make family activities special.

Growing up in the same house with a grandparent can be special, but it isn't always easy. At times your grandparent may not understand or like what you do, the way you dress, or the music you play. When you have a problem with an extended family member, stop and think. Why do the two of you disagree? Why do you suppose your grandmother doesn't like your music? What can you do to help solve the problem?

Solving problems with extended family members may be hard work, but it's worth it. You feel good when everyone gets along.

Did you know?

People don't stop exercising as they get older. Many runners in the Masters Track and Field Championships are more than sixty years old!

▶ Outdoor activities such as fishing, hiking, and camping are fun for people of all ages.

LESSON CHECKUP

Check Your Facts

1. Name four kinds of families.

2. What do nearly all families have in common?

3. CRITICAL THINKING How does a child's role in a family change over time? How do you think a parent's role changes over time?

Use Life Skills

4. COMMUNICATE Think about how you will change over the years. Make a chart with columns labeled 20 Years, 40 Years, and 60 Years. Tell in words and in pictures what you think you'll be like at each of those ages. What responsibilities will you have within your family?

MAIN IDEA It is important that family members cooperate and respect and support each other.

WHY LEARN THIS? When family members respect each other and can work and have fun together, it is easier to learn from each other.

VOCABULARY
• values
• cooperate
• generations

Family Tradition

On Your Own
Look in the library for books about family traditions. Write about one of the traditions, and share what you learned with the class.

○ ○ ○

Families Work Together

A family teaches its members important things. Families pass along **values**, or strong beliefs about how people should live. In your family you learn many values, such as honesty, that will guide you through life. You also learn how to **cooperate** (koh•AH•puh•rayt), or work together and get along with other people.

What do you learn from your family?

You may think of your family as the people who live in your home. You may also think of aunts, uncles, and cousins. However, you also have **generations** of family members who came before you. Besides your parents, these generations include your grandparents, great-grandparents, great-great-grandparents, and so on. If you have children when you grow up, you will be adding a new generation to your family.

Values, traditions, and stories are passed down through the generations by parents and grandparents to their children and grandchildren. When you grow up, you may pass down many of your family's values, traditions, and stories to the next generation.

Activity **Identify Values** Look at the drawings of values on these pages. Think of three other values that are important in your family. Show an example of each one in words or pictures.

Parents and grandparents teach many values by example. If you see that your mother makes it a point to be truthful, you will probably grow up to be truthful, too. If you see your parents helping others, you will learn from their example. If your grandparents teach you respect for nature, you will probably grow up to respect Earth's resources. If your family respects your belongings, it is likely that you will respect other people's belongings, too.

▲ What values do you think these family members share?

Families also pass down values through spiritual beliefs and teachings. The spiritual teachings you learn when you are young will continue to be an important part of your life when you are grown.

Another way to learn values is through stories. If your grandfather tells you about an event in his life that called for courage, you may remember his story at a time when you need courage. If your parents tell you about a time when they stood up for something they believed in, you too may decide to be that kind of person.

Family stories also help family members know more about their own history. The stories help you feel connected to earlier generations of your family long after those people have died.

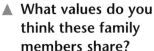

LIFE SKILLS
FOCUS

COMMUNICATE
Emily and Shannon see a girl neither of them knows. Shannon points at the girl's shoes and laughs. Emily's family has taught her that teasing hurts people's feelings. Use the steps for communicating shown on page *xii* to help Emily explain her feelings to Shannon.

• • •

How can families cooperate and work together?

ART CONNECTION

Make a Comic Strip

On Your Own Create a comic strip showing what could happen if a family member does not keep up with his or her chores. Display your comic strip in a place where your family will see it.

You and your family will spend many years together. It's important for everyone to find ways to respect and cooperate with each other. When you knock before entering your mother's room, and say "please" and "thank you," you are showing respect. When you ask before you borrow your brother's bike, you are showing respect. When you take time to listen to your little sister and treat her with kindness, you are also showing respect.

Helping out in your family is one way to cooperate. If you do your jobs around the house without being told, you show the people in your family that they can count on you. When you see something that needs to be done, you can do it instead of waiting for someone else to take care of it. If towels are left on the bathroom floor, pick them up. If the trash can is full, empty it. It feels good to be a responsible member of your family.

Everyone needs encouragement from time to time. Sometimes just a word, a hug, or a pat on the back is all it takes to let someone in your family know you care. And it's nice to know you can count on family members to be there for you when you need support.

Families cooperate at both work and play. How do you cooperate with your family?

58

Every family has conflicts and problems at times. You can help solve problems in your family. You can control your anger. You can use words to tell people how you are feeling and work toward solutions that everyone agrees on. When you can deal with conflict without whining or exploding in anger or tears, you know you are growing up.

When family members get along well together, even work can be fun. But people in families need to take time to play together, too. What do you and other members of your family do to have fun together?

Some families enjoy making pizza, ice-skating, and playing games together. Families can enjoy many different activities. Whatever your family does together, it's important to choose activities that everyone in the family can take part in.

Good times with your family can become new traditions. One Friday of pizza and movies with your family can turn into a weekly family night. A Saturday spent decorating a surprise birthday cake can turn into a tradition that each member of the family will look forward to.

By working cooperatively and having fun together, a family stays strong. A strong family can withstand the big and small changes that families may experience.

LIFE SKILLS
FOCUS

Resolve Conflicts
You want to watch a video. Your parents want to go on a bike ride. Your brother wants to play a game. How can your family choose a fun activity that satisfies everyone? Use the steps for resolving conflicts shown on page *xiii*.

● ● ●

Activity **Plan Family Fun** Look over the pictures of families on pages 48 through 59. Then make a list of activities *your* family could do together. List as many as you can. Put the list where everyone in the family can add to it. Then, as a family, choose one activity to do together.

Why are rules important?

Does the word *rules* make you groan? It probably reminds you of things you want to do, but can't. Rules might mean you have to go to bed early or that you can't ride your bike at night. Rules also might mean you have to finish your homework before you watch TV.

But have you ever thought about how important rules are in families? Along with values, rules provide a firm base that everyone in a family can count on.

Some rules may apply to everyone in a family. Your family may have a rule that everyone helps clear the table after meals. Some rules may be different for children of different ages. Younger children may have an earlier bedtime than older children.

Rules help you make decisions. If your family has a rule that you must call if you'll be late, you don't have to spend time thinking about whether or not you should call. You know the rule.

There may be times when you are even grateful for a family rule. If your friends want you to do something that you don't feel is right, you can truthfully state, "My family has a rule against that, so I can't." That's all you need to say. Understanding and following rules also ensures safety.

Family members don't always agree on rules. If this happens in your family, you should talk to your parents. Sometimes you may have to accept a decision you don't like. Even though accepting a rule that cannot be changed isn't always easy, understanding why a rule is important helps everyone obey it.

It may help to remember that rules in your family show you that you are loved. Your parents care enough to make rules to help keep you safe and healthy. As you get older and show that you are responsible, some of these rules may change.

▲ Many families have a rule that family members must call home if they will be late.

Career

Family Counselor

What They Do

Family counselors work with all members of a family. They help each person learn to express feelings in a safe way and to listen respectfully to others. They help family members learn how to work together and have fun together. They also help families learn to negotiate and solve problems.

Training

Family counselors must have a bachelor's degree. They also must have a master's degree or a doctorate in counseling or psychology. Many states also require one or two years of training in counseling.

JOURNAL

In your Health Journal, make a list of your family's rules. Then write the purpose of each. Put a star next to the rules that apply to you. How do you think the rules may change as you get older?

Sometimes families have trouble working out their differences. Some family members may have trouble obeying family rules. When this happens, some families get help from a counselor. A counselor listens to all family members and helps them reach a compromise they can all live with.

LESSON CHECKUP

Check Your Facts

1. Name three things you learned from family members.

2. How are values taught in families?

3. CRITICAL THINKING Why is it important to show respect for family members?

4. Name three good things about rules.

Set Health Goals

5. Think about ways you can cooperate in your family. Make a list of your ideas. Try to do one thing on your list each day.

COMMUNICATE
with Your Family

Family members must respect and support each other. Working on your communication skills will help you get along with family members.

Learn This Skill

Cynthia and her new best friend call each other every evening. Sometimes they are on the phone for a long time. Cynthia's family has put a ten-minute limit on phone conversations. Cynthia doesn't think this new rule is fair. What should she do?

1. Understand your audience.

Cynthia knows that she needs to talk to the whole family about the phone rules. She asks her dad to plan a family meeting.

2. Give a clear message.

Cynthia tells her family that she and her new friend don't have enough time to talk at school. She explains that ten minutes isn't long enough to say everything she wants to say.

3. Listen actively.

"If the phone is always busy, we might miss important calls," Cynthia's mom explains.
"I need to use the phone to plan my activities, too," says her brother.

4. Gather feedback.

Cynthia realizes that everyone else feels the new rule is fair, so she agrees to the ten-minute limit. Then the family thinks of other ways Cynthia can spend more time with her friend.

Practice This Skill

Use this summary as you solve the problems below.

Steps for Communicating

1. Understand your audience.
2. Give a clear message.
3. Listen actively.
4. Gather feedback.

A. Miguel has a new baby sister, and now he's feeling left out. How can he communicate his feelings to his parents?

B. As Peter and Vanessa were racing through the house, Vanessa broke her mother's favorite vase. Vanessa knows that running in the house is against the family rules. How can she use communication skills to explain to her mom what happened?

MAIN IDEA As you grow, your body will change and you will continue to develop as a special person.

WHY LEARN THIS? Learning what causes growth helps you understand the changes that you experience.

VOCABULARY
- inherited traits
- cell
- acquired traits
- cell membrane
- nucleus
- cytoplasm
- tissue
- organs
- body systems

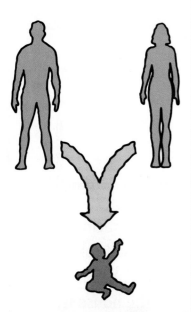

▲ Traits from both parents combine to make a unique human being.

You Are Growing Cell by Cell

You've probably heard that no two snowflakes are exactly alike. That's really true of people. No one else is exactly like you. Your special interests, skills, and talents come together to make you a special person.

▲ Musical talent can run in a family. A talent may be inherited, but a skill must be practiced.

How did you get your traits?

You have your own special combination of **inherited traits** (in•HAIR•uh•tid TRAYTS), or characteristics that were passed on to you from your parents. You may have red hair like your mother and a nose that looks like your father's. You may have blue eyes like both your parents. You may even have curly hair like your grand-mother's because she passed that trait to your father and he passed it on to you.

Each cell in your body contains a plan for inherited traits from your parents. A **cell** is the smallest working part of your body. Part of the plan came from your mother. Another part came from your father. The plans from your parents joined to make a new plan just for you. Look at the members of your family. You may see traits that many of your family members share.

Inherited traits also affect what happens inside your body. Your inherited body plan tells your cells when and how to divide and multiply. This message system affects when and how your brain will grow. It controls how fast your body grows and how tall you will become.

Not all of your traits are inherited. **Acquired traits** (uh•KWYRD TRAYTS) are things about you that did not come from either your mother or your father. You develop acquired traits as a result of your life experiences.

If you join a 4-H club and learn about animal care, you may develop an ability to raise and care for animals. If you grow up near a lake, you may become comfortable around water or skilled at swimming. If your family reads and enjoys books, you may be a good reader who also likes books. Acquired traits change as you learn and develop new interests and skills.

Some scientists are studying inherited and acquired traits. They sometimes disagree about which human traits are inherited and which are acquired. Scientists now think that some traits, such as musical and artistic abilities, are both inherited *and* acquired. For example, identical twins may share inherited artistic talent, but the twin who takes art lessons and practices drawing and painting will probably become the better artist.

Twins

When a mother has two babies at the same time, the children are called twins. Identical twins have the same plan for inherited traits. They look exactly alike and are either both boys or both girls. Fraternal twins may not look alike at all because they don't have identical plans for inherited traits. Fraternal twins can be girls, boys, or a girl and a boy.

▲ Inherited and acquired traits work together to make each person different from any other.

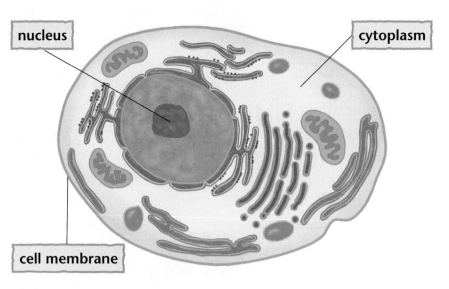

nucleus

cytoplasm

cell membrane

What happens inside a cell?

Living things are made up of cells. Cells take in food and get rid of waste. They grow, reproduce, and die. There are trillions of cells inside a human being. Each of your cells holds the plan for your growth.

Most cells are so small that they can be seen only through a microscope. Scientists call these tiny units the "building blocks of life." That's because cells combine to make all the parts of your body. Cells make millions of copies of themselves to help you grow.

The cells in your body come in many shapes and sizes. Each cell's shape helps it do its work. Nerve cells have long, wirelike parts that carry signals throughout the body. Red blood cells look like tiny, flat disks. Their flexible shape helps them pass through small spaces as they carry oxygen to the body. Each cell is designed to help your body stay alive.

If you looked at a cell under a microscope, you would see that it has many parts. The **cell membrane** holds the cell together. Its structure only lets certain materials into the cell. The **nucleus** (NOO•klee•uhs) is the control center of a cell. It contains your body's inherited plan. It tells the cell when and how to do its job. The **cytoplasm** (SY•tuh•pla•zuhm) is the jellylike fluid inside a cell. It contains many tiny structures, including the nucleus. All the parts of a cell work together.

HUMAN BODY CONNECTION

Organs in Body Systems

Body systems have important jobs to do. Each system helps keep you alive and healthy. Pick three body systems from pages 2 through 15. List the organs that make up each system.

• • •

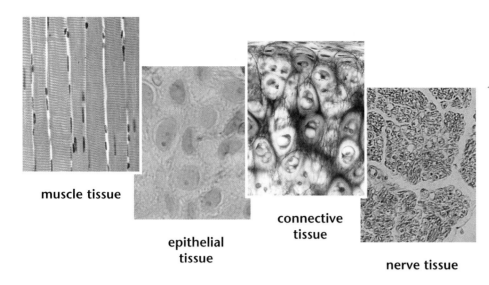

muscle tissue

epithelial
tissue

connective
tissue

nerve tissue

◀ Cells join together to
form four types of
tissues. Muscle, epithelial,
connective, and nerve
tissues all have different
jobs to do.

You grew from a single cell. This cell made millions of copies of itself. As the number of cells grew, cells began to form groups. A **tissue** is a group of cells that work together to do a job in the body.

Your body contains four kinds of tissues. Each is specially designed to do its job. Muscle tissue is made up of long, narrow cells. Muscle tissue cells contract and relax to make your body parts move. Epithelial tissue lines the surfaces inside your body. It also forms the outer layer of your skin. The wide, flat shape of epithelial tissue cells helps protect the outside of your body. Connective tissue, including bone, holds your body up and connects all its parts. Nerve tissue carries messages throughout your body.

Groups of tissues join together in structures called **organs**. Your organs include your heart, stomach, and lungs. Each organ has a special job to do. Your heart is a complex organ made of mainly muscle tissue. Its job is to pump blood throughout your body. Even your tongue is an organ made of special tissues that work together to help you eat, talk, and taste.

Some jobs inside your body are so big that several organs need to work together to get the job done. These groups of organs form **body systems**. Body systems help you breathe, digest food, carry messages from the brain to other parts of the body, and fight off disease.

Making the Skeletal System

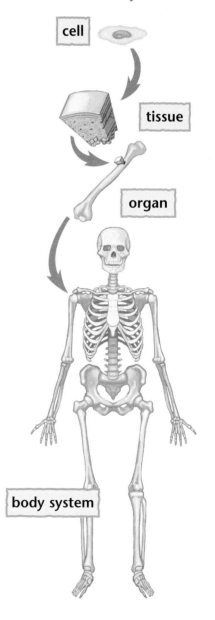

cell

tissue

organ

body system

Are you really "growing like a weed"?

Has anyone ever told you that you've "grown like a weed"? This means you grew taller in a short time. You grew like a weed before the age of two. This time of quick growth was your first growth spurt. At other times you will grow more slowly. As an adult you won't grow taller at all. When and how much you grow are part of the body plan you inherited from your parents.

▲ Look around! People come in all different shapes and heights. You will grow at your own rate until you reach the height you are supposed to be.

Between the ages of two and eleven, children grow about 2 or 3 inches each year. As young children, girls and boys are about the same size. This changes when girls have their second growth spurt at about age eleven. Then girls grow faster than boys for about two years, or until boys start their own growth spurt.

As you change and grow from a child to an adult, your looks will change in many ways. Every part of you will grow and develop. During your second growth spurt, the shape and size of your body will change as different body parts grow at different times and rates. For example, some boys' legs get longer before their arms start to grow. Your body shape and size will change many times until you become an adult and stop growing.

Your bones grow in a special way. Growing bones cause your body to change from your nose to your toes. When you were a baby, some bones in your body were made of a soft tissue. Your ears and the tip of your nose are still made of this material, which bends easily. When you were learning to walk, this soft material made it possible for you to fall without breaking a bone. As you grew taller, your bones became longer, harder, and thicker to support your growing body.

As you get older, you may be curious or even worry about the way you are growing. "Am I ever going to get taller?" "Is my nose too long?" "Why are my feet so big?" Worrying about growth is normal. Remember that everyone grows at his or her own rate. Growth differences are part of what makes you special.

CONSUMER FOCUS

Access Valid Health Information
Find out more about how bones grow. Research "bone turnover" in children. Also find out which minerals your bones store. Note where you find the information. Is it all valid? Use the steps for accessing valid health information on page *xvi* in the front of this book.

• • •

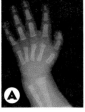
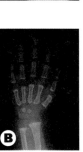
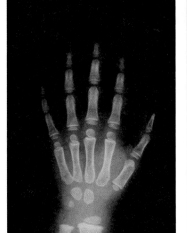
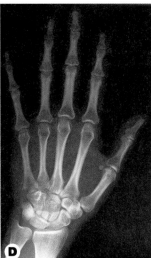

▲ The bones of your hands develop as you grow. These X-ray photos show the hands of (A) a newborn, (B) a six-month-old, (C) a two-year-old, and (D) a sixty-year-old. Look at how the wrist bones change over time.

LESSON CHECKUP

Check Your Facts

❶ Give two examples of inherited traits.

❷ CRITICAL THINKING How can you tell if twins you know are identical or fraternal?

❸ What is the job of a cell nucleus?

❹ Explain what a growth spurt is.

Set Health Goals

❺ List as many special qualities as you can about one or more members of your family. Underline the qualities that you would like to develop as acquired traits.

Your Brain and Nervous System: The Control Center for Growth

HUMAN BODY CONNECTION

The Nervous System

Find the nervous system on pages 14 and 15. Locate the central nervous system as well as some of the sense organs that form the peripheral nervous system.

• • •

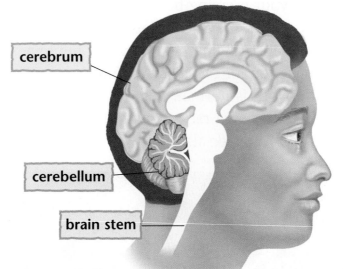

cerebrum

cerebellum

brain stem

How does your brain control your body?

How do you remember the way to school? Why do your eyes blink even though you don't think about it? How does your body know when it's time to grow faster? Your amazing brain manages these and many more activities.

Your brain and your nerve cells make up your nervous system. Your **nervous system** is a communication network that coordinates all your body's activities. Millions of messages are traveling around your body all the time to keep you alive, growing, and able to adjust to change.

The nervous system has two main parts, the central nervous system and the peripheral (puh•RIH•fuh•ruhl) nervous system. The brain and spinal cord make up the central nervous system. The peripheral nervous system is made of nerves that carry messages to and from the central nervous system.

The brain is the master control center of the nervous system. It has three main parts: the cerebrum, the cerebellum, and the brain stem.

The **cerebrum** (suh•REE•bruhm) is the biggest part of the brain. It is where all your thinking takes place. The **cerebellum** (sair•uh•BEH•luhm) is located in back of the cerebrum. It controls your movements. Without the cerebellum you couldn't keep your balance or stand up straight. Other parts of the brain are in the **brain stem**, which connects the cerebrum with the spinal cord.

The **hypothalamus** (hy•poh•THA•luh•muhs) is in the brain stem. It controls growth. When it's time for a growth spurt, the hypothalamus sends a message to the pituitary gland at the base of the brain. The **pituitary gland** (puh•TOO•uh•tair•ee GLAND) releases chemicals that make cells multiply quickly, causing you to grow.

MATH CONNECTION

Brain Race

On Your Own Nerve messages to the brain can travel at about 248 miles per hour. A thought travels at about 150 miles per hour. If you stubbed your toe, how much faster would your nerves tell your brain about it before you started thinking about how much your toe hurt?

▼ Different parts of the brain control different body functions.

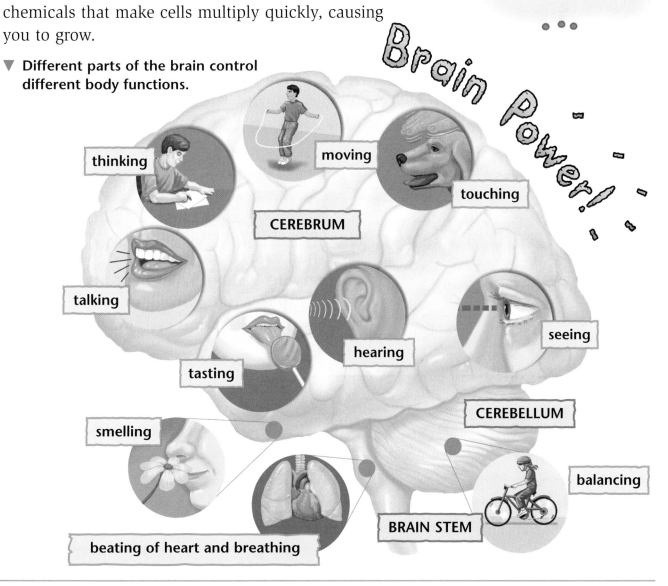

thinking

moving

touching

CEREBRUM

talking

tasting

hearing

seeing

CEREBELLUM

smelling

balancing

BRAIN STEM

beating of heart and breathing

Brain Power!

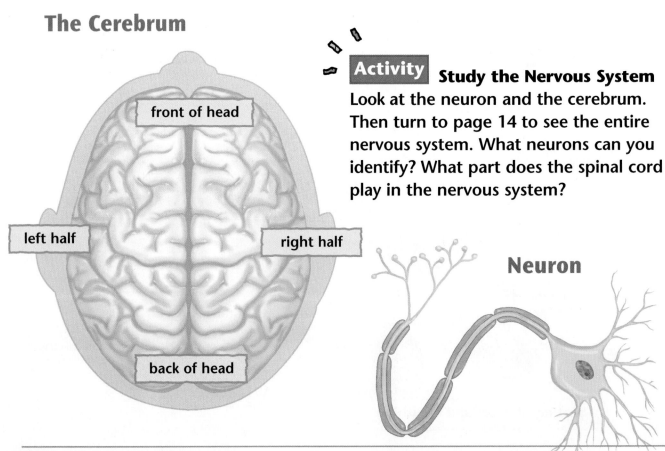

What else does your brain do?

To keep you alive, your brain has to know everything that affects you. Thanks to the millions of messages the nervous system sends, your brain knows how to react when something happens. If you have a cold, if a car is coming toward you, or if the temperature drops, the brain orders the nervous system to tell the right parts of the body to rest, get out of the way, or put on a jacket.

Your nervous system uses nerve cells called **neurons** (NOO•rahnz) to carry its messages. You have millions of neurons in your body. Each neuron has tiny branches that allow it to connect to other neurons. When you were born, you had the same number of neurons that you have now. In order for you to learn something new, like riding a bike, the messages had to travel from one neuron to another, over and over again. In time the brain made pathways between the neurons. Then riding your bike became easier, and you could do it without falling. Your brain builds more new pathways as you continue to learn new things.

Did you know?

The brain's nearly 10 billion nerve cells use more than 100,000 chemical reactions a second to send, receive, and process information while coordinating the body's activities.

The Cerebrum

front of head

left half

right half

back of head

Activity **Study the Nervous System**
Look at the neuron and the cerebrum. Then turn to page 14 to see the entire nervous system. What neurons can you identify? What part does the spinal cord play in the nervous system?

Neuron

The brain makes it possible for you to learn new things and to remember what you already know. Scientists have found that memories are stored in many parts of the brain. When you remember a trip to the beach, for example, the memory of the smell of salt water is stored in a different place from the memory of the sound of the waves.

You build memory power through practice. Memorizing chess moves or songs on the piano helps improve your memory. Connecting something you want to remember with something else that is interesting helps memory. You may have learned songs to help you memorize the alphabet or the names of all the states.

The brain is also the center of your emotions. When a barking dog surprises you, your brain produces feelings of fear. When someone breaks a toy you like, you feel anger.

You need your brain to live. It controls your body systems, growth, ability to think, memory, and emotions. It is important to make choices that help your brain stay healthy and do its many important jobs.

▶ **The nervous system allows us to respond to changes in our environment. When it rains, people respond by opening their umbrellas.**

LESSON CHECKUP

Check Your Facts

1. Which body system controls your memory and emotions?
2. What functions does your brain control?
3. CRITICAL THINKING How does practicing a skill help your brain do its job?
4. Where does the brain store memories?

Set Health Goals

5. Like all other parts of your body, your brain is affected by the way you take care of it. Think about the choices you make every day that affect your health. List two choices that help you take care of your brain. Name one choice that would put your brain at risk.

USE VOCABULARY

acquired traits (p. 65)	cerebrum (p. 71)	inherited traits (p. 64)	single-parent
blended family (p. 51)	cooperate (p. 56)	nervous system (p. 70)	family (p. 50)
body systems (p. 67)	cytoplasm (p. 66)	neurons (p. 72)	tissue (p. 67)
brain stem (p. 71)	extended family	nuclear family (p. 50)	traditions (p. 54)
cell (p. 64)	(p. 54)	nucleus (p. 66)	values (p. 56)
cell membrane (p. 66)	generations (p. 56)	organs (p. 67)	
cerebellum (p. 71)	hypothalamus (p. 71)	pituitary gland (p. 71)	

Use the terms above to complete the sentences. Page numbers in ( ) tell you where to look in the chapter if you need help.

1. A family with children, parents, and a grandparent is one kind of ____.

2. A cell is held together by the ____.

3. Repeated customs that are passed from generation to generation are called ____.

4. Your ____ develop from your life experiences.

5. The control center of a cell is called the ____.

6. Honesty is one of the ____ that many parents teach by example to their children.

7. The ____ is the part of your brain that makes you able to keep your balance.

8. A group of cells that work together to do a job is called a ____.

9. If you can work together and get along with other people, it shows that you know how to ____.

10. Each ____ in your body contains a plan for inherited traits.

11. The name for a family made up of one parent and one or more children who live together is ____.

12. Blue eyes and curly hair are examples of ____.

13. Nerve cells are called ____.

14. Your heart and stomach are body ____.

15. Grandparents, parents, and children make up three ____ of family.

16. Organs that work together to do a complex job form ____.

17. The ____ at the base of your brain releases chemicals that cause your body to grow.

18. The ____ in the brain stem sends out a message when it's time for a growth spurt.

19. A family with stepparents and two stepbrothers is one kind of ____.

20. The jellylike fluid inside a cell is called ____.

21. The _____ is a communication network that coordinates all your body's activities.

22. Parents, brothers, and sisters form a _____.

23. The _____ is connected to the spinal cord.

24. The biggest part of your brain is your _____.

CHECK YOUR FACTS

25. List five things you could learn from a grandparent. (pp. 54–55)

26. Name three ways you can learn values from family members. (pp. 56–57)

27. Give two examples of how a cell's shape helps it do its job. (p. 66)

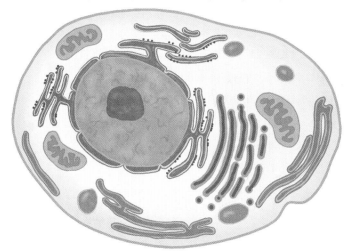

28. List the two main parts of the nervous system. (p. 70)

THINK CRITICALLY

29. If you could plan a perfect evening with your whole family, what would you do together?

30. If you were to meet a scientist who studies the brain, what questions would you ask him or her about the brain?

APPLY LIFE SKILLS

31. **Communicate** Suppose you wanted to volunteer at a local wildlife shelter. What positive traits would you list on your application to show you could do a responsible job in this position?

32. **Resolve Conflict** Suppose you want your parents to let you stay up one hour later on Friday nights, but you don't think they will agree. List what you think their concerns will be. Keeping those concerns in mind, how will you convince them that a later bedtime would be OK? When would be the best time to talk with them? What will you do if you do not get your way?

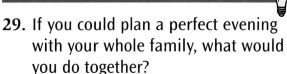

Promote Health — Home and Community

1. Tell family members what you learned about the importance of respecting and appreciating each other. Let each person in your family know what you appreciate about him or her. Give each family member a chance to do the same thing.

2. For your school library, design a poster titled "Boost Your Brain Power!" What kinds of activities will you include on it?

Activities

Mending Bones

With a Team • Research why bones sometimes break. What do doctors do to help repair breaks? How do bones grow back together? How do you think therapy and nutrition help the healing process?

My Favorite Tradition

On Your Own • Think of your favorite family tradition. Ask your parents where it came from. Describe it in words and in drawings.

It's All in the Family

At Home • Make a list of questions for your parents and other family members about physical traits that have been shared by your family for generations. List the traits. Beside each one, write the names of family members who have the trait.

Families at Play!

With a Partner • Look through magazines to find as many examples of families having fun together as you can. Combine your pictures to make a poster entitled Families at Play.

Multiple Choice

Choose the letter of the correct answer.

1. A blended family could be ____.
   a. a parent and children
   b. children, parents, and grandparents
   c. one parent, a child, and a cat
   d. a parent, stepparent, and children

2. A(n) ____ family is *not* a family group.
   a. complex   b. blended
   c. nuclear   d. extended

3. Twins who are different sexes or who do not look alike are called ____.
   a. acquired   b. blended
   c. fraternal   d. identical

4. Tissue that covers your body is called ____ tissue.
   a. epithelial   b. muscle
   c. nerve   d. connective

5. The ____ holds the cell together.
   a. cytoplasm   b. neuron
   c. cell membrane   d. nucleus

Modified True or False

Write *true* or *false*. If a sentence is false, replace the underlined term to make the sentence true.

6. Your <u>role</u> in the family changes as you get older.

7. Your body has <u>millions</u> of cells.

8. An <u>extended family</u> is made up of two parents and their children.

9. The parts of your personality you developed from your own experiences are called <u>inherited traits</u>.

10. <u>Values</u> are taught by parents through example, stories, and spiritual beliefs.

11. You grow because your cells <u>subtract</u>.

12. The <u>nucleus</u> is the jellylike fluid inside a cell.

13. Calling home when you will be late is an example of a family <u>rule</u>.

14. You have <u>two</u> major growth spurts in your lifetime.

15. The <u>cerebrum</u> is the part of your brain that controls growth.

Short Answer

Write a complete sentence to answer each question.

16. How does the brain send its messages throughout the body?

17. Name three ways a family can cooperate at mealtimes.

18. What helps you remember things you don't want to forget?

19. Why do you think cells are called the building blocks of life?

20. Why is it important to respect and appreciate each family member?

21. Tell how an organ is different from a tissue.

22. How do the shape and size of your body change as you grow?

23. Why is it sometimes helpful to have a rule to fall back on? Give an example.

Writing in Health

Write paragraphs to answer each item.

24. Think of a time when you stood up for yourself. Now imagine you are a grandparent. Write the story as you would tell it to your grandchild.

25. Explain how your cells, tissues, organs, and body systems work together to keep you alive.

Your Health and Fitness

MAKE A PERSONAL HEALTH BROCHURE
Use colored paper and markers to make a brochure that shows how to take good care of your skin, teeth, gums, eyes, and ears. Share your brochure with your family.

For other activities, visit the Harcourt Learning Site. www.harcourtschool.com

MAIN IDEA
Taking care of your skin is important for your health.

WHY LEARN THIS? Understanding how your skin protects you can help you make good choices about caring for it.

VOCABULARY
• epidermis
• dermis
• oil glands
• sweat glands
• pores
• sunscreen

MATH CONNECTION

Count Hairs

On Your Own Cut a one-inch square hole in a sheet of paper. Hold the paper on top of your forearm. Use a hand lens to count the hairs on your arm visible inside the square hole. Measure your whole arm and use the count to estimate how many hairs are on your arm.

• • •

Your Skin and Its Care

Your bones hold you up. Your muscles help you move. Your heart pumps your blood. All these important organs are enclosed and protected by your largest organ—your skin. Taking care of your skin helps your skin take care of you.

What is your skin?

As the diagram at right shows, skin has two main layers. The top layer is called the epidermis. The **epidermis** (eh•puh•DER•muhs) is a tough, waterproof barrier. It holds moisture inside your body and keeps germs out. Germs can't pass through your skin unless the epidermis is broken. That's why it's important to wash cuts and scrapes and keep them clean until they heal.

The top of the epidermis is made of dead skin cells that flake off easily. This hardened layer of cells prevents germs from entering your body. The lower cells of the epidermis rapidly divide to make new cells. In time the lower cells die and are pushed toward the surface. As the top skin cells flake off, the new cells from below replace them.

The bottom layer of skin is called the dermis. The **dermis** (DER•muhs) is thicker than the epidermis, and it contains blood vessels and nerve endings.

I'm hot!

▶ How will sweating help this girl cool off?

It also contains oil glands. **Oil glands** make oil that helps soften your skin. Oil reaches the surface of your skin through openings called follicles.

Sweat is produced by structures called **sweat glands** in the dermis. Sweat reaches the skin's surface through openings called **pores**. You sweat the most when you are hot because sweat helps cool your body. Sweat changes from a liquid to a gas in a process called evaporation. Evaporation takes energy. The energy for sweat evaporation comes from the heat of your body. So your body loses heat and cools as sweat evaporates.

You might be surprised to learn that your hair and nails are also made of dead skin cells. Hair and nail cells form deep inside your skin. A strand of hair is a narrow stack of dead skin cells piled one on top of the other. A fingernail or toenail is a broad, flat sheet of dead skin cells. Your hair and nails grow because new cells push against the dead cells from below.

SCIENCE CONNECTION

Examine Your Skin

On Your Own Use a hand lens to examine the skin on the back of your hand. Compare what you see with the skin cross-section shown below. List the parts of the skin you can see.

○ ◉ ○

The Skin

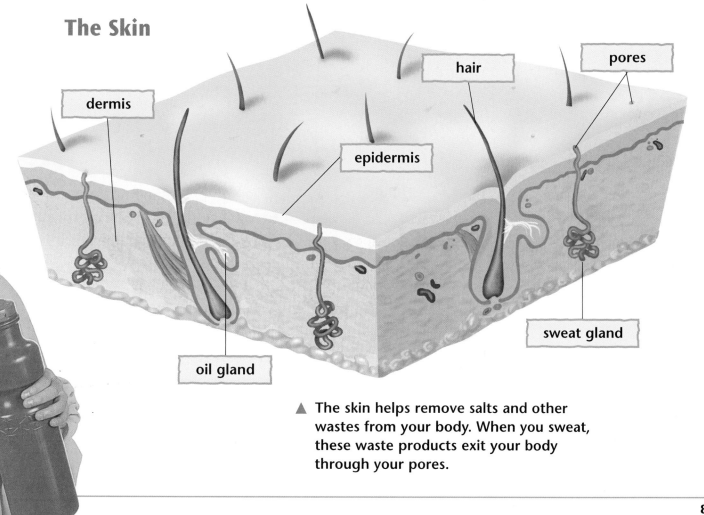

dermis

hair

pores

epidermis

oil gland

sweat gland

▲ The skin helps remove salts and other wastes from your body. When you sweat, these waste products exit your body through your pores.

How can you take care of your skin?

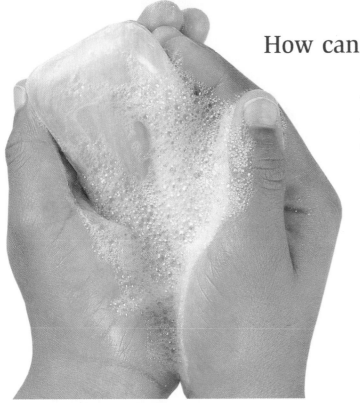

▲ Any kind of soap will loosen dirt and germs from your hands. For thorough cleaning, scrub for 20 seconds or longer before rinsing.

Myth: Antibacterial soap is the best soap for everyday use.

Fact: Regular soap and water are fine for everyday use. Overuse of antibacterial soap has been linked to the possible production of dangerous, drug-resistant bacteria.

Keeping your skin clean is one of the best ways to help it stay healthy. If your hands and face are dirty, germs might enter your body when you touch your eyes, nose, or mouth. Germs that cause colds and flu are often spread this way.

When you wash your hands, germs you have picked up from things you've touched are rinsed away. It's important to wash your hands after blowing your nose and after sneezing or coughing into your hands. Also, wash your hands after you go to the bathroom or handle anything that is dirty. If you touch an animal, wash your hands afterward. Always wash your hands just before you handle or eat food.

When you wash your hands, rub them all over with soap and warm water. Squeeze the suds between your fingers. Wash the skin on your knuckles and around your fingernails. Get underneath your nails, too, because dirt and germs tend to build up there. Use a nailbrush to do a thorough job. Then rinse your hands well to wash away the dirt and germs. You can use lotion if your hands feel tight and dry after washing.

Wash your face at least twice a day. Most people wash their faces before going to bed and after waking up. Use soap, warm water, and a clean washcloth. Having a clean face helps you look good and feel good about yourself.

Bathing also helps you look and feel refreshed. If you are very active, take a bath or shower every day. When the weather is cold and dry, you might bathe every few days instead so your skin won't get too flaky or itchy. Wash your hair with shampoo when it begins to look or feel dirty. Some people need to wash their hair daily. Others can go for several days without shampooing.

Washing is not the only way to take care of your skin. You also need to protect your skin from the sun.

Sunlight can harm your skin. It can cause your skin to burn, dry out, and wrinkle. Over time, too much sun can cause a serious disease called skin cancer.

Sunscreen is a lotion or cream that protects your skin from the sun's harmful rays. Sunscreen containers list the Sun Protection Factor (SPF), a number between 2 and 50. The higher the number, the more protection the sunscreen will give you. If possible, stay out of the strongest sun, between 10:00 A.M. and 3:00 P.M., to protect your skin. Protecting your skin from sun now will help you have healthy skin all your life.

JOURNAL

Record the times you wash your hands this week. When the week is over, look at your record. Do you think you should change your hand-washing habits? Give reasons to explain your answer. Remember, your journal is private and need not be shared with others.

▼ Wearing a hat, covering up with a shirt or other clothing, and using sunscreen are all ways to protect your skin from the sun.

LESSON CHECKUP

Check Your Facts

1 What does your skin do for you?

2 CRITICAL THINKING Why might biting your fingernails lead to infection?

3 Why is it important to protect your skin from the sun, and how can you do it?

Set Health Goals

4 List the skin, hair, and nail products you use. Are there any additional products you should be using? Do you think the products you've listed are all necessary?

MAIN IDEA Taking care of your teeth and gums is important for your health.

WHY LEARN THIS? Knowing about your teeth and gums will help you make good choices about caring for them.

VOCABULARY
• plaque
• cavities
• decay
• fluoride

Your Teeth and Their Care

Here's a riddle. You talk with them. You eat with them. They are small, sharp, and white. Can you guess what they are? They are your teeth. Caring for your teeth helps you stay healthy and look your best. If you take care of your teeth, they will last your whole life.

What causes tooth and gum problems?

You use your teeth to chew food. Chewing is one of their main functions. However, the food you chew can also cause problems for your teeth. Leftover bits of food and bacteria can stick to your teeth. The bacteria are part of a sticky natural material called **plaque**.

Bacteria in plaque break down sugars in food and form acids. The acids can make holes called **cavities** (KA·vuh·teez) in the outer surfaces of your teeth. Cavities can grow and grow. They sometimes reach deep inside a tooth and cause pain. The process of forming cavities is called tooth decay. **Decay** (dih·KAY) happens when things rot. If a decaying tooth is not treated in time, it can die.

Many people have tooth decay problems because plaque is constantly forming in the mouth. Clinging to teeth, plaque's bacteria go to work on food that remains in the mouth. Sticky, starchy, or sugary foods—such as candy, chewing gum, and even raisins—can mean trouble. Frequent snacking on these types of foods keeps sugar in the mouth all the time. As bacteria break down the sugars, the teeth come under constant attack from acids.

◀ A disclosing tablet can help you see plaque on your teeth. As you chew the tablet, plaque turns purple. Then you can floss and brush until no purple remains.

If left on teeth, plaque hardens. Hardened plaque is called tartar. Tartar rubs against the gums and can make them bleed. It can lead to an infection that destroys the bone holding teeth in place. With serious gum disease even healthy teeth can fall out.

Fortunately, preventing dental problems is easy. One way to prevent decay is to avoid sugary and sticky snacks. Brushing your teeth or at least rinsing your mouth with water after you eat such foods is a good idea. You need to brush twice a day and floss once a day to keep your teeth and gums healthy.

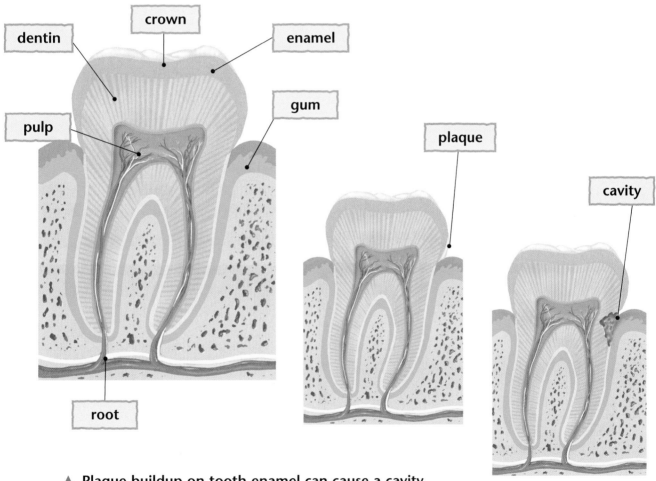

dentin
crown
enamel
pulp
gum
root
plaque
cavity

▲ Plaque buildup on tooth enamel can cause a cavity to form. You can't feel a cavity in its early stages because tooth enamel has no nerves. If the cavity reaches the dentin, bacteria can travel through it to the pulp. Nerves in the pulp may swell with infection, causing pain.

How can you prevent tooth and gum problems?

Proper flossing and brushing help prevent tooth and gum problems. To floss, cut off about 18 inches of dental floss. Wind the floss around your two middle fingers, with most of it around the middle finger of one hand. Leave 2 to 3 inches of floss stretched between your fingers. Insert the floss between two teeth. Gently raise and lower the floss, moving it back and forth against one tooth to scrape away plaque.

At the gum line, curve the floss around the lower part of one side of the tooth. Rub the floss against the lower edge of that tooth. Do the same to the other tooth. Gently remove the floss. Unwind a clean section for the next pair of teeth. Continue until you have flossed all your teeth, including the far edges of your back teeth.

When you brush, use a fluoride toothpaste. **Fluoride** (FLAWR•yd) is a mineral that helps prevent cavities. Brush all the surfaces of your teeth. Brush the fronts and sides with gentle circular strokes. Be sure to brush the chewing surfaces of your back teeth thoroughly. Plaque can build up in the pits of these teeth, so take extra time brushing them.

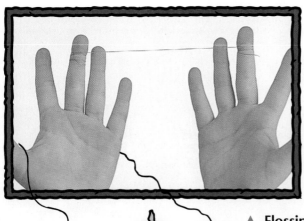

Floss daily!

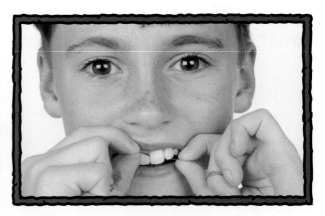

▲ Flossing removes plaque from between your teeth. Many dentists recommend that you floss before brushing. Your toothbrush will remove stray bits of plaque and food scattered by flossing. Check with your dentist to see what he or she recommends.

Don't forget to brush the inner surfaces of all your teeth. You will have to turn your toothbrush different ways to clean these surfaces well. When you've finished brushing, rinse your mouth with water. Rinsing removes the food and plaque you loosened by brushing.

Flossing and brushing aren't the only ways to prevent problems with teeth and gums. You also need to choose healthful snacks. Milk products and fruits help build strong teeth and are a good choice if you can brush your teeth soon after eating. Crunchy vegetables are the best choice if you can't brush right away.

Visiting a dentist twice a year is another important way to prevent tooth and gum problems. The dentist or a dental hygienist will remove tartar and check for cavities and signs of gum disease. The dentist may coat your teeth with extra fluoride to strengthen them or apply dental sealants to back teeth to keep cavities from growing on chewing surfaces. Your dentist will work with you to help keep your teeth and gums healthy.

▲ When would be the best time to choose each of these foods as a snack?

▲ Use your toothbrush to remove plaque from the tooth surfaces you can reach. To clean along the gum line, hold the brush at an angle. You can then brush in a circular pattern, or flick the toothbrush away from the gum line to remove plaque and food. Use the tip of your toothbrush to reach the inner surfaces of your front teeth.

How can you choose dental care products?

The next time you visit a grocery store, look for toothpaste. How many different kinds can you find? When you choose a toothpaste, look for the word *fluoride* on the label. Or, look for the American Dental Association (ADA) Seal of Acceptance. Any toothpaste with this seal has fluoride. Brush twice a day with a fluoride toothpaste that has the ADA Seal of Acceptance.

Some toothpastes have a chemical that can kill some bacteria in your mouth. But the chemical doesn't replace daily flossing. You need to floss daily to reach the spaces between your teeth.

You can buy dental floss that is waxed or unwaxed. Waxed floss may be easier to use if your teeth are very close together. You can also buy flavored or plain floss.

▼ **Any toothpaste with the ADA Seal will help remove plaque and fight cavities—and it may be a better buy. The ADA Seal is given by the American Dental Association.**

ADA ACCEPTED American Dental Association ®

Tartar control. These toothpastes help prevent tartar buildup, but only your dentist can remove tartar below the gum line.

Baking soda. Make sure the baking soda toothpaste also contains fluoride to fight cavities. It should have the ADA Seal.

Whitening toothpaste. Ask your dentist about whitening toothpastes. Many regular toothpastes are just as effective.

88

Dental Hygienist

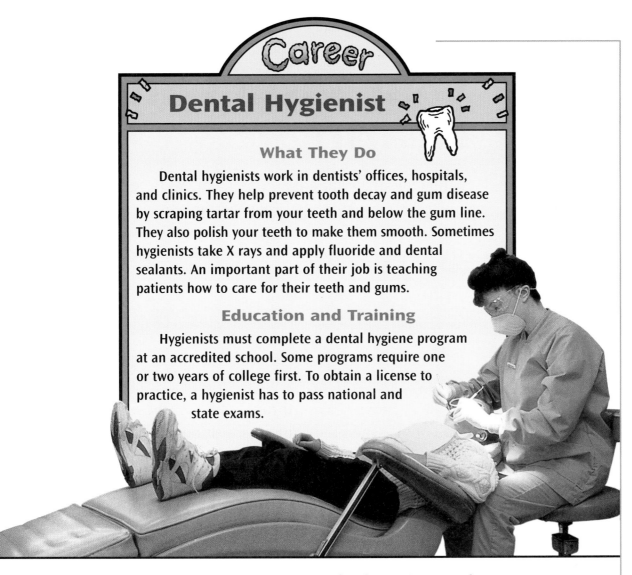

What They Do

Dental hygienists work in dentists' offices, hospitals, and clinics. They help prevent tooth decay and gum disease by scraping tartar from your teeth and below the gum line. They also polish your teeth to make them smooth. Sometimes hygienists take X rays and apply fluoride and dental sealants. An important part of their job is teaching patients how to care for their teeth and gums.

Education and Training

Hygienists must complete a dental hygiene program at an accredited school. Some programs require one or two years of college first. To obtain a license to practice, a hygienist has to pass national and state exams.

Toothbrushes come in a variety of colors, sizes, and shapes. Choose a toothbrush with soft bristles. It will remove plaque without hurting your gums. Look for the ADA Seal on toothbrushes and dental floss. You can also ask your parents, dentist, or dental hygienist to help you choose a good toothpaste, dental floss, or toothbrush. A dentist or dental hygienist can show you how to use these tools to take good care of your teeth.

LESSON CHECKUP

Check Your Facts

❶ How can plaque cause dental problems?

❷ CRITICAL THINKING Does your own flossing and brushing routine need to be changed? Explain.

❸ How does visiting the dentist help you have healthy teeth and gums?

Use Life Skills

❹ REFUSE Imagine that a friend wants you to eat a candy bar as a snack. Write how you might refuse the candy bar without hurting your friend's feelings. Include a list of snacks you could eat that are more healthful choices.

Your Vision and Hearing

Imagine that you are at a carnival. You see a funny clown walk by. You hear the cheerful tune of a merry-go-round. You enjoy all the sights and sounds. Your vision and hearing help you appreciate the world around you.

What are some problems people have with vision?

To understand how vision works, look at the diagram of the eye below. Light bounces off objects, like the bird. The light enters the eye through a hole called the **pupil** (PYOO•puhl). Then the light passes through a clear, curved structure called the **lens** (LENZ). The lens bends the light to form an image on the back part of the eye. This back part of the eye is called the **retina** (REH•tuhn•uh). Nerves carry the image from the retina to the brain. When the image reaches your brain, you see the object.

Your Eyes

The colored part of the eye is the iris. The iris may be blue, green, brown, or a mixture of those colors. Turn to page 2 of The Amazing Human Body to learn more about your eyes.

▼ Your eyes adjust to different conditions. In a dark place, your pupils get bigger to let in more light. Your lenses change shape to help you focus on both nearby and distant objects.

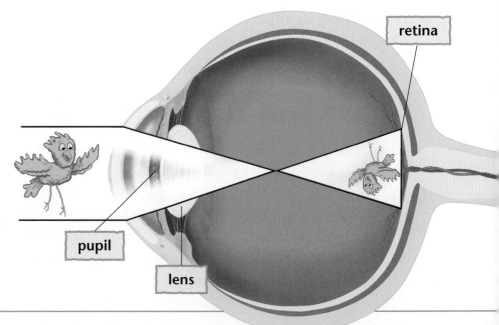

retina

pupil

lens

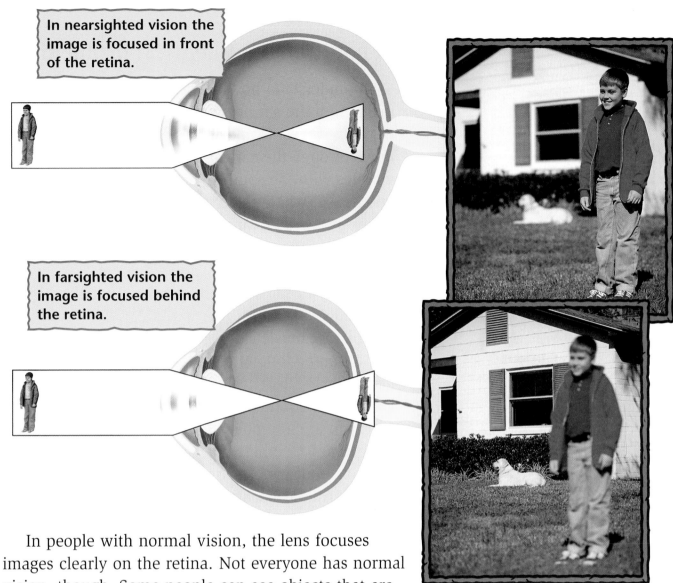

In nearsighted vision the image is focused in front of the retina.

In farsighted vision the image is focused behind the retina.

▲ The photos show how the same scene might appear to a nearsighted person (top) and a farsighted person (bottom).

In people with normal vision, the lens focuses images clearly on the retina. Not everyone has normal vision, though. Some people can see objects that are close to them, but they have a hard time seeing things that are far away. These people are **nearsighted**. In nearsighted people the eye focuses images in front of the retina. This causes a blurry image on the retina.

Other people can see things well when they look into the distance, but they have a hard time seeing things that are close to them. These people are **farsighted**. In farsighted people the eye focuses images behind the retina. The image from the retina that travels to the brain is blurry, too.

People who are nearsighted or farsighted may wear glasses or contact lenses. These artificial lenses focus images correctly on the retina. Glasses and contacts allow most nearsighted or farsighted people to see as clearly as people who have normal vision.

What are some hearing problems?

To understand how hearing works, look at the diagram of the ear below. Sounds, like the bird's song, travel in waves. Sound waves enter your outer ear and move through the ear canal. They hit the eardrum, which vibrates with the sound. The vibrations pass into the middle ear, where three tiny bones vibrate, too. These bones pass the vibrations to the inner ear. In the inner ear the vibrations are changed into nerve signals that travel to the brain. When your brain receives the nerve signals, you hear the sound.

Loud sounds from heavy traffic, noisy machines, and blaring music can permanently damage your inner ear. Listening to loud sounds is a main cause of hearing loss. **Hearing loss** has occurred when a person can no longer hear sounds that he or she was once able to hear.

If you are in a noisy place where you must shout to be heard by others, the sounds around you may be harming your ears. If your ears ring when a noise stops, some harm has occurred already. Your ears probably will recover from hearing loud sounds once, but listening to loud sounds again and again will cause hearing loss.

Your Ears

The tiniest bone in your body is in your middle ear. To learn the name of this bone and other interesting facts about your ears, turn to page 2.

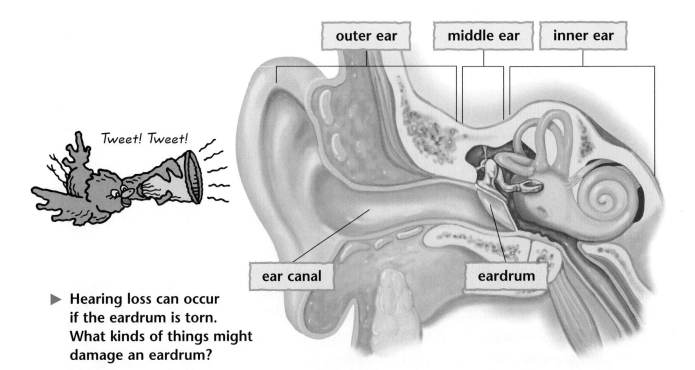

Tweet! Tweet!

▶ Hearing loss can occur if the eardrum is torn. What kinds of things might damage an eardrum?

How can you protect your eyes and ears?

You can't prevent all vision and hearing problems. For example, some people are born with vision and hearing problems. But you can prevent many injuries. Follow these safety rules:

- Keep sharp objects away from your eyes and ears. Even cotton swabs can poke holes in the eardrums.
- Wear safety goggles when using hammers or other tools.
- Protect your ears from loud sounds. Turn down the volume on radios and headphones. Wear earplugs, or leave noisy places.
- Wear sunglasses to shield your eyes from sunlight.
- Get an eye exam every two years if you wear glasses or contacts. Get an exam every three to five years if you have normal vision.
- Wear a helmet with ear protection when you play sports.
- Have your ears checked by a doctor if they hurt or leak fluid or if you have hearing loss.

Protection Poster

With a Partner Make a poster showing how to protect the eyes or ears. Draw pictures and write one or more slogans. Share your poster with younger students.

▶ A hard hit on the ear can damage hearing. Be sure to protect your ears when playing baseball, hockey, and other sports.

LESSON CHECKUP

Check Your Facts

1. Describe how ears work.

2. CRITICAL THINKING Name three sounds that could possibly damage your hearing. How can you protect yourself from each sound?

3. Describe how eyes work.

Set Health Goals

4. How can you protect your eyes? Make a list of things you can do, and share your list with the class.

Your Posture

MAIN IDEA
Having good posture is important for your self-image and your health.

WHY LEARN THIS? Learning how to hold your body correctly will help you take pride in your appearance and stay healthy.

VOCABULARY
• posture

Picture yourself receiving an award from the President of the United States. The award might be for doing good work in school or for your athletic skills. It might be for helping others in your community. You would stand tall and walk proudly to get your prize. Standing tall and walking with pride are not just for receiving special awards. Good posture is important every day.

What is good posture?

Your **posture** (PAHS•cher) is the way you hold your body. Having good posture helps you feel good about yourself. It also helps prevent problems with your bones, muscles, and joints, especially as you get older. Good posture gives your inner organs room to function. It helps your whole body work at its best.

The pictures here show how to stand and walk with good posture.

HUMAN BODY CONNECTION

Moving Along
Your spine and the muscles attached to it allow you to bend, twist, and move in different ways. Turn to pages 4–7 to learn more about how your skeletal and muscular systems work together.

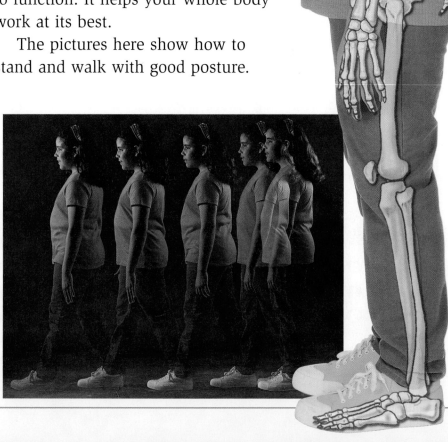

Activity **Practice Good Posture**

Practice standing, walking, sitting, and lifting the way the pictures show. Ask a friend to look at your posture and suggest improvements. Listen to your friend's suggestions and try them. Then switch roles.

When you have good posture, your ears, shoulders, and hips are in a straight line. Your chin is parallel to the floor. Your shoulders are level, and your knees are relaxed. Your spine is as straight as possible with only a slight *S*-shaped curve. Hold this posture when you walk. It helps to imagine that a string is pulling gently upward on the center of your head.

You should also have good posture when you sit down. Always sit with your back straight. This is important whether you are sitting in a hard or a soft chair. When you write at a desk, pull your chair close to the desk. You should not lean over your work. Rest your feet flat on the floor or on a footstool to help prevent backaches.

Good posture is also important when you lift heavy things. Never bend over to lift something heavy. Instead, bend your knees and squat so the object is in front of you. Grasp the object close to your body and keep your back straight. Lift the object by slowly straightening your legs. Let your legs, not your back, do the hard work.

FOCUS

Communicate

Isaac's cousin Josh carries four books home each night, even if he isn't going to use them. Josh uses one shoulder strap to wear his backpack. How can Issac communicate in a positive way the benefits of properly wearing a backpack? Use the steps for communicating shown on page *xii*.

• • •

How can you have good posture when using a computer?

It is important to practice good posture when you sit at a computer. Good posture at the computer lets you work or play longer without getting tired or achy.

When you sit at a computer, sit up straight. Use the picture below as your model. Use the same good posture you use when writing at a desk. Sit back in your chair, and relax your shoulders. Let the chair support your shoulders and back.

Whenever you can, work at a computer with an adjustable keyboard rack that you can raise and lower. You should be able to type without having to reach up or bend forward over the keyboard. Keep your wrists straight when you type. When you use the mouse, hold it loosely to prevent cramps in your hand.

An adjustable chair is also important. Adjust the seat to a good height so that the monitor is at eye level and the keyboard is at wrist level. Adjusting the chair may mean your feet don't touch the floor. If this happens, find a footrest. Your feet should rest flat on it.

Good lighting also is important when you work at a computer. Working in poor light can strain your eyes, making them feel tired or sore. Things may begin to look blurred, or you may get a headache. Work in a well-lit room. Make sure that the lights don't shine directly on the screen. Glare from the screen can cause eyestrain. Also, try to avoid working at a computer in front of or opposite an uncovered window. The outside light can make it hard to read the screen. A filter placed over the screen can help lessen the glare.

You can do other simple things to prevent eyestrain and muscle soreness when you work at a computer. Blink your eyes often to moisten them. Look away from the screen every few minutes. Looking into the distance gives your eyes a chance to rest and refocus. Sitting at a computer can tire you as much as some sports. Your muscles can feel tired from lack of movement. Standing up and stretching at least once every half hour allows your muscles to relax.

Myth: Reading or using a computer in a room with only dim light will ruin your eyesight.

Fact: Bad lighting cannot ruin your eyesight. It can, however, make your eyes get tired faster.

LESSON CHECKUP

Check Your Facts

❶ CRITICAL THINKING If a person has bad posture for years, what problems might he or she develop?

❷ Describe the correct way to lift something heavy.

❸ What are three tips for preventing eyestrain when working at a computer?

Use Life Skills

❹ COMMUNICATE Draw three cartoons of people working at computers. In each cartoon, show a different posture problem. Share your cartoons with a classmate. Discuss how the people in the cartoons could avoid or correct their posture problems.

The Muscular System

Your muscles work
in groups to move
different parts of
your body. Turn to
pages 6–7 of The
Amazing Human
Body to learn more
about your
muscular system.

Your Physical Fitness

On Monday you go swimming. On Tuesday you carry a big stack of books to the library. On Wednesday you walk to your music lesson. On Thursday you play softball. On Friday you help your parents clean the house. Over the weekend you play active games. If you follow a schedule like this one, you have the energy to do the things you want to do. In other words, you are physically fit. Exercising—doing activities that make your body work hard—helps you become fit and stay that way.

How can different exercises help your muscles?

Different exercises do different things for muscles. Some exercises build **muscle strength**. When your muscles are strong, they can apply a lot of force. Exercises that build muscle strength include rope climbing, pull-ups, push-ups, and abdominal crunches, also called curl-ups.

Some exercises build **flexibility** (flek•suh•BIH•luh•tee). If you are flexible, you can bend and twist comfortably. Exercises that stretch your muscles make you flexible. Standing on your toes and reaching toward the ceiling is one stretching exercise. Touching your toes is another. The picture on page 99 shows a stretching exercise that builds flexibility.

Other exercises build **endurance** (in•DUR•uhnts). Your muscles have endurance when they can work hard for a long time. The muscles may get a little tired, but you can still keep going. To build endurance, you must exercise for at least twenty minutes at a time. Jogging, bicycling, and jumping rope are activities that build endurance.

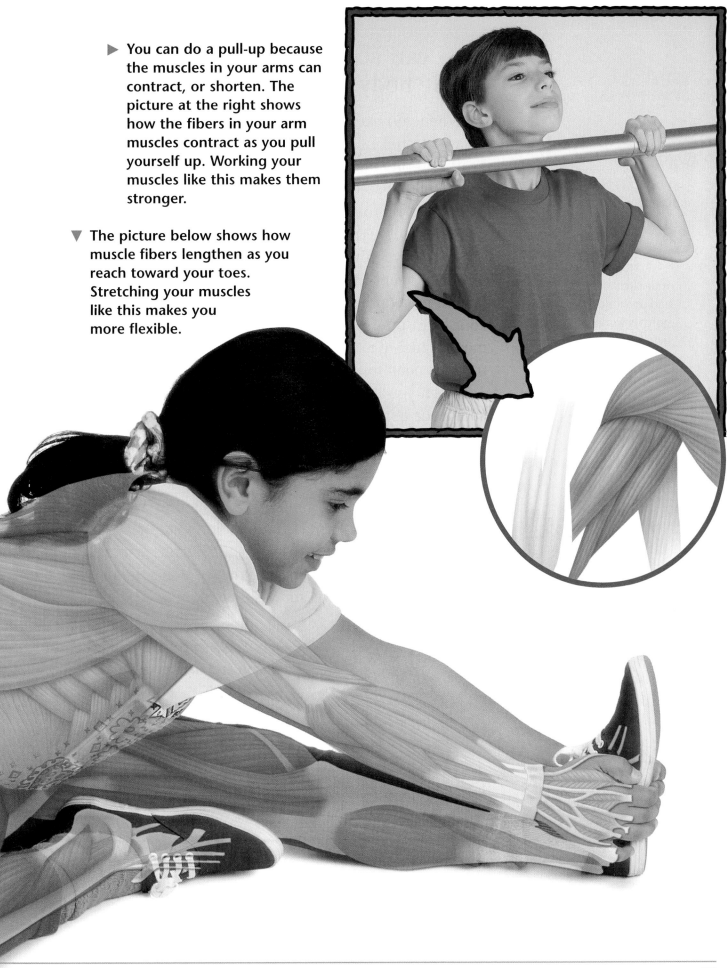

▶ You can do a pull-up because the muscles in your arms can contract, or shorten. The picture at the right shows how the fibers in your arm muscles contract as you pull yourself up. Working your muscles like this makes them stronger.

▼ The picture below shows how muscle fibers lengthen as you reach toward your toes. Stretching your muscles like this makes you more flexible.

How can aerobic exercise help your whole body?

HUMAN BODY CONNECTION

The Heart and Lungs

Your circulatory and respiratory systems work together when you exercise. You can learn more about these systems by turning to pages 10–13.

When you exercise hard, your heart beats fast. You breathe fast, too. Hard exercise that speeds up your heart and breathing rates is called **aerobic exercise** (air•OH•bik ek•ser•syz). Aerobic exercise should last at least twenty minutes.

The word *aerobic* means "with oxygen." Your muscles get extra oxygen when you do aerobic exercise. Here's how it happens. As your breathing speeds up, your lungs take in more air. Oxygen from that air enters your blood. Your heart pumps your blood at a fast pace. The blood moves quickly to your muscles, bringing the oxygen that muscles need to keep working hard.

When you do aerobic exercise, be active enough to keep your heart and breathing rates up. However, you need to be able to continue exercising for at least twenty minutes. If you can't talk to a friend while you exercise, you are probably exercising too hard.

Sports with lots of running such as tennis and field hockey are aerobic exercises if you don't stop often to rest. Some other aerobic exercises are skating; cross-country skiing; fast rowing, walking, or dancing; and even digging, raking, or snow shoveling.

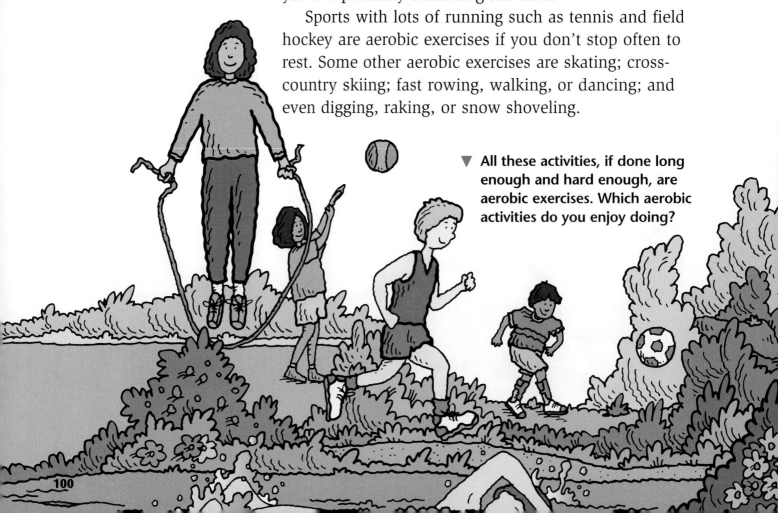

▼ All these activities, if done long enough and hard enough, are aerobic exercises. Which aerobic activities do you enjoy doing?

Doing aerobic exercise three or more times a week helps your body in many ways. Aerobic exercise increases your endurance. Also, your lungs become able to take in more air with each breath. In this way, aerobic exercise strengthens your respiratory system.

Aerobic exercise also strengthens your circulatory, or **cardiovascular system** (kar•dee•oh•VAS•kyuh•ler SIS•tuhm). Your cardiovascular system includes your heart and your blood vessels. Your heart is a muscle that works like a pump. When you do aerobic exercise, you work your heart muscle hard to make it stronger. A strong heart can pump more blood with each beat. A strong heart can then beat more slowly when you are resting. A low resting heart rate is usually a sign of a strong heart.

Aerobic exercise also keeps blood vessels from getting clogged with fats. Blood flows more easily through clean blood vessels than through clogged ones. Having a strong heart and healthy blood vessels benefits your whole body. Your muscle cells and all other body cells get more oxygen to help them work well.

Exercising regularly also can help you deal with stress. Exercise takes your mind off things that bother you. It helps you let go of anger and other strong feelings. It relaxes you and helps you sleep well at night. It also can energize you if you feel tired or bored during the day.

▼ Compare the two blood vessels. The heart must strain to pump blood through clogged vessels.

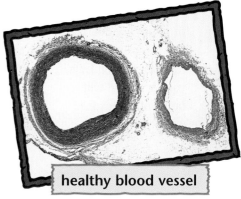

healthy blood vessel

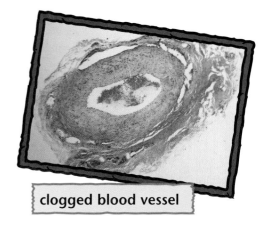

clogged blood vessel

How can you plan an exercise program?

You may already do exercises that keep you physically fit. Writing a plan for an exercise program can help you make sure you are doing the right exercises for the right amount of time. A good exercise plan includes doing aerobic activities you enjoy at least three times each week. On the other days your plan should have exercises that build muscle strength and flexibility.

Each exercise session in your plan should last twenty to thirty minutes. You also need to allow for a warm-up before the session and a cool-down afterward. Each warm-up and cool-down should have at least five minutes of stretching and slow activity. This time prepares your heart and other muscles to start and stop exercising. If you warm up and cool down, you will be less likely to injure yourself.

MY EXERCISE PLAN

Monday	Swim after school. Goal—do 20 lengths. Warm-up—stretches, walking in the pool. Cool-down—slow swimming, stretches.
Tuesday	Play baseball with friends and do extra pitching practice to build arm strength. Warm-up—arm stretches.
Wednesday	Jump rope before supper. Goal—see how many jumps I can do in twenty minutes.
Thursday	Play baseball with friends and do extra batting practice. Warm-up and cool-down—stretches and walking around bases.
Friday	Jog with Dad. Goal—try to keep up with him for twenty minutes. Cool-down—walking and stretches.
Weekend	Help dig in the garden and maybe play baseball or go swimming, depending on the weather.

Activity **Evaluate an Exercise Plan**
Look over this exercise plan. Is anything missing? How would you change it if it were your plan? What wouldn't you change? Make a list of your changes.

How do rest and sleep keep you healthy?

Exercising each day is a great way to stay fit and healthy. But you can't be active all the time. You also need to rest. Resting after a busy day is good for your body. It gives your heart and other muscles a chance to slow down. Resting also is good for your mind. Quiet activities, such as reading, drawing, and listening to music, help you relax. Listen to your body. It will tell you when you are tired and need to rest.

Sleep is another way to rest your body. When you sleep, your heart rate slows down even more than when you are awake and resting. Your breathing rate slows down, too. Your muscles relax almost completely. Even your brain rests. When you sleep, your body repairs damaged cells and makes new cells to help you grow. During sleep your body stores up energy from the food you have eaten. You need to get ten or eleven hours of sleep every night. When you do, you will wake up with the energy to enjoy a new day.

Exercise and Sleep

On Your Own Research has shown that people who exercise regularly sleep better. For a week, keep a log of your daily exercise and your sleep patterns. Did you sleep better or worse on the days you exercised?

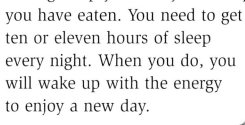

▶ Relaxing helps give you energy for times when you are more active.

LESSON CHECKUP

Check Your Facts

❶ How do pull-ups and toe touching help your muscles?

❷ What does aerobic exercise do for your lungs and heart?

❸ CRITICAL THINKING How could one type of exercise, such as dancing, build strength, flexibility, and endurance?

Set Health Goals

❹ Write down everything you did for fun and relaxation yesterday. Also, record how long you slept. Look over your record. What would you change to have a more healthful day? List activities you should do more of as well as those you should do less of.

SETTING GOALS
About Fitness

Exercise helps keep your body healthy, but you need to get enough rest to help your muscles rebuild after physical activity. Use the goal-setting steps to help you get enough rest.

Learn This Skill

Janice loves to play active sports. She can't wait to ride her bike or to skate after school. She plays on several sport teams and is always eager to try new sports. How can Janice use goal setting to make sure she gets the rest her body needs?

1. Set a goal.

2. Plan steps to help you meet the goal.

Janice decides to set a goal to relax at least 30 minutes each evening and to get 10 to 11 hours of sleep each night.

Janice lists some other things she can do to relax. Then she chooses the time to go to bed each night so she can sleep 10 hours.

3. Monitor progress toward the goal.

Each night Janice writes in her journal about a restful activity she did and how it made her feel. She checks her journal once a week to see if she is meeting her goal.

4. Evaluate the goal.

When Janice checked, she found that she was meeting her goal. She felt more rested, and she was performing better in sports than she had been.

Practice This Skill

Use this summary as you solve the problems below.

> ### Steps for Setting Goals
>
> **1.** Set a goal.
>
> **2.** Plan steps to help you meet the goal.
>
> **3.** Monitor progress toward the goal.
>
> **4.** Evaluate the goal.

A. Kevin doesn't like sports, but he knows that he should exercise at least three times a week for twenty minutes. How can he use goal setting to help him get the exercise he needs?

B. On many nights Olivia is so tired that she doesn't have the energy to do what she needs to do. How can she set a goal to help her get enough rest?

USE VOCABULARY

aerobic exercise (p. 100)
cardiovascular system
   (p. 101)
cavities (p. 84)
decay (p. 84)
dermis (p. 80)

endurance (p. 98)
epidermis (p. 80)
farsighted (p. 91)
flexibility (p. 98)
fluoride (p. 86)
hearing loss (p. 92)

lens (p. 90)
muscle strength (p. 98)
nearsighted (p. 91)
oil glands (p. 81)
plaque (p. 84)
pores (p. 81)

posture (p. 94)
pupil (p. 90)
retina (p. 90)
sunscreen (p. 83)
sweat glands (p. 81)

Use the terms above to complete the sentences. Page numbers in ( ) tell you where to look if you need help.

1. The top layer of skin is the ____.

2. ____ is the sticky, natural material that forms constantly in the mouth.

3. Light enters the eye through the ____.

4. The way you hold your body is called ____.

5. The ____ is the bottom layer of skin.

6. Holes in the teeth made by acids are called ____.

7. The ____ is the clear, curved structure that bends light in the eye.

8. The ability of muscles to apply a lot of force is called ____.

9. ____ in the dermis make a substance that softens skin.

10. The process of rotting is called ____.

11. The ____ is found in the back part of the eye.

12. Bending and twisting comfortably are signs of ____.

13. Sweat reaches the skin's surface through openings called ____.

14. A mineral that strengthens tooth enamel is ____.

15. If you have a hard time seeing distant objects, you may be ____.

16. The ability of muscles to work hard for a long time is called ____.

17. ____ in the dermis help keep you cool.

18. People who have a hard time seeing nearby objects may be ____.

19. Hard exercise that speeds up your heart and breathing rates is ____.

20. ____ protects skin from the sun's harmful rays.

21. A person who can no longer hear certain sounds may have ____.

22. Your ____ includes your heart and blood vessels.

CHECK YOUR FACTS

Page numbers in ( ) tell you where to look if you need help.

23. Name two ways to protect your hearing. (p. 93)

24. Describe what your body looks like when you stand with good posture. (pp. 94–95)

25. List four situations in which you should wash your hands. (p. 82)

26. Tell three ways that aerobic exercise can help you. (p. 101)

27. Use the pictures below to describe the correct way to floss. (p. 86)

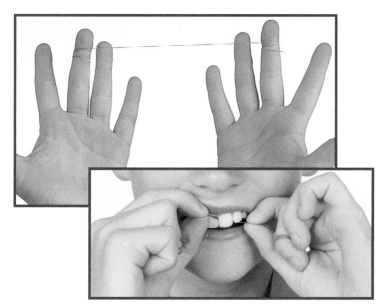

28. Why do you suppose young people need more sleep than adults do?

29. When planning an exercise program, why is it important to include activities that you really enjoy?

30. How might a nearsighted person's refusal to have an eye exam be dangerous?

APPLY LIFE SKILLS

31. **Manage Stress** It's a rainy Saturday. You and your friends are bored, restless, and irritable. Someone suggests watching TV. Someone else suggests a nap. Offer two better ideas for breaking the boredom and helping your bodies at the same time.

32. **Make Decisions** Now it's a sunny Saturday. You want to play outdoors, but there's no sunscreen in the house and no way to get to the store. Use what you know about protecting your skin to decide what to do.

Promote Health **Home and Community**

1. Work with your family to make "healthful reminder" signs for your home. A sign on the refrigerator might read, "Don't open me until you've washed those hands!" A sign near the TV might read, "Do your ears a favor. Turn me down!" Decorate the signs with funny drawings.

2. With one or more classmates, create a puppet play about keeping teeth and gums healthy. Get permission to perform your play for a group of preschoolers or kindergartners.

Activities

Eye Model, Ear Model

With a Team • Make a model of the human eye or ear. Use the diagrams in this book to help you. You can also get more information from an encyclopedia. Label the parts, and display your model in class.

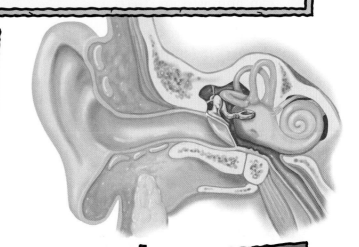

Go for Your Goal

On Your Own • Choose an aerobic activity that you enjoy. Set a goal for the activity—for example, a distance you want to ride on your bicycle without having to rest. Decide how many weeks it will take to reach your goal. Keep records to show your progress. Make a medal for yourself when you achieve the goal.

So Many Choices

With a Partner • Visit a store that sells toothpaste. Make a list of brand names and note which toothpastes have the ADA seal. Also, note the ingredients, price, tube size, flavor, and anything else you think is important. Which toothpaste would you choose? Why?

This Family Stands Together

At Home • Demonstrate good posture for your family. Show how to hold your body correctly when standing, walking, sitting, and lifting heavy objects. Discuss things family members could do to improve their posture.

Multiple Choice

Choose the letter of the correct answer.

1. Washing your hands is a way to keep
   ____ out of your body.
   a. germs   b. sunlight
   c. soap   d. pores

2. Brush teeth after ____.
   a. shampooing   b. eating
   c. exercising   d. shopping

3. What should you wear to protect your
   vision when using tools?
   a. safety goggles b. sunglasses
   c. baseball cap   d. helmet

4. When at a computer, try to ____.
   a. squeeze the mouse
   b. lean forward
   c. sit up straight
   d. reach upward

5. Exercises that shorten or contract your
   muscles help build ____.
   a. posture   b. bones
   c. flexibility   d. strength

Modified True or False

Write *true* or *false*. If a sentence is false, replace the underlined term to make the sentence true.

6. You should wash your face at least
   twice a <u>week</u>.

7. The higher its SPF number, the <u>more
   protection</u> a sunscreen will give you.

8. Avoiding <u>sugary snacks</u> is important
   for preventing tooth decay.

9. For healthy teeth and gums, visit your
   dentist <u>every two years</u>.

10. A person who must sit close to the
    board may be <u>nearsighted</u>.

11. To help your hearing, <u>raise the volume</u>
    when you listen to music.

12. When you stand, your ears, shoulders,
    and hips should <u>form a sharp curve</u>.

13. When lifting something heavy, let <u>your
    legs</u> do the hard work.

14. Running and bicycling are examples
    of <u>aerobic exercise</u>.

15. A person your age needs <u>six or seven
    hours</u> of sleep every night.

Short Answer

Write a sentence to answer each item.

16. What are three ways to protect your
    skin from the sun's harmful rays?

17. How can hardened plaque, or tartar,
    affect your gums?

18. Why should you use a toothpaste that
    has the ADA seal?

19. What can a farsighted person do to
    see clearly?

20. How does noise cause hearing loss?

21. Why should you do computer work in
    a well-lighted room?

22. What is the difference between muscle
    strength and endurance?

23. How does aerobic exercise help the
    heart and blood vessels?

Writing in Health

Write paragraphs to answer each item.

24. Describe the features of a good weekly
    exercise plan.

25. Suppose a friend says that you're both
    too young to bother with things like
    sunscreen, floss, earplugs, and aerobic
    exercise. How might you respond?

Food and Your Health

Project

YOU'RE THE CHEF People often make a weekly plan for what they are going to eat. By planning ahead, they can make sure that they have all the groceries they need and that they are eating a healthful diet. Plan a week's worth of healthful lunches. As you work through this chapter, use the Food Guide Pyramid and the information about food labels to help you plan well-balanced meals.

For other activities, visit the Harcourt Learning Site. www.harcourtschool.com

MAIN IDEA
Food contains six kinds of nutrients that are important to good health.

WHY LEARN THIS? You can use what you learn to help you choose healthful foods.

VOCABULARY
- carbohydrates
- fats
- proteins
- vitamins
- minerals
- digestive juices
- water
- fiber

Nutrients and Your Digestive System

You skate, you swim, you run. You grow and get taller. You read and study. You sleep. Food gives your body all the substances it needs to grow, work, and be active. Food also gives your body the materials it needs to build and repair itself. No wonder you get hungry!

What are the energy nutrients?

Nutrients are the substances in food you need for growth, energy, and good health. Foods contain six important nutrients: carbohydrates, proteins, fats, vitamins, minerals, and water. You need to eat a variety of foods to get all the nutrients necessary to stay healthy.

Carbohydrates (kar•boh•HY•drayts) are your body's main source of energy. You need large amounts of carbohydrates each day because your body uses them quickly. You can get carbohydrates from breads, potatoes, cereals, beans, fruits, and desserts such as cookies and raisins.

Vegetables such as carrots and peas and grains such as rice and pasta are also good carbohydrate choices. They contain many other nutrients as well and not too much sugar.

Fats give your body more energy than any other kind of nutrient. Your body stores extra fat when you don't use all the food energy you take in. You use this stored energy when you don't get enough energy from other foods. A layer of fat helps keep you warm. It also protects your body's insides.

Oils, margarine, butter, meat, cheese, whole milk, and nuts all have fats. Cakes, pastries, and fast foods also are high in fat. It's easy to eat more fat than your body needs, so choose foods carefully.

Energy!

▲ What provides these skaters with energy?

Proteins (PROH•teenz) are another kind of nutrient that gives you energy. They also help build and repair your cells. Without protein your body would not grow. You would not get better if you were ill. Cuts you might have on your skin would not heal. You can get protein by eating eggs, meat, poultry, fish, oatmeal, and peanut butter. Some vegetables, seeds, and beans also have a lot of protein.

Why is breakfast important?

Would you like to feel better when you start your day? Would you like to do better in school, too? Here's a tip: eat a good breakfast. Sound strange? It's true!

Your body and brain need nutrients to work their best. When you wake up, it likely has been about twelve hours since you last ate. If you don't eat breakfast, you will begin to run out of energy. About mid-morning you will start to slow down. You won't be able to think well. You may even get tired and grouchy.

To avoid this, you need to refuel each morning with a healthful breakfast. You may not want to get up extra early. That's fine. Breakfast doesn't need to take long. You can quickly perk up cereal with chopped nuts or fresh, canned, or dried fruit. You can add fruit to cottage cheese or yogurt.

For a change of pace, try filling celery with peanut butter or a meat or cheese spread. Eat it with a glass of milk. Or, have cheese and crackers with vegetable juice or instant breakfast mix. All these foods will keep you—and your brain—going strong until lunch.

▼ Why is it important to eat a good breakfast?

Access Valid Health Information You may think all fats are unhealthful. Your body does need fats. But, are all fats the same? Use the steps on page *xvi* to find out the differences between saturated and unsaturated fats.

Why do you need vitamins and minerals?

Not all nutrients give you energy. **Vitamins** (vy•tuh•muhnz) are nutrients that help your body perform specific functions. You need only small amounts of each vitamin. Too much of some vitamins can be harmful.

Each vitamin has one or more jobs in the body. For example, vitamin A keeps your skin and eyes healthy. Vitamin D keeps bones and teeth strong. You need vitamin C for healthy gums and teeth. Vitamins B_1 and B_2 help you use the energy in carbohydrates. Vitamin B_{12} helps keep your blood and nerves healthy.

▲ Can you get all your vitamins from one kind of food? How can you tell?

Activity **Analyze Foods** List each food shown. Make a chart of the vitamins each contains and the jobs these vitamins do. Show on your chart which of these foods you eat.

MINERALS FOR GOOD HEALTH

Mineral	Sources	Role in the Body
Calcium	milk, cheese, yogurt, dark green leafy vegetables	Builds strong bones and teeth, helps muscles and nerves work, helps blood clot
Iron	dark green leafy vegetables, peas, beans, meat	Helps blood carry oxygen throughout the body, helps cells use energy, protects against infection
Phosphorus	meat, peas, beans, whole grains, dairy products	Builds strong bones and teeth, helps cells function
Potassium	potatoes, lima beans, oranges, bananas	Helps nerves and muscles work, helps cells use energy and keep water balance, helps build proteins
Zinc	eggs, seafood, grains, nuts, beef	Helps the body grow, helps heal wounds, maintains the senses of smell and taste

Minerals (MIN•ruhlz) are nutrients that help your body grow and work. Like vitamins, minerals do not give you energy and are needed in only small amounts. In fact, too much of some minerals can be harmful.

Minerals are found in many foods. Fruits, vegetables, and milk products are good sources of minerals. So are meats, poultry, and fish. The jobs of some minerals are described in the chart above.

Minerals help keep the water inside and outside your cells in balance. They make chemical reactions occur. They help build body parts such as bones and blood cells.

Some minerals are added to prepared foods. For example, sodium is added as salt to many foods as a preservative or for flavor. And because so many foods contain added salt, eating too much salt is a common problem.

SCIENCE CONNECTION

Research Minerals

On Your Own How do minerals get into foods? Minerals are the most common solid materials found on Earth. Plants get minerals from the soil, which is formed from rocks. Find out more about how rocks turn into soil.

○ ○ ○

How does food move through the body?

Your body cannot use a whole bite of cheese. The cheese, or other food, must be broken down. This happens in your digestive system.

In your digestive system food first breaks down into smaller pieces. Next, large nutrients break down into smaller building blocks. **Digestive juices** (dy•JES•tiv JOO•suhz) are substances that break down large nutrients. Your body then takes in the smaller building blocks, along with vitamins, minerals, and water.

You take in two important substances each time you eat a piece of celery or an apple. These substances are water and fiber. Water and fiber are in many foods. They help your body use the food you eat.

HUMAN BODY CONNECTION

Your Digestive System

Food can take from three to eight hours to go from your mouth to your large intestine. Look at the diagram of the digestive system shown below. Trace the path of food through the body. For more information, turn to pages 8 and 9.

Stages of Digestion

1 In your **mouth** your teeth break food into smaller pieces. Saliva, a digestive juice, begins breaking down carbohydrates.

2 Food moves through the food tube, or **esophagus**, from your mouth to your stomach.

3 In the **stomach** more digestive juices mix with the food. The food gets churned and broken down. The digestive juices begin breaking down proteins.

4 In the **small intestine** digestive juices finish breaking down proteins, carbohydrates, and fats. Your blood takes in the building blocks from these nutrients.

5 Undigested food moves into the **large intestine**. Here water is removed from the undigested food.

6 Solid wastes pass from the large intestine into the **rectum**. They move out of the body through the anus.

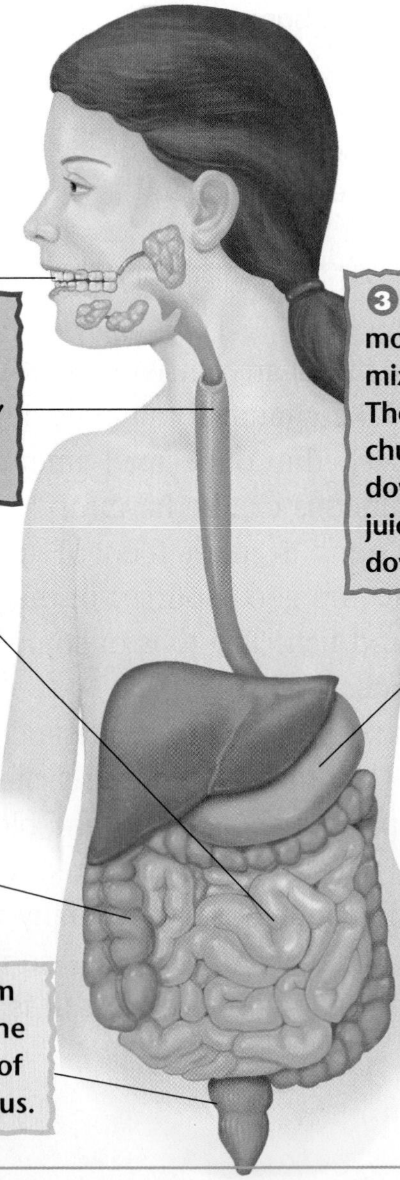

Did you know that water makes up more than half of your body? **Water** is a nutrient necessary for life. It helps break down foods. It carries digested nutrients to your cells. It also carries away wastes.

Foods such as lettuce, melons, and raw carrots have a lot of water. But drinking water is the best way to get the water your body needs. You should drink six to eight 8-ounce glasses of water every day.

Fiber is the woody substance in plants. Your body cannot digest fiber, but it needs fiber to work well. Fiber helps move food and wastes through your digestive system. It sweeps your body like a broom.

Oatmeal and brown rice are good sources of fiber. Apples, pears, and other fruits with skins you can eat give you fiber, too. Vegetables such as broccoli, corn, peas, and beans also have a lot of fiber.

▼ These foods provide fiber. Which would you like to eat?

LESSON CHECKUP

Check Your Facts

❶ Which nutrients provide energy?

❷ How do water and fiber help you stay healthy?

❸ What are the stages of digestion?

❹ CRITICAL THINKING How can breakfast help you have a good day at school?

Set Health Goals

❺ Think about what you ate for breakfast this morning. What can you do to improve your breakfasts?

MAIN IDEA
The Food Guide Pyramid is a tool to help you achieve a balanced diet.

WHY LEARN THIS? You can use what you learn to achieve a balanced diet.

VOCABULARY
• Food Guide Pyramid
• serving
• balanced diet

Food and the Nutrients It Contains

If you like bananas and broccoli, you eat two healthful foods. But if you eat nothing but bananas and broccoli, you do not have a healthful diet. To have a healthful diet you need to eat a variety of healthful foods. You also need to eat foods in the right amounts.

What are the food groups?

You need to eat a variety of foods from the first five groups on the Food Guide Pyramid each day. That doesn't mean you should eat foods from only one group at each meal! The most healthful diet includes foods from several groups at each meal or snack.

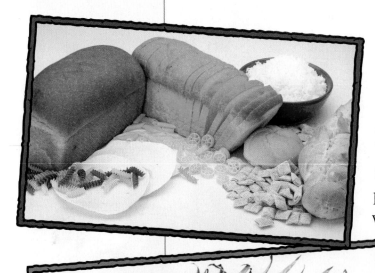

Bread, Cereal, Rice, Pasta Group

Foods in this group are grains or are made from grain. They include tortillas, cereals, rice, breads, pasta, and crackers. These foods contain carbohydrates, proteins, fiber, minerals, and vitamins. Most are low in fat.

Fruit Group

Fruits include peaches, strawberries, bananas, and pineapples. These foods are rich in minerals, vitamins, carbohydrates, and fiber. They have little or no fat.

Vegetable Group

Broccoli, cauliflower, carrots, corn, lettuce, and celery are in this group. Vegetables are rich in minerals, vitamins, fiber, and carbohydrates. Many have small amounts of protein or fat.

Meat, Poultry, Fish, Dry Beans, Eggs, Nuts Group

Nuts, dry beans, eggs, fish, poultry, and meat are all good protein sources. These foods also contain vitamins and minerals. Many of these foods are high in fat.

Milk, Yogurt, Cheese Group

Cottage cheese, yogurt, ice cream, and all kinds of hard cheeses are made from milk. Milk and foods made from milk are good sources of protein, vitamins, and minerals. Some of these foods are also high in fat.

Fats, Oils, Sweets Group

Doughnuts, chocolate bars, cookies, cakes, and chips are just a few of the foods in this group. These foods give you very few nutrients. They may also contain large amounts of salt, fat, and sugar.

How can you have a healthful, balanced diet? Eat a combination of foods from each of the first five groups every day. When you eat, don't choose too many foods from the Fats, Oils, and Sweets group. You get plenty of these nutrients from foods in the other groups.

The Food Guide Pyramid

Fats, Oils, Sweets Group
Use sparingly, or in only small amounts.

Meat, Poultry, Fish, Dry Beans, Eggs, Nuts Group
You need **2–3 SERVINGS.** One serving equals 3 ounces of cooked meat, poultry, or fish, $\frac{1}{2}$ cup cooked dry beans, 1 egg, or $\frac{1}{2}$ cup nuts.

Milk, Yogurt, Cheese Group
You need **2–3 SERVINGS.** One serving equals 1 cup of milk or yogurt or 2 ounces of cheese.

Vegetable Group You need **3–5 SERVINGS.** One serving equals 1 cup of raw spinach or $\frac{1}{2}$ cup cooked or chopped raw vegetables.

Bread, Cereal, Rice, Pasta Group You need **6–11 SERVINGS.** One serving equals 1 slice of bread, $\frac{1}{2}$ bun or muffin, 5 small crackers, or $\frac{1}{2}$ cup cereal, rice, or pasta.

How can you be sure you're getting all the nutrients you need?

The **Food Guide Pyramid** is a tool that can help you have a healthful diet. The Food Guide Pyramid divides foods into groups. It tells you how many servings you should eat from each food group each day. A **serving** is the measured amount of a food you would probably eat during one meal or as a snack.

If you look at the shape of the pyramid, you will see that its base is the largest part. This tells you that the foods from this group—the bread group—should form the largest part of your diet. These foods include pasta, rice, bread, and cereal. The foods from the tip of the pyramid—the fats and sweets group—should form the smallest part of your diet. Eat these foods only in small amounts.

No matter what foods you like, the Food Guide Pyramid will work for you. It shows you that no one food group gives you all your nutrients. It can help you choose a healthful balance of foods. It reminds you not to eat too many unhealthful foods. By using the Food Guide Pyramid, you can be sure to get a balanced diet. A **balanced diet** (BA•luhnst DY•uht) is made up of a healthful amount of foods from each of the food groups. Eating a balanced diet gives your body the nutrients it needs.

MATH CONNECTION

Menu Planning

With a Partner Plan a menu for a family of four for one day. Calculate how much of each food you'll need so that everyone will get enough servings from each food group.

Fruit Group You need **2–4 SERVINGS.** One serving equals 1 medium orange, apple, or banana, $\frac{1}{2}$ cup berries or chopped fruit, or $\frac{3}{4}$ cup fruit juice.

LESSON CHECKUP

Check Your Facts

1. Name the food groups.
2. CRITICAL THINKING How does the Food Guide Pyramid help you choose a balanced diet?
3. What kinds of foods should you eat the most of? The least of?

4. What is a food serving?

Use Life Skills

5. MAKE DECISIONS Decide on a menu for one day. Use foods you enjoy. Check your menu against the Food Guide Pyramid. Make sure you have used the correct number of servings from each food group.

Using the Food Guide Pyramid

MAIN IDEA
The Food Guide Pyramid can help you choose healthful snacks.

WHY LEARN THIS? Making wise food choices at snack time will help you develop healthful eating habits.

VOCABULARY
• habit

4:02 P.M. "I get hungry at this time every day!" says Ramón. He opens the refrigerator, looking for a snack. Cheese, carrots, cupcakes. He opens the cupboard. Chips, soup, cookies, popcorn. Ramón sees a bowl on the table. Plums, grapes, pears. "What am I going to eat?" cries Ramón. "I can't decide!"

Does this story sound familiar? Do you often want a snack when you get home from school? If so, you know that choosing a healthful snack is not always easy.

How can you make wise food choices?

Learning to choose foods wisely now will help you stay healthy all your life. It will help you form healthful eating habits. A **habit** is something you do so often that you don't even think about it. Healthful eating habits are formed by using the Food Guide Pyramid to help you plan your meals and snacks. The more often you choose healthful foods, the easier making healthful choices will become. You also can use the other food guide pyramids on pages 302–303 to try new foods.

▶ Ramón will use these steps and the Food Guide Pyramid to choose a healthful snack. You can practice using these steps on pages 123 and 126 and 127.

Steps for Making Decisions

1 Find out about the choices you could make.

2 Imagine the possible result of each choice.

3 Make what seems to be the best choice.

4 Think about what happened as a result of your choice.

It won't hurt to eat foods from the tip of the Food Guide Pyramid now and then. But habits can last a long time, and breaking bad ones isn't easy. If you choose unhealthful foods often, you'll soon have a habit that's hard to break!

Ramón wants to make a wise food choice. He thinks about what he's already eaten today. He asks himself, "Will I have a balanced diet if I choose that food?"

Ramón wants a cupcake. But he decides he has not eaten enough foods from the fruit and milk groups. He chooses the grapes and cheese. He knows they are healthful and will provide him with the nutrients he needs.

5:02 P.M. Ramón isn't hungry. He feels good. He has gotten the nutrients he needed.

Common Snack Choices

LIFE SKILLS FOCUS

Make Decisions
Several common snack foods appear in the photo. Choose three foods you would enjoy eating that also are healthful snacks. Use the four steps listed on page 122 to help make your choices. These steps also appear on pages 126 and 127 and *ix*.

CONSUMER FOCUS

Analyze Advertisements and Media Messages A fad is something that is very popular for a short time. Often certain foods and special diets are fads. Relying on food fads can lead to an unhealthful diet. Find three examples of food fads. Explain how they are influenced by advertising and media messages. Use the steps on page *xv* to analyze messages about food fads.

What are some hints for choosing a healthful snack?

You're hungry. It's not yet dinnertime. What do you choose for a snack? Do you want cookies or fruit? A glass of milk or a doughnut?

When you choose a snack, think of the guidelines for a healthful diet (see page 304). Try not to eat too much sugar, fat, or salt. Foods high in these substances fill you up, but they don't give you the nutrients you need.

How you are feeling can affect what you want to eat. Do you want something warm? Cold? Crunchy? Soft? Smooth? There is a healthful food for every mood.

Sometimes you might be hungry, but you don't feel like eating. Remember, a snack doesn't have to be solid food. Try having a glass of orange, grapefruit,

Peanut butter on whole wheat bread?

Baked tortilla chips dipped in salsa?

A mix of unbuttered popcorn, unsalted pretzels, and sunflower seeds?

Sliced cucumbers and celery dipped in plain yogurt?

A glass of chocolate milk and a granola bar?

◀ What other healthful choices could Ramón have made?

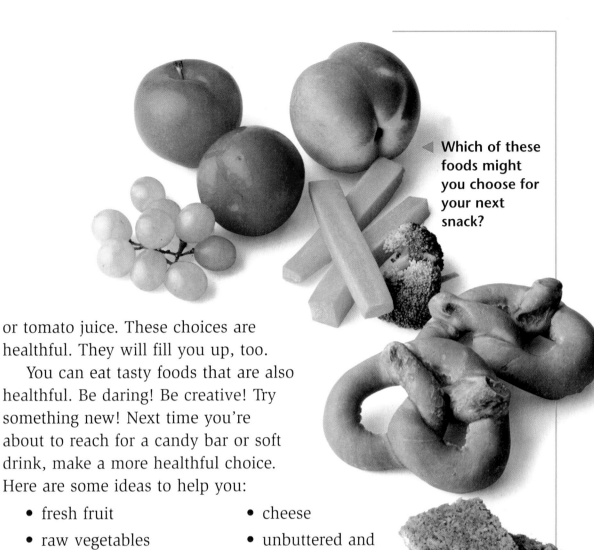

▶ **Which of these foods might you choose for your next snack?**

or tomato juice. These choices are healthful. They will fill you up, too.

You can eat tasty foods that are also healthful. Be daring! Be creative! Try something new! Next time you're about to reach for a candy bar or soft drink, make a more healthful choice. Here are some ideas to help you:

- fresh fruit
- raw vegetables
- nuts and seeds
- whole grain cereal
- rice cakes
- unsweetened juice
- plain granola bars
- lowfat yogurt

- cheese
- unbuttered and unsalted popcorn
- dried fruit
- animal crackers
- peanut butter sandwich
- whole wheat crackers

LESSON CHECKUP

Check Your Facts

❶ Use the Food Guide Pyramid to help you name four healthful snacks.

❷ How can you develop healthful eating habits?

❸ What kinds of food do not make healthful snacks?

❹ **CRITICAL THINKING** What do you need to do to make healthful food choices?

Set Health Goals

❺ Make a list of healthful snacks that you enjoy. Include foods for every mood. How can eating these foods help you develop healthful snacking habits?

MAKE DECISIONS
About Breakfast

You make decisions about what to eat every day. But do you really think through the decisions you make? Using the steps for making decisions can help you make healthful breakfast choices.

Learn This Skill

Li's alarm didn't work this morning. Li doesn't have time for her favorite breakfast of eggs, toast, and juice. What should she do?

1. **Find out about the choices you could make.**

2. **Imagine the possible result of each choice.**

Li can skip breakfast or she can prepare juice and toast with jelly.

If Li skips breakfast, she may be sleepy at school. If she eats breakfast, she may have more energy.

3. Make what seems to be the best choice.

Li decides to eat breakfast so she will have the energy she needs.

4. Think about what happened as a result of your choice.

Li has the energy she needs for a successful day at school.

Practice This Skill

Use this summary as you solve the problems below.

Steps for Making Decisions

1. Find out about the choices you could make.

2. Imagine the possible result of each choice.

3. Make what seems to be the best choice.

4. Think about what happened as a result of your choice.

A. Suppose you have a soccer game on Saturday. Decide what to eat that morning.

B. You will be taking a nature hike during a class field trip. What snack will you take?

4

Understanding a Food Label

Yoshi enjoys reading cereal boxes. Today he has played a game and read all the fun facts. He looks at the nutritional information. He can't believe how much information there is! As he reads, Yoshi wonders, "What does it all mean?"

What's on a food label?

Food labels are on all packaged foods. Cereals, pastas, crackers, soups, and many other foods have labels. The labels show how **nutritious** (nu•TRIH•shuhs) the food is, or how much nutritional value it has.

One part of a food label tells how much protein, carbohydrate, and fat the food contains. It shows the amount of fiber. It also lists some vitamins and minerals in the food. Calcium and iron are among the minerals listed on Yoshi's cereal. The listed vitamins include vitamins A and C.

Cereal

Nutrition Facts

Serving Size	1 cup (29g)
Servings Per Package	8

Amount Per Serving

Calories 140	Fat Calories 25

	% Daily Value
Total Fat 3.0g	5%
Cholesterol 0mg	0%
Sodium 110mg	5%
Total Carbohydrate 27g	9%
Dietary Fiber 1g	10%
Sugars 11g	
Protein 2g	

Vitamin A	15%	Niacin	25%
Vitamin C	0%	Vitamin B₆	25%
Calcium	0%	Folate	10%
Iron	10%	Phosphorus	4%
Thiamin	25%	Magnesium	2%
Riboflavin	25%	Zinc	10%

*Percent Daily Values are based on a 2,000-Calorie diet. Your daily values may be higher or lower depending on your Calorie needs:

		Calories:	2,000	2,500
Total Fat	Less than		65g	80g
Sat. Fat	Less than		20g	25g
Cholesterol	Less than		300mg	300mg
Sodium	Less than		2,400mg	2,400mg
Total Carbohydrate			300g	375g
Dietary Fiber			25g	30g

Calories per gram
Fat 9 • Carbohydrate 4 • Protein 4

serving size, number of servings in the package

Calories per serving

amounts of proteins, fats, carbohydrates, sodium (salt), and dietary fiber

vitamins and minerals the food contains

explanation of percent daily value

JOURNAL

Keep track of everything you eat for one week. Compare your diet to a healthful diet. Is your diet balanced? If not, what foods should you change to balance your diet?

Another part of a food label is the ingredients list. The **ingredients** (in•GREE•dee•uhnts) are all the things used to make a food. On a food label the ingredients are listed in order from greatest amount to least amount. By looking at the list, you can see everything that's used to make a food product.

Yoshi is surprised when he reads the list of ingredients in his cereal. There are so many things in it!

Activity **Analyze Ingredients** Read the ingredients list. Find the four main ingredients. Decide which nutrients they provide. Think about what you know about the Food Guide Pyramid. Is this food a good nutritional choice? Explain why or why not.

INGREDIENTS: Cornmeal, rice flour, oat flour, wheat flour, sugar, salt, corn syrup, malt flavoring, baking soda.
VITAMINS AND MINERALS: Vitamin C, zinc, iron, Vitamin B₆, Vitamin B₂, Vitamin A, Vitamin B₁, Vitamin B₁₂, Vitamin D.

Make Buying Decisions Keep a log of cereal ads shown on TV. Write what the ads claim, and write details about what they show. Find and copy nutrition labels for the same cereals. Make a buying decision using the steps on page *xiv* in the front of this book.

• • •

How is a food label useful?

Food labels give you information about a food. Reading a food label can help you decide if a food is healthful. You can use food labels to make better decisions when you choose foods.

Suppose you want to buy popcorn. You find bags labeled "POPCORN" and "CARAMEL POPCORN." You want to know what you are eating, so you look at the ingredients lists on the two bags. What differences do you think you'll see?

What can you learn by comparing foods?

When you buy a food such as popcorn, you might expect the bag to contain more popcorn than anything else. As you read the "POPCORN" bag, you learn the food has no butter, no salt, and no sugar. It has just one ingredient—popcorn.

Plain Popcorn

INGREDIENT:
Popcorn.

This popcorn tastes great without any added salt or butter!

INGREDIENTS: Brown sugar, popcorn, corn syrup, molasses, sodium bicarbonate, vanilla flavor.

Caramel Popcorn

LIFE SKILLS
FOCUS

Communicate

Joyce went shopping for breakfast cereal. She made a choice after reading the food labels on all the boxes. She believes she made a wise choice. How can she show her mother that it is a good choice? Use the steps for communicating shown on page *xii*.

When you look at the caramel popcorn label, you can't believe it. Brown sugar is the first ingredient! Popcorn is the *second* ingredient. The fact that brown sugar is first tells you that this bag has more brown sugar in it than popcorn!

As you read more, you see that the third ingredient is corn syrup. The fourth is molasses. These are other forms of sugar!

"I am trying to eat a healthful diet," you say. You put back the caramel popcorn and take the plain popcorn. You munch happily, knowing you are eating a healthful snack of popcorn, not a snack of sugar!

LESSON CHECKUP

Check Your Facts

1. How can you identify a nutritious food?
2. List three things a food label can tell you.
3. What does the ingredients list on a packaged food tell you?
4. **CRITICAL THINKING** How can you use ingredients lists to help you make healthful food choices?

Set Health Goals

5. Think about the foods you often eat as snacks. Have you read the ingredients lists on these foods? Which have sugar, salt, or fat as one of the first three ingredients? Which do not? Set a goal as to how often in one week you will eat the more healthful foods. Can you meet your goal?

MAIN IDEA
You must handle food properly in order to avoid illness.

WHY LEARN THIS? You can use what you learn to help you handle and prepare foods safely.

VOCABULARY
• food poisoning

Preparing Foods Safely

Ari and his dad prepare dinner. Ari puts the dog outside. They both wash their hands. Dad thaws meat in the microwave. Ari checks vegetables for spoilage. He looks for fuzz or mold or soft spots. They both want their food to be safe to eat.

How can you be sure the foods you prepare are safe to eat?

Foods don't have to be spoiled to be dangerous. Germs can come from many places. Some fresh foods, including eggs, raw meat, and raw poultry, carry germs. Even when you are healthy, your body carries germs that can get onto food.

Food poisoning (FOOD POYZ•ning) is an illness caused by eating food that contains germs. To avoid food poisoning, you need to take precautions. Here are some tips to make sure the foods you prepare will be safe to eat.

- Wash your hands with soap and warm water before handling food.

- Wash all work surfaces and utensils with hot water and soap, especially after working with eggs, meat, or chicken.

- Cook eggs until the yolks are hard.

- Cook meat and chicken until no red or pink shows.

- Use a wood or plastic cutting board when cutting raw meat or chicken.

- Never eat foods made with raw or under-cooked meat, chicken, or eggs. This includes cookie dough and frosting made with uncooked egg whites.

- Don't handle food when you are ill.

- Always wash a cutting board used to cut raw meat or raw chicken with soap and hot water before using it for other foods.

- Thaw food in the refrigerator or micro-wave, not on the kitchen counter.

- Keep pets away from food, cooking surfaces, and equipment.

Activity **Identify What's Wrong** Study the picture of the boy and his mother making a meal. What unhealthful practices can you find? Discuss what they should do instead.

It is important to check food carefully before you buy it. Cracked or broken eggs should not be bought.

SCIENCE
CONNECTION

Watch Bacteria Grow

On Your Own Put a little milk in two containers that you can seal tightly. Put one container of milk on a windowsill and the other in the refrigerator. After one day, look at the containers of milk side by side. Describe the milk that has been stored on the windowsill. Check the containers every day for a week.

○ ○ ○

How can you tell if a food has spoiled?

Did you ever smell sour milk? Have you ever seen fuzz or mold growing on breads, fruit, or cottage cheese? Sometimes it's easy to tell a food has spoiled. The food looks or smells bad. Breads, fruits, and vegetables may be covered with white or gray fuzz. Meat or milk may smell strange. It's always best to play it safe. If you think there's a problem, throw out the food.

You can help prevent food spoilage. When returning from shopping, put fresh foods in the refrigerator right away. After eating, wrap leftovers and store them in the refrigerator. Freeze bread and meat to keep them longer. Throw out bent cans or cracked eggs. The dents or cracks may let germs get into the food.

Who else helps make sure the food you eat is safe?

You are not alone when you try to keep food safe. On farms, boats, and in processing plants, workers and food inspectors check the safety of food.

Food inspectors test foods as they are grown, caught, processed, and stored. They test foods during shipping. They check foods in stores, hospitals, and restaurants. Every kind of food is checked—meat, poultry, fish, fresh fruits and vegetables, eggs, dairy products, and grains.

Food inspectors stop shipments of foods that are unsafe. They find the causes of large outbreaks of food poisoning. Food inspectors want you to enjoy your food and feel safe, too.

Career

Fish Inspector

What They Do

Some fish inspectors work for the government. Some work for private companies such as fish processing plants. They also work in warehouses and public storage freezers. They inspect the color, texture, smell, and taste of fish. They make sure fish processing and storage areas are clean.

Education and Training

Fish inspectors usually have a high school diploma. They learn on the job or are trained in schools. Many fish inspectors have a college degree in chemistry or microbiology. To work for the federal government, they must pass a special test.

LESSON CHECKUP

Check Your Facts

1. **CRITICAL THINKING** Why is it important to wash cooking utensils and surfaces with soap and hot water?

2. Name four ways you can help keep the foods you prepare safe.

3. Why should you throw out any food that you think might be spoiled?

4. What does a food inspector do?

Set Health Goals

5. Think about and describe the safety steps you follow in your kitchen. Then list other ways you could help keep your food safe. If you carry a bag lunch, consider it as well.

USE VOCABULARY

balanced diet (p. 121)	**fiber** (p. 117)	**habit** (p. 122)	**proteins** (p. 113)
carbohydrates (p. 112)	**Food Guide**	**ingredients** (p. 129)	**serving** (p. 121)
digestive juices (p. 116)	**Pyramid** (p. 121)	**minerals** (p. 115)	**vitamins** (p. 114)
fats (p. 112)	**food poisoning** (p. 133)	**nutritious** (p. 128)	**water** (p. 117)

Use the terms above to complete the sentences. Page numbers in ( ) tell you where to look in the chapter if you need help.

1. Nutrients that perform specific functions in the body are ____.

2. The substances in your body that break down large nutrients are ____.

3. The measured amount of a food you would likely eat during one meal is a ____.

4. The things used to make a food are its ____.

5. A plant substance that helps food move through the digestive system is ____.

6. ____ is a nutrient needed to sustain life.

7. Eating a healthful amount of food from each food group provides you with a ____.

8. Nutrients the body uses for growth and repair are ____.

9. A food that has value in the diet is ____.

10. The nutrients that should be your main source of energy are ____.

11. An illness caused by eating food that has germs is ____.

12. The ____ is a tool to help you achieve a balanced diet.

13. Nutrients such as calcium and iron are ____.

14. Something you do often without thinking about it is a ____.

15. The nutrients that have the greatest amount of energy are ____.

CHECK YOUR FACTS

Page numbers in ( ) tell you where to look in the chapter if you need help.

16. Why is water important for your body? (p. 117)

17. Study the ingredients label for the cereal shown here. What ingredient makes up most of this food? The smallest amount? (p. 129)

> **INGREDIENTS:** Cornmeal, rice flour, oat flour, wheat flour, sugar, salt, corn syrup, malt flavoring, baking soda.
> **VITAMINS AND MINERALS:** Vitamin C, zinc, iron, Vitamin B6, Vitamin B2, Vitamin A, Vitamin B1, Vitamin B12, Vitamin D.

18. What are three things you can do at home to help avoid food poisoning? (p. 133)

19. Which ingredients should you avoid in order to eat healthful snacks? (p. 124)

20. Name two foods from each food group in the Food Guide Pyramid. (p. 120)

THINK CRITICALLY

21. Some people suffer from an illness caused by not eating enough protein. What kinds of foods might help improve their health?

22. You buy raw chicken for tomorrow night's dinner. How would you safely store and handle the chicken before you cook it?

23. The ingredients list of a snack food shows molasses, corn syrup, vegetable oil, and salt as the first four ingredients. What does this information tell you about the healthfulness of the snack?

APPLY LIFE SKILLS

24. **Make Decisions** When you get home from school, you're tired. But you have to study for a test tomorrow. Use what you know about nutrition to help you name a healthful snack that will give you the energy you need to study.

25. **Make Decisions** You live in a cold area and your family doesn't buy much fresh fruit. Use what you know about nutrition to suggest how you might get the servings of food you need from the fruit group.

Promote Health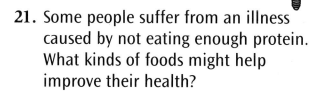

1. Talk with your family about how you can change the types of snacks you eat to make them more healthful.
2. Make a poster that encourages people to use the Food Guide Pyramid as a guideline for proper nutrition. Display your poster in your classroom or cafeteria or in a local hospital.

Activities

Nutrition Sayings

On Your Own • Research the facts behind the saying "an apple a day keeps the doctor away." Display what you learn on a poster. Draw a picture that shows what the saying means.

Good and Nutritious

With a Partner • Go to the frozen food section of a grocery store to find out what packaged meals are available. List the food groups included in three of these meals and the number of servings of each group.

Eating Right

At Home • Use the Food Guide Pyramid to make a list of healthful snacks. Be sure your list includes foods from all the food groups.

Make Your Own Food Guide Pyramid

With a Team • Create a large Food Guide Pyramid that includes pictures of foods from each group that you have cut from food labels or magazines. Arrange the pictures, and add labels to the pyramid that list the name of each food group and the number of servings from the group a person should eat each day.

Test

Multiple Choice

Choose the letter of the correct answer.

1. What do carbohydrates, fats, and proteins give your body?
   a. fiber
   b. energy
   c. vitamins
   d. minerals

2. Fiber and water are usually found in
   a. fruits and vegetables
   b. meats
   c. eggs
   d. cheese

3. Calcium is one of many _____ that your body needs.
   a. proteins
   b. vitamins
   c. minerals
   d. fibers

4. A food _____ checks the color, texture, smell, and taste of food to make sure it is safe.
   a. checker
   b. processor
   c. inspector
   d. worker

5. The Food Guide Pyramid recommends numbers of _____, or portions.
   a. nutrients
   b. snacks
   c. proteins
   d. servings

Modified True or False

Write *true* or *false*. If a sentence is false, replace the underlined term to make the sentence true.

6. <u>Minerals</u> are your body's main source of energy.

7. The <u>Food Guide Pyramid</u> is a picture of a balanced diet that shows the major food groups.

8. The foods you need to eat most are at the <u>top</u> of the Food Guide Pyramid.

9. You should eat 6 to 11 servings each day of foods from the <u>fruit</u> group.

10. Washing fruits and vegetables is important because it helps get rid of harmful <u>vitamins</u>.

11. Most of your body is made up of <u>fiber</u>.

12. One slice of bread is considered one <u>serving</u>.

13. Careful handling and storage of food can help prevent <u>food poisoning</u>.

14. You should limit the sugar, salt, and <u>carbohydrates</u> in your diet.

15. Your body needs six to eight glasses of <u>juice</u> each day.

Short Answer

Write a complete sentence to answer each question.

16. Why is it important to eat foods from all the food groups?

17. Name three ways you can tell that a food might be spoiled.

18. How are Nutrition Facts labels important?

19. How can reading ingredients lists help you choose nutritious foods?

20. Why are vitamins important to health?

21. Name two foods high in calcium.

22. What does water do for the body?

23. Why is an apple with peanut butter more healthful than a piece of cake?

Writing in Health

Write paragraphs to answer each item.

24. Juan can choose a candy bar or fresh fruit as a snack. Describe how he uses the steps for making decisions to make a healthful choice.

25. Explain why eating healthful foods now can help you when you are an adult.

CHAPTER 5

Guarding *Against* Disease

Project

DISEASE PREVENTION SKIT As you read through this chapter, you will be learning about how to prevent diseases from spreading. Write and perform a skit about pathogens that cause disease. Use the information from this chapter to help you explain how to destroy these pathogens.

For other activities, visit the Harcourt Learning Site.
www.harcourtschool.com

Why People Become Ill

MAIN IDEA
People get ill with diseases that can be spread from person to person and diseases, that cannot be spread. All people get ill sometimes.

WHY LEARN THIS? When you understand diseases, it is easier to deal with being ill yourself and to help others who are ill.

VOCABULARY
• disease
• infectious disease
• noninfectious disease
• chronic
• acute

Think about the last time you were ill. How did you feel? You might have had a stomachache, a fever, or a sore throat. You probably felt weak and wanted to stay in bed. You had a disease. A **disease** (dih•ZEEZ) is an illness. When you have a disease, your body doesn't work normally. You don't feel well.

What are some kinds of diseases?

Ben is ill today. His body temperature is higher than usual. Ben also has a cough and a sore throat. Ben tells his dad that some other children at school have been ill. Ben's dad says that Ben has probably caught a disease from the other kids.

Ben has an infectious disease. An **infectious disease** (in•FEK•shuhs dih•ZEEZ) is an illness that can be spread from person to person. Someone at school spread the disease to Ben. Ben can spread the disease to someone else. Colds, flu, chicken pox, pinkeye, and strep throat are common infectious diseases.

Not all diseases are spread from person to person. A **noninfectious disease** is an illness not caused by pathogens, so it cannot be

◀ Average normal body temperature is about 98.6° F (37° C). A higher-than-normal temperature means the body is fighting disease.

142

▲ These children have cancer. Cancer is a noninfectious disease. You can't "catch" cancer from someone else. The treatment this girl is having for cancer has caused a temporary hair loss. Her hair will grow back soon.

spread from person to person. Some noninfectious diseases are allergies, cancer, asthma, and diabetes.

Noninfectious diseases have many causes. Certain diseases, such as type 2 diabetes, are common in some families. Cancer and other noninfectious diseases can be caused by harmful things in the air and water. Sometimes people get noninfectious diseases because they have habits that are not healthful. This is why it's important to eat healthful foods and get plenty of exercise and rest.

Chronic (KRAH•nik) diseases are diseases that last a long time. Many noninfectious diseases last for months or even years. Cancer and heart disease are chronic diseases. Most infectious diseases, like colds, are acute diseases. An **acute** (uh•KYOOT) disease lasts only a short time. Even though it seems as if a cold lasts forever, most acute illnesses last for only a few days or a few weeks.

Who can become ill?

The last time Emma had an earache, she went to the doctor. There were many people in the doctor's waiting room. Emma wondered why all of the people were there.

Just like Emma, everyone gets ill from time to time. Most people have at least one cold during the winter. Many also have the flu. These are acute illnesses. They do not last very long.

Not everyone in the waiting room has a disease that can spread to others. Some people in the waiting room may have noninfectious or chronic diseases, such as asthma or cancer. But they all are there because their bodies are not working properly.

Another type of health condition that cannot spread to other people is a disability—a mental or physical problem that keeps the body from working as it should. Emma's friend Lisa has a disability that prevents her from walking. She uses a wheelchair.

You should respect the needs and feelings of people who have illnesses or disabilities. Get to know them. Imagine how an illness or disability would affect you and how you would want to be treated.

► **Everyone gets ill at one time or another.**

When it was Emma's turn to see the doctor, a medical assistant named Jeff led her and her mother into the exam room. Jeff weighed Emma and took her temperature. He also asked Emma questions to find out why she had come to see the doctor. After Emma saw the doctor, Jeff cleaned up the exam room for the next patient. He also made sure Emma's medical record was updated.

▼ This clinical medical assistant is filling out a patient's medical history.

Career

Medical Assistant

What They Do

Medical assistants work in clinics, hospitals, and doctors' offices. There are different types of medical assistants.

A **Clinical Medical Assistant** fills out medical histories, prepares exam rooms, takes vital signs (pulse rate, breathing rate, blood pressure), and does simple lab tests.

An **Administrative Medical Assistant** schedules and greets patients, answers phones, fills out insurance forms, and sends out bills and reminders.

Education and Training

A medical assistant is usually required to have a high school education and complete a program in medical assisting at a vocational or community college. Before working in a doctor's office, the medical assistant must pass a test to be certified.

LESSON CHECKUP

Check Your Facts

❶ What is the difference between an infectious disease and a noninfectious disease?

❷ Compare and contrast an acute disease with a chronic disease.

❸ List three types of acute diseases and describe the symptoms of each.

❹ CRITICAL THINKING Why should you stay home from school if you have an infectious disease?

Use Life Skills

❺ COMMUNICATE Joe has a fever, a sore throat, and a cough. How can Joe tell everyone how he feels? In your answer, include whether his disease is infectious or noninfectious, and chronic or acute.

Infectious Diseases

MAIN IDEA
Infectious diseases are
spread by pathogens.

**WHY LEARN
THIS?** You can use
what you learn to
reduce the spread of
pathogens.

VOCABULARY
• pathogen
• viruses
• bacteria
• infection
• contaminated water

You have learned that infectious diseases are spread
from person to person. But *how* are these diseases
spread? They are spread by pathogens. A **pathogen**
(PATH•uh•juhn) is an organism or virus that causes
disease. You probably have never seen a pathogen
because most are very small. People who are ill may
spread pathogens to other people, causing those people
to become ill.

What kinds of pathogens cause disease?

There are several kinds of pathogens. **Viruses**
(VY•ruh•suhz) are the smallest pathogens. Viruses cause
colds, flu, chicken pox, and measles. Viruses cannot
live by themselves. They must
live inside the cells of
other living things.
Cells are the tiny
building blocks
that make up
living things.

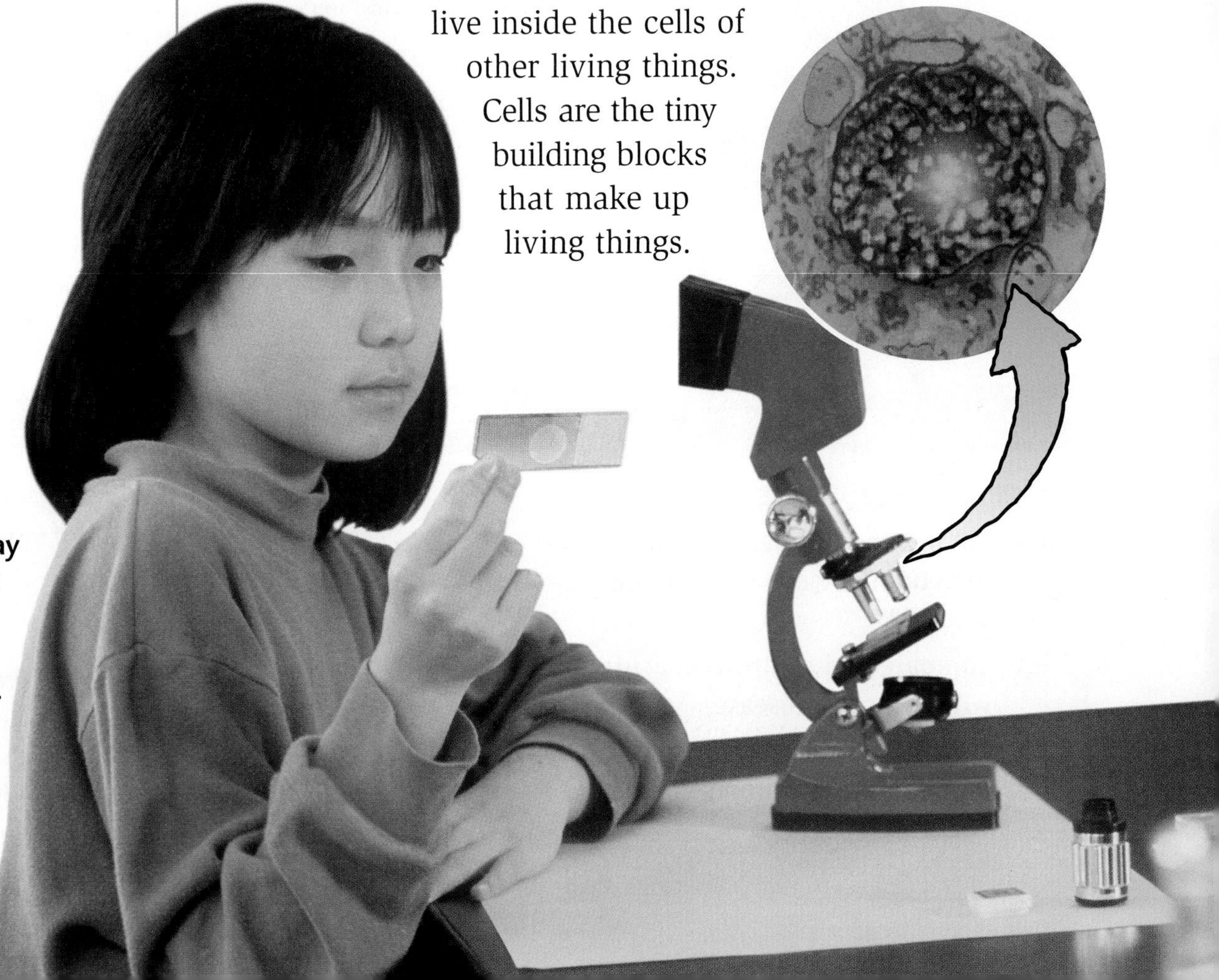

▶ The only way
to see most
pathogens
is with a
microscope.

146

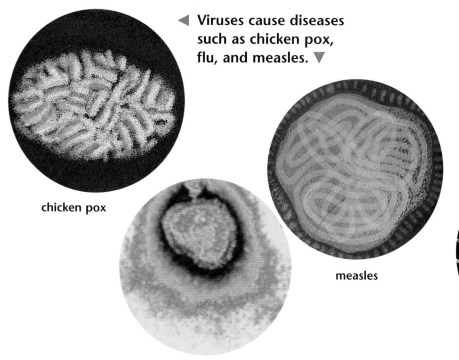

◀ Viruses cause diseases such as chicken pox, flu, and measles. ▼

chicken pox

measles

flu

▲ The bacteria that cause strep throat are round. Other kinds of bacteria are rod- or spiral-shaped.

Viruses cause disease when they enter cells in your body. A virus causes a cell to stop working in its normal way. The cell then starts making more viruses. When the cell is full of viruses, it bursts open and the viruses spread to other cells in the body. The viruses can also spread from one person to another.

Another kind of pathogen is bacteria. **Bacteria** (bak•TIR•ee•uh) are one-celled living things that can cause disease. Bacteria live in all kinds of places. Some live in dry places. Others live in wet places. Some need light. Others must live in the dark. Because bacteria are living cells, they need food and water. Bacteria are different shapes and sizes, but almost all bacteria are so small that they can be seen only with a microscope.

Most bacteria don't harm people. In fact, your body needs some kinds of bacteria to work normally. A few kinds of bacteria, however, do cause diseases in people. Pinkeye, ear infections, and strep throat can be caused by bacteria.

When viruses or bacteria grow in the body, they cause infections. An **infection** (in•FEK•shuhn) is the growth of pathogens somewhere in the body. When your body has an infection, you may become ill with a disease.

SCIENCE
CONNECTION

Good Bacteria

On Your Own
Not all bacteria cause diseases in people. Some bacteria can actually help you. Find out two ways in which bacteria are helpful to people. Share your findings with your class.

○ ○ ○

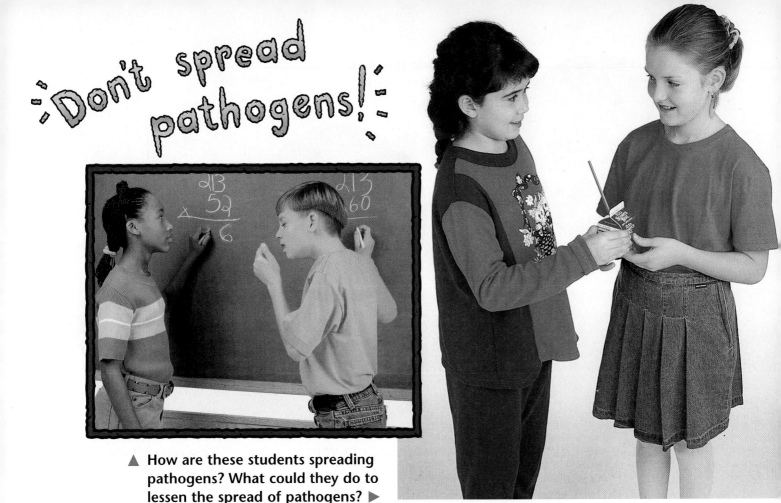

Don't spread pathogens!

▲ How are these students spreading pathogens? What could they do to lessen the spread of pathogens? ▶

How are pathogens spread?

Pathogens can be spread from person, insect, animal, food, or water to a person. Pathogens may spread to you if you kiss someone who is ill or touch skin that is infected. Some pathogens can be spread through the air. When someone coughs or sneezes, droplets with pathogens can be sprayed into the air. If you are nearby, you may breathe in those pathogens and develop a disease.

Some pathogens remain on objects after a person who is ill has touched or used them. If you use a drinking glass that someone else has used, you can get pathogens from it. You can get pathogens from objects, such as pencils, books, doorknobs, and handrails, if someone who is ill with a respiratory or intestinal illness has touched them without washing his or her hands.

Sometimes animals, such as insects and birds, spread pathogens to people. People also can get pathogens from eating food that isn't prepared properly or drinking water that isn't clean.

How do food and water spread pathogens?

As you read in Chapter 4, even foods that aren't spoiled can spread pathogens. Always wash your hands with warm water and soap before you handle food. That way you prevent any pathogens that may be on your hands from getting onto your food. You must also wash your hands after handling food to avoid spreading pathogens that may be on the food.

Pathogens in certain foods can grow and make poisons. Beef, pork, chicken, and fish left outside the refrigerator for just a few hours can spoil. Eggs, milk, and foods made from eggs or milk can spoil quickly too. You must handle and prepare these fresh foods very carefully in order to avoid the spread of pathogens.

Water is another source of pathogens, especially water that is not moving or flowing. Water that is warm, shallow, and dirty may be filled with pathogens.

Water that has dangerous pathogens in it is called **contaminated water** (kuhn•TA•muh•nay•tid WAW•ter). You will probably become ill if you drink contaminated water. Some water is so contaminated that even swimming or standing in it can make you ill. The pathogens in the water can get into your mouth, any breaks in your skin, or on your hands. Staying away from such water can help prevent you from getting a disease.

▲ Standing water, even a puddle, contains pathogens.

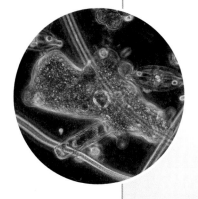

LESSON CHECKUP

Check Your Facts

❶ How are infectious diseases spread?

❷ Name three illnesses caused by viruses and three caused by bacteria.

❸ CRITICAL THINKING If your best friend has a cold, what are three ways that the pathogens in your friend's body could spread to you?

❹ Why is it important to wash your hands before and after you handle food?

Set Health Goals

❺ Review what you know about how pathogens are spread from one person to another. Then describe two ways you could reduce the spread of pathogens.

MAIN IDEA
Your body can protect itself from diseases. You can help protect your body from diseases too.

WHY LEARN THIS? You can use what you learn to help avoid getting diseases.

VOCABULARY
- symptoms
- immune system
- white blood cells
- mucus
- cilia
- antibodies
- immunity
- vaccines

Fighting Infectious Diseases

Aleesha is ill. She has a sore throat, a cough, a fever, and body aches. Aleesha has symptoms of the flu. **Symptoms** (SIMP•tuhmz) are signs or feelings of a disease. A fever, or above-normal body temperature, is a common symptom of many diseases. A fever is one way the body fights off pathogens.

How does the body fight disease?

Pathogens are around you all the time. Yet you get ill only now and then. What protects you from pathogens?

Your body defends itself against pathogens. The first defenses help keep pathogens from entering your body. These defenses include skin, cilia, mucus, saliva, and digestive juices. Find these defenses in the figure on the next page, and read how each keeps pathogens out of the body.

Sometimes pathogens get past these first defenses. Then your immune system goes to work. The **immune system** (ih•MYOON SIS•tuhm) is the body system that fights disease. An important part of the immune system is **white blood cells**, blood cells that kill pathogens. Some white blood cells are large enough to surround pathogens and destroy them.

◀ **Cilia are found in the nose and other air passages. They help fight disease by preventing pathogens from entering the body.**

◀ **White blood cells find and destroy pathogens that get past cilia and the body's other first defenses.**

"The Body's Defenses"

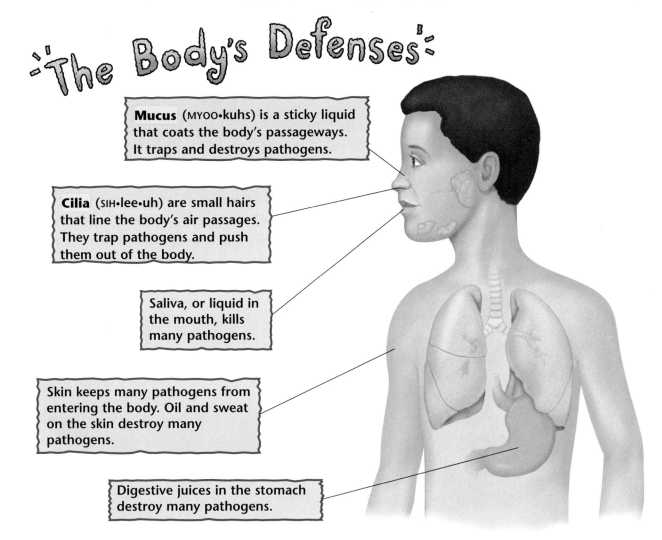

Mucus (MYOO•kuhs) is a sticky liquid that coats the body's passageways. It traps and destroys pathogens.

Cilia (SIH•lee•uh) are small hairs that line the body's air passages. They trap pathogens and push them out of the body.

Saliva, or liquid in the mouth, kills many pathogens.

Skin keeps many pathogens from entering the body. Oil and sweat on the skin destroy many pathogens.

Digestive juices in the stomach destroy many pathogens.

Other white blood cells fight pathogens by making antibodies. **Antibodies** (AN•tih•bah•deez) are chemicals made by the body to help fight disease. Your body makes a different antibody for each kind of pathogen that enters it. An antibody sticks to a pathogen and either destroys it or marks it. If the antibody marks the pathogen, the large white blood cells come and destroy the pathogen.

Once your body has made an antibody for a certain pathogen, your body can have immunity to that pathogen. **Immunity** (ih•MYOO•nuh•tee) is the body's ability to defend itself against certain kinds of pathogens. For example, if you have chicken pox, your body will make an antibody just for the chicken-pox virus. This antibody can stick only to the chicken-pox virus. It will protect you from the chicken-pox virus for the rest of your life.

HUMAN BODY CONNECTION

Systems of Defense

Study the digestive system on page 8 and the respiratory system on page 12 of The Amazing Human Body. Match each of the body's defenses shown above to the correct body system.

● ● ●

How can you avoid disease?

Stacy has an eye infection called pinkeye. Bacteria cause this disease. Stacy's eyes feel itchy, so she rubs them. The pinkeye bacteria in her eyes get on her hands and fingers. When Stacy touches the checkers, the bacteria get on the checkers. When Jared picks up a checker, he gets pinkeye bacteria on his fingers. Then he touches his face and eyes. Bacteria get into his eyes. In a few days Jared will have pinkeye too.

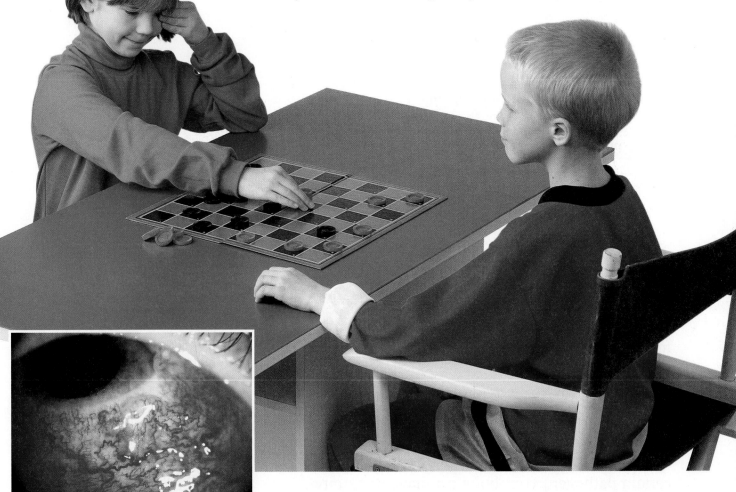

▲ **Pinkeye can spread easily to others when people share objects like checkers.**

Even though your body is good at fighting pathogens, you can do some things to help your body avoid disease. One thing you can do is to stay away from people when they have an infectious disease. You can get some pathogens by touching infected people or objects they have touched. You can breathe in pathogens their bodies have released into the air.

Kill those pathogens!

Activity **Kill Pathogens** Describe how these people are killing pathogens. List other ways to kill pathogens.

You can avoid disease by not touching objects that could have pathogens on them. For example, don't put your mouth on the spout of a drinking fountain.

Of course, you touch hundreds of items every day. All of these items are likely to have pathogens on them, which then get on your hands. So one of the best ways to avoid disease is to wash your hands often during the day with soap and warm water. Always wash your hands before eating and after using the bathroom. If Jared had washed his hands before he touched his face and eyes, he probably wouldn't have gotten pinkeye. If you can't wash your hands, keep them away from your eyes, nose, and mouth.

If you cut or scrape your skin, pathogens can easily enter your body. To stop pathogens, wash the cut carefully with soap and warm water. Then cover the cut with a sterile bandage.

Some cleaning products can help you avoid disease. For example, you can spray a disinfectant—a chemical that kills pathogens—on light switches, doorknobs, and other objects in your home. Using hot, soapy water to wash surfaces that come into contact with food also helps you kill or remove pathogens.

JOURNAL

Think about your daily habits. How might you change your habits if a family member or classmate had an infectious disease? In your Health Journal, make a list of things you could do to avoid getting the disease. Remember that your journal is private.

How can vaccines protect you against disease?

Chris is getting a flu shot. Chris doesn't like getting the shot, but she knows it will probably keep her from getting the flu this year. The nurse has told Chris that the flu shot is a vaccine. **Vaccines** (vak•SEENZ) are substances made to prevent and control certain diseases. Most vaccines are given as shots. Some are taken by mouth.

Each vaccine protects you from one kind of disease. For example, one vaccine protects you from measles, another from polio, and another from mumps. Some different vaccines can be mixed and given together in one shot. There are no vaccines for some diseases, such as colds.

IMMUNIZATION SCHEDULE

Vaccine	When Needed
Hepatitis B Protects against hepatitis B virus	birth–2 months, 1–4 months, 6–18 months
DTP Protects against diphtheria, tetanus, and pertussis bacteria	2 months, 4 months, 6 months, 15–18 months, 4–6 years, 11–16 years and every 10 years lifelong (tetanus and diphtheria only)
MMR Protects against measles, mumps, and rubella viruses	12–15 months, 4–6 years
Hib Protects against <u>Haemophilus influenzae</u> bacterium	2 months, 4 months, 6 months, 12–15 months
IPV Protects against polio virus	2 months, 4 months, 6–18 months, 4–6 years
Pneumococcal Conjugate Protects against pneumococcal bacteria	2 months, 4 months, 6 months, 12–15 months
Varicella Protects against chicken pox	12–18 months

A vaccine used to prevent a disease is made from the pathogen or part of the pathogen that causes that illness. The pathogen is changed, however, so that it will not cause the disease when the vaccine is given. When the changed pathogen is put into your body, your body makes antibodies to fight the pathogen. The antibodies then give you immunity to the disease. If that pathogen ever spreads to you from another person, your body quickly destroys it. This prevents you from getting the disease.

Some vaccines give you immunity to a disease for life. Others give you immunity for only a short time. More vaccine is needed to boost your immunity, so you must be vaccinated again. If you don't get a booster, your body has weak immunity and you can get the disease. Look at the table on page 154. Which vaccines need boosters?

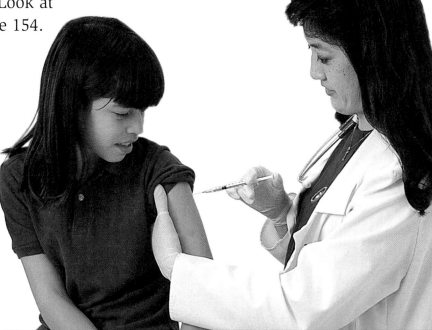

▶ Doctors suggest that children more than six months old who have chronic diseases such as asthma or heart disease get flu shots each year.

LESSON CHECKUP

Check Your Facts

1 CRITICAL THINKING What are some symptoms you recognize and what diseases do they signal?

2 Name five of your body's first defenses against disease.

3 How do white blood cells fight infectious diseases?

4 CRITICAL THINKING Suppose your mother has a cold. What are three things you can do to avoid getting a cold too?

Use Life Skills

5 MAKE DECISIONS What would you do if you started having symptoms of a disease? Describe how your decision would help you get the treatment you need.

Noninfectious Diseases

MAIN IDEA
Some diseases are not infectious. They can't be spread from person to person.

WHY LEARN THIS? Choices you make can affect whether or not you develop noninfectious diseases.

VOCABULARY
• cancer
• allergy
• arthritis
• diabetes
• asthma

You have learned about infectious diseases that spread from one person to another. These diseases are caused by pathogens. Many other diseases, though, are not caused by pathogens. They are noninfectious. Noninfectious diseases can't be spread from one person to another.

What are some heart diseases?

Heart diseases are the leading cause of death for adults in the United States. Some people are more likely than others to have heart diseases.

Some people are born with heart disease. Their hearts don't work normally because specific parts aren't shaped correctly. One sign of this kind of heart disease is a heart murmur. A murmur is a sound that isn't usually made by a healthy heart. Many of these types of heart disease are treated with surgery.

Some adults get heart diseases because they have poor health habits. Poor health habits include eating high-fat diets, not exercising regularly, and using tobacco. Heart diseases often are present in the body for a long time before symptoms develop. When symptoms develop, they seem to appear without warning. Some symptoms include chest pain, weakness, and shortness of breath. Sometimes the heart suddenly stops, which causes death. This is why heart diseases are so dangerous.

▶ An EKG is a test used to find heart damage and skipped or irregular heartbeats. It can show if a heart is diseased.

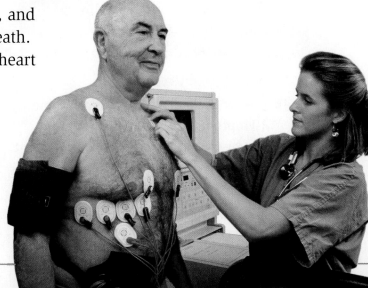

What is cancer?

Meg's father is putting sunscreen on her face. Sunscreen will protect her skin from the harmful rays of the sun. Even in winter, sun rays can damage skin. Over time such damage can lead to skin cancer.

Cancer is a noninfectious disease that happens when one kind of cell grows out of control. Cancer cells are different from normal body cells. Cancer cells grow faster than normal cells. Sometimes cancer cells form lumps. These lumps can grow in place of other body cells. Cancer cells can keep body cells from working normally. Symptoms of cancer vary, depending on which body cells are not working properly. Many kinds of cancer can be treated and cured if the cancer is found early.

▲ Using sunscreen helps protect your skin. It can help prevent skin cancer.

Cancer can grow in people of any age. But some people are more likely to get cancer than other people are. Certain kinds of cancer, such as breast cancer, run in families. Some people who work with dangerous chemicals get cancer of the liver. People who use tobacco often get cancer of the mouth, throat, or lungs. Exposure to the sun can lead to skin cancer. Other kinds of cancer are brain tumors and leukemia. Leukemia is a kind of cancer in which white blood cells grow out of control.

You can help prevent some kinds of cancer. Using sunscreen and not using tobacco products are two things you can do to help prevent cancer.

Communicate

Tyrone is having dinner at his best friend's house. Tonight they're having lasagna made with cheese. Tyrone is allergic to all dairy products. How can he communicate that he cannot eat the lasagna? Use the steps for communicating shown on page *xii*.

▼ **Things that cause allergies include dust, tiny parts of plants, bee stings, certain foods, and animal dander, or skin cells.**

What are allergies?

Kevin liked to go to his Aunt Sue's farm to ride the horses, milk the cows, and play with her dog and cat. But Kevin sneezed and had itchy eyes every time he went. Aunt Sue said Kevin probably had an allergy to something on the farm. Kevin went to the doctor and found out he has an allergy to cats.

An **allergy** (A•ler•jee) is a noninfectious disease in which a person has a reaction to a certain thing. Some of the things that cause allergic reactions are animals, plants, medicines, dust, and bee stings. Foods, such as eggs, peanuts, and milk, also can cause allergic reactions. Not all people have allergies. Those who do can be allergic to only one thing or to many things.

Usually allergic reactions have symptoms like sneezing, itchy and watery eyes, a runny nose, or an itchy rash. Some allergic reactions to bee stings and to foods like eggs and peanuts are dangerous. People with these kinds of reactions need medical help right away.

If you have allergies, your doctor may give you medicine to help your symptoms go away. Your doctor also may tell you to avoid the things to which you are allergic. Kevin's doctor told him to stay away from cats. Your doctor may give you allergy shots. Allergy shots make the body less sensitive to the things that cause the allergies. With allergy shots Kevin might even be able to have a cat for a pet.

► A health-care worker helps a young girl who has arthritis exercise her joint. Proper exercise helps keep the joint working normally.

What is arthritis?

Arthritis (ar•THRY•tuhs) is a noninfectious disease in which the body's joints become swollen and painful. Joints are the places, such as your wrists and knees, where your body bends. Both adults and children can get arthritis. But the form of arthritis children get is different from the type adults get. In children the disease usually starts between the ages of two and five years.

Arthritis most commonly affects the knees, wrists, ankles, and elbows. Joints affected with arthritis can be red, swollen, stiff, and painful. Over time the joints stop working normally. Often a child with arthritis has bones that don't grow normally. For example, one leg may grow to be longer than the other. Sometimes arthritis causes a child's growth to slow down or stop. Children with arthritis miss school when it is too painful to move.

There is no cure for arthritis, but doctors can give medicines to help the pain and swelling go away. Often children must do special exercises to help their joints move normally. Sometimes they must wear braces at night to keep their joints from moving. If necessary, doctors can replace nonworking joints with artificial joints.

CONSUMER FOCUS

Access Valid Health Information
Many medicines and treatments are sold for arthritis. Look for treatment ads in newspapers and magazines, and on TV. Use library resources to learn more about each treatment. Is all the information in the ads valid? Where can you find valid information about arthritis treatments? Use the tips for accessing valid information on page *xvi* in the front of this book.

• • •

Myth and Fact

Myth: People with asthma should never exercise.

Fact: Although exercise can cause asthma attacks, exercise is important for good health. People with asthma usually can avoid such attacks by exercising mildly or by taking medicine before exercising.

What is diabetes?

Diabetes (dy•uh•BEE•teez) is a noninfectious disease in which the body cannot make enough insulin or properly use sugar from food. Too much sugar stays in the blood, causing many problems. A person with untreated diabetes feels thirsty and tired. He or she may lose weight. If diabetes is not treated, the extra sugar in the blood damages blood vessels as well as the heart, kidneys, and eyes.

▲ Children with diabetes must learn how to balance daily meals and snacks. All of the foods shown here, eaten in proper amounts, can be part of a diabetes diet.

Diabetes cannot be cured. However, it can be treated with medicine, diet, and exercise. A hormone called *insulin* allows the body to properly use the sugar in food. People with diabetes may need insulin injections or other medicines if their bodies don't make enough insulin. A balanced diet controls the amount of sugar that is eaten. Exercise helps the bodies of people with diabetes use sugar better. Exercise also helps control weight.

What is asthma?

Jamal wears a scarf over his face in cold weather. He always carries his fast relief inhaler in case he starts coughing. The inhaler sends medicine directly to Jamal's lungs. He also uses one medicine each day to prevent breathing trouble. Jamal has asthma.

Asthma (AZ•muh) is a noninfectious disease that sometimes causes difficulty in breathing. People who have asthma do not feel ill all the time. They have attacks during which they cannot breathe easily. These asthma attacks are caused, or triggered, by different things. Some of these triggers are allergies, cigarette smoke, dust, exercise, cold air, and diseases like colds and flu that affect the lungs.

An asthma attack begins with a feeling of tightness in the chest. Then it becomes difficult to breathe. A person may begin to cough or wheeze. Wheezing may be loud, or hard to hear.

Doctors cannot cure asthma. Sometimes children grow out of the disease. If you have asthma, your doctor will order a medicine to keep your airways from swelling on most days. Your doctor will also give you medicine to take when you are having an attack. Your doctor will help you identify things that trigger your asthma.

▶ Breathing in cold air can trigger asthma. Wearing a scarf or mask helps warm the air before it moves into the lungs.

LESSON CHECKUP

Check Your Facts

1. What is cancer?

2. Name some things that can cause an allergic reaction.

3. CRITICAL THINKING If you were planning a snack for yourself and a friend who has diabetes, what foods would you recommend?

4. CRITICAL THINKING Why might a person with arthritis have difficulty playing sports?

Set Health Goals

5. Choose one of the noninfectious diseases from the lesson. Imagine that one of your classmates has this disease. Describe one or two things you could do to help your classmate feel better.

MAIN IDEA
Making healthful choices helps reduce disease.

WHY LEARN THIS? You can use what you learn to have a healthful lifestyle.

VOCABULARY
• resistance
• abstinence

Staying Well

Have you ever stood in front of the refrigerator trying to decide what to eat? The food you choose may affect how your body fights disease. Every day you make choices like this that affect your body. These choices make up your lifestyle. A *lifestyle* is the way a person lives. A healthful lifestyle will help your body stay well.

What can you do to stay well?

You can do many things to stay well. Exercise helps prevent heart diseases and helps your body fight off pathogens. Getting enough rest helps your body grow and repair itself. Healthful foods give your body building blocks but keep it at a healthy weight.

A healthful lifestyle also includes regular checkups. Having vaccinations at the times listed in the chart on page 154 is also important. So is not using harmful substances like alcohol, tobacco, and other drugs.

Managing stress is another important part of a healthful lifestyle. Some stress is good for you, but too much stress can make you ill. Knowing what causes too much stress is the first step. For example, you may feel stress because you don't plan your time so you can finish all your homework.

▼ Look at the pictures on these two pages. How does each activity help you stay well?

Always wash your hands before you eat.

The next step in managing stress is to decide how to handle the situation. You can probably make time to do your homework by cutting out another activity. Learning to relax is another way to manage your stress. Think about a fun activity you can do *after* your homework is done.

Remember that you also can stay well by avoiding pathogens. One way to avoid pathogens is to keep clean. You should wash your hands often and your body daily. Wash your hands before and after preparing food.

By making healthful lifestyle choices, you help your body have resistance to disease. **Resistance** (rih•ZIS•tuhnts) is the ability of the body to fight pathogens by itself. If you choose good health habits, you will have a better chance of staying well.

Some people think that taking large amounts of vitamins will improve their resistance. However, too much of some vitamins can cause problems. If you aren't sure whether you need vitamins or don't know which vitamins to take, ask your doctor.

▼ A doctor or nutritionist can help you decide if you need to add vitamins or minerals to your diet.

Why should you avoid tobacco?

Sarah and her grandmother are eating lunch together. While they are eating, a person at a nearby table begins smoking a cigarette. The smoke smells bad. It makes Sarah cough. She does not like breathing in cigarette smoke.

Sarah knows that using tobacco is not a good choice for a healthful lifestyle. Using tobacco can lead to many health problems and may lead to death. Smoking can cause cancer of the lungs, throat, and mouth. Smoking also can cause heart disease and asthma. Using chewing tobacco can cause problems with teeth and gums. It can cause cancer of the mouth. Smoking also causes the body to have less resistance to pathogens. That is why smokers are ill more often than people who do not smoke.

Smoking cigarettes has been around for a long time. Now all cigarette packages are labeled with warnings about the health problems that smoking can cause. Many people quit smoking when they learned about these health problems.

▼ Cigarette smoke can harm your lungs. To stay well, try to avoid people who are smoking.

Activity **Avoid Smoke** Think about Sarah's situation. She and her grandmother are sitting in the no-smoking area of the restaurant when a person at a nearby table starts smoking. What should Sarah do? What should her grandmother do? Act out the situation.

Other people quit smoking because of the high cost of cigarettes or because smoking is no longer allowed in many public places and workplaces. People who choose not to use tobacco are practicing **abstinence** (AB•stuh•nuhnts)—they are avoiding a behavior that will harm their health.

When you know about the health problems caused by smoking, you may wonder why anyone still smokes. Smoking is a hard habit to stop. Once someone starts smoking cigarettes, his or her body wants more cigarettes. Often the person feels uncomfortable for a while when he or she tries to stop smoking.

Some people start smoking when they are young. They smoke to fit in with certain groups, or they may want to appear grown up. Neither of these is a good reason to smoke. The most healthful choice you can make is to never start smoking.

Calculate the Cost

On Your Own If one pack of cigarettes costs $2.00, how much would it cost to smoke one pack of cigarettes every day for one year? For two years? How much would it cost to smoke two packs of cigarettes every day for one year? For two years?

● ● ●

▼ Smoking is so dangerous that cigarettes carry warning labels. Would you start smoking if you read this label first?

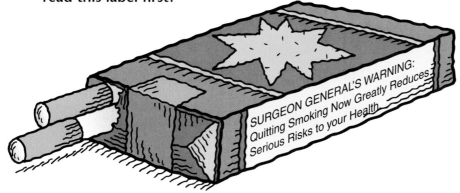

SURGEON GENERAL'S WARNING: Quitting Smoking Now Greatly Reduces Serious Risks to your Health.

LESSON CHECKUP

Check Your Facts

1. Name four things you can do to stay well.
2. CRITICAL THINKING What things could you do to improve your body's resistance?
3. How can tobacco smoke harm the body?
4. CRITICAL THINKING If you know someone your age who smokes, what can you say to persuade and help that person to quit?

Use Life Skills

5. MAKE DECISIONS Susie's family likes to have dessert after dinner every evening. Susie would like to make more healthful choices and not eat as many sweets. Help Susie plan healthful desserts.

MANAGE STRESS *at the Doctor's Office*

We all feel stress from time to time. Learning to manage stress is an important part of staying healthy.

Learn This Skill

Sylvia stepped on a board with a nail in it during a family vacation. The nail went through the sole of her shoe and punctured her foot. Sylvia knows she needs to see the doctor, but she's afraid the doctor will give her a shot. How can she handle her stress?

1. Know what stress feels like and what causes it.

Sylvia's heart is pounding. She is breathing faster than usual. Her mouth feels dry, and her muscles are tense. She is worried about getting a shot.

2. When you feel stress, think about ways to handle it.

Sylvia has had shots before. She knows they sting for just a minute. She thinks about what she did the last time she got a shot.

3. Focus on one step at a time.

Sylvia decides she will look away when the nurse approaches her.

4. Learn to release tension.

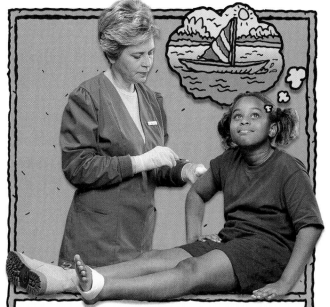

Sylvia thinks about the rest of her vacation. She feels a slight sting. The nurse says, "That's it! You did a great job!"

Practice This Skill

Use this summary to help you solve the problems below.

Steps for Managing Stress

1. Know what stress feels like and what causes it.

2. When you feel stress, think about ways to handle it.

3. Focus on one step at a time.

4. Learn to release tension.

A. Carlos has butterflies in his stomach and can't get to sleep. Tomorrow he gets his report card, and he's worried about his grades. How can Carlos manage his stress?

B. Carol is involved in many after-school activities. Sometimes she is so busy that she can't keep up with her schoolwork. How can she manage her stress?

USE VOCABULARY

abstinence (p. 165)	cancer (p. 157)	immunity (p. 151)	pathogen (p. 146)
acute (p. 143)	chronic (p. 143)	infection (p. 147)	resistance (p. 163)
allergy (p. 158)	cilia (p. 151)	infectious	symptoms (p. 150)
antibodies (p. 151)	contaminated water (p. 149)	disease (p. 142)	vaccines (p. 154)
arthritis (p. 159)	diabetes (p. 160)	mucus (p. 151)	viruses (p. 146)
asthma (p. 161)	disease (p. 142)	noninfectious	white blood cells
bacteria (p. 147)	immune system (p. 150)	disease (p. 142)	(p. 150)

**Use the terms above to complete the sentences. Page numbers
in ( ) tell you where to look in the chapter if you need help.**

1. The body's system that fights disease
   is the ____.

2. One-celled living things that may
   cause disease are ____.

3. An illness not caused by pathogens is
   a ____.

4. ____ is a noninfectious disease caused
   by cells growing out of control.

5. Avoiding behavior that will harm your
   health is called ____.

6. Chemicals made by the body to
   help fight disease are ____.

7. ____ diseases last a long time.

8. Signs or feelings of disease are ____.

9. An illness that can be spread from
   person to person is an ____.

10. Shots containing substances made
    to prevent certain diseases are
    called ____.

11. A noninfectious disease in which the
    body's joints become swollen and
    painful is ____.

12. Any organism or virus that causes
    disease is a ____.

13. ____ diseases last a short time.

14. A sticky liquid that covers the body's
    passageways is ____.

15. ____ is a noninfectious disease in
    which the body can't properly
    use sugar.

16. Blood cells that destroy pathogens
    are ____.

17. Small hairs that line the body's air
    passages are called ____.

18. The growth of pathogens somewhere
    in the body is an ____.

19. An illness is a ____.

20. A noninfectious disease that
    sometimes causes difficulty in
    breathing is ____.

21. Once your body has made an anti-
    body for a certain pathogen, your
    body usually has ____ to that
    pathogen.

22. By making healthful lifestyle choices, you help your body have _____ to disease.

23. A noninfectious disease in which a person has a reaction to a certain thing is an _____.

24. The smallest pathogens are called _____.

25. Water that has harmful substances in it is called _____.

CHECK YOUR FACTS

Page numbers in ( ) tell you where to look in the chapter if you need help.

26. Identify five of the body's defenses in the diagram below. Describe how each defense helps the body fight disease. (p. 151)

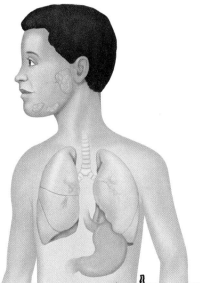

27. Contrast infectious and noninfectious diseases. (pp. 142–143)

28. Name two kinds of pathogens, and describe how they are spread. (pp. 146–148)

29. List six noninfectious diseases, and describe how each affects the body. (pp. 148–149)

30. List five lifestyle choices that will help you stay well. (pp. 162–165)

THINK CRITICALLY

31. Chicken pox is spreading through your class. You have had the chicken pox vaccine. Will you get chicken pox? Explain your answer.

32. Claire has allergies. If Claire sneezes on Robert, will he get allergies too? Explain your answer.

APPLY LIFE SKILLS

33. **Manage Stress** Suppose you are nervous about playing in your first piano recital. Explain what you could do to feel more relaxed.

34. **Communicate** Kevin's friend Anna offers him a piece of cake. Kevin has diabetes. How can Kevin use communication skills to explain that he can't eat the cake?

Promote Health  Home and Community

1. Talk with your family about what you've learned about good health habits and how they can prevent the spread of pathogens.
2. Make a poster that encourages people to wash their hands frequently to kill pathogens and to keep from spreading pathogens. Display it in a restroom at school.

Activities

Disease Detective

At Home • List all the ways you could have spread disease to your family members during the day. Decide how you can change your habits so that you don't spread pathogens to your family.

Speedy Diseases

On Your Own • Find out about epidemics. An epidemic is the very fast spread of a disease through a group of people. Choose one epidemic to learn more about. Write a paragraph that describes how the disease spread, what its symptoms were, and how it might have been prevented from spreading.

Disease-Fighting Kit

With a Team • Make a list of things that can be used to help people avoid spreading or getting pathogens. You might include tissues, paper cups, disinfectant spray, paper towels, and soap. Write instructions that tell how and when to use these things.

Food Gone Bad

With a Partner • Observe what happens to food that isn't stored properly. Choose two different foods, and place them in sealed zip-type bags. Keep the bag at room temperature. Check the foods every day for one week. Record your observations. Explain how you could prevent the foods from spoiling.

Multiple Choice

Choose the letter of the correct answer.

1. What are chemicals made by the body to help fight disease?
   a. cilia
   b. antibodies
   c. bacteria
   d. vaccines

2. Which of the following is an infectious disease?
   a. asthma
   b. diabetes
   c. arthritis
   d. flu

3. A _____ is an organism or virus that causes disease.
   a. pathogen
   b. symptom
   c. vaccine
   d. cilia

4. A noninfectious disease caused by cells growing out of control is _____.
   a. diabetes
   b. asthma
   c. heart disease
   d. cancer

5. One way to improve resistance is to _____.
   a. eat high-fat foods
   b. smoke cigarettes
   c. get plenty of rest
   d. stop exercising

Modified True or False

Write *true* or *false*. If a sentence is false, replace the underlined term to make the sentence true.

6. Signs of a disease are called <u>infections</u>.

7. An <u>infectious disease</u> is an illness that can be spread from person to person.

8. <u>Viruses</u> are one-celled living things that may cause disease.

9. <u>Asthma</u> is a disease in which the body cannot properly use sugar.

10. An <u>acute</u> disease lasts for a short time.

11. Washing your hands helps get rid of harmful <u>antibodies</u>.

12. Choosing not to <u>exercise</u> is an example of abstinence.

13. <u>Bee stings</u> can cause allergic reactions.

14. <u>White blood cells</u> are a part of your immune system.

15. A vaccine will <u>lessen</u> your immunity to a certain disease.

Short Answer

Write a complete sentence to answer each question.

16. Name two chronic diseases.

17. Name three things you can do to avoid disease.

18. Name three diseases caused by viruses.

19. What are some symptoms of arthritis?

20. Name three ways in which pathogens may be spread.

21. How does the skin help the body fight disease?

22. How does cigarette smoke affect the body?

23. Name four things you can do to stay well.

Writing in Health

Write paragraphs to answer each item.

24. Micha is moving to a new town. Describe how he could use the steps for managing stress to help him get used to his new environment.

25. Explain how living a healthful lifestyle helps your body avoid or control disease.

Organs Affected by Drugs

Medicines, Drugs, and Your Health

MAKE A DRUG POSTER

This chapter talks about how medicines and drugs affect your health. Make a poster that shows how using drugs can be harmful to your body. Choose one drug, and show all the organs it affects. Use information from this chapter and from pages 1–15 to help you.

For other activities, visit the Harcourt Learning Site. www.harcourtschool.com

173

Medicines Affect the Body

MAIN IDEA
Medicines can be helpful if they are used properly.

WHY LEARN THIS? Learning to use medicines safely will help you stay healthy.

VOCABULARY
- medicine
- drug
- side effects
- pharmacists
- prescription
- prescription medicines
- over-the-counter medicines
- dose

Have you ever taken medicine to bring down a high fever? Have you ever put first-aid cream on a cut to help it heal? Medicines can help you in these ways and in many other ways too.

What are medicines?

A **medicine** (MEH•duh•suhn) is a drug used to treat or cure a health problem. Pain relievers and cough syrups are types of medicines. A **drug** is a substance other than food that changes the way the body works. Marijuana and cocaine are types of drugs. All medicines are drugs, but not all drugs are medicines.

Medicines come in many forms—pills, liquids, sprays, and creams. The way a medicine is used depends on its purpose. Creams and some sprays are put directly on the area being treated. Other sprays are breathed in. Liquids and pills are swallowed. Some are given as shots. They enter the bloodstream and then are carried throughout the body. All drugs can cause changes in many parts of the body.

▼ There are thousands of kinds of medicines. The pictures on these two pages show a few ways medicines are used. Can you think of others?

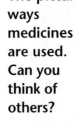
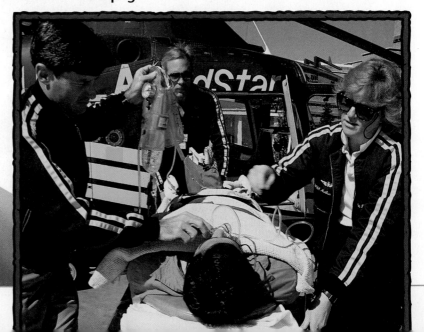

Medicines are powerful drugs that should be used only if absolutely needed. Good health habits can help prevent the need to use medicines. If you eat well, exercise, and get enough rest, you probably will stay healthy. You seldom will need medicines.

When you do not feel well, medicine should not be the first choice to make you feel better. You might not need it. If you have a mild headache, for example, take a walk or relax for a few minutes before asking a parent or another trusted adult for medicine.

If you do need medicine, it's important to use it carefully. When medicines are used correctly, they can make you feel better. But when medicines are not used correctly, they can harm you.

Even when used properly, all medicines have side effects. **Side effects** are unwanted changes in the body caused by a medicine. Adults take aspirin to relieve pain or reduce fever. But aspirin also can irritate or upset the stomach. That is one of its side effects. Doctors know the side effects of each medicine. So do **pharmacists** (FAR•muh•sists), people trained to prepare medicines. Most side effects are not harmful. But if you feel worse after taking a medicine, always tell an adult.

LIFE SKILLS
FOCUS

Make Decisions

Sally has a mild headache. She doesn't want to take medicine if she doesn't need to. What other things could Sally do to help her feel better? Which one seems like the best choice? Use the steps for making decisions shown on page *ix*.

• • •

What are prescription medicines?

There are many kinds of medicines. Some medicines can be found on a store shelf. Other medicines are available only through a doctor's order.

A **prescription** (prih•SKRIP•shuhn) is a doctor's order for a medicine. It has information such as the name of the medicine, how much you should take, and how often you should take it. The doctor writes the prescription. Then an adult takes the prescription to a pharmacist. The pharmacist fills the order for the medicine.

Medicines that an adult can buy only with a doctor's order are called **prescription medicines**. Each prescription medicine is meant for just one person. Never take another person's prescription medicine. This can be dangerous to your health.

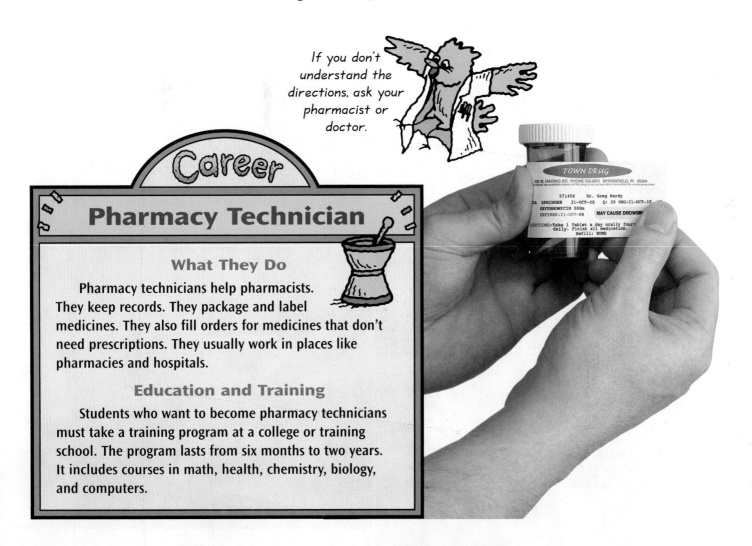

If you don't understand the directions, ask your pharmacist or doctor.

Career

Pharmacy Technician

What They Do

Pharmacy technicians help pharmacists. They keep records. They package and label medicines. They also fill orders for medicines that don't need prescriptions. They usually work in places like pharmacies and hospitals.

Education and Training

Students who want to become pharmacy technicians must take a training program at a college or training school. The program lasts from six months to two years. It includes courses in math, health, chemistry, biology, and computers.

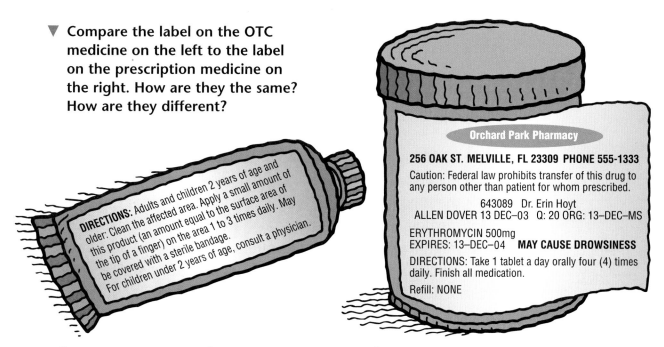

▼ Compare the label on the OTC medicine on the left to the label on the prescription medicine on the right. How are they the same? How are they different?

Orchard Park Pharmacy

256 OAK ST. MELVILLE, FL 23309 PHONE 555-1333

Caution: Federal law prohibits transfer of this drug to any person other than patient for whom prescribed.

643089 Dr. Erin Hoyt
ALLEN DOVER 13 DEC–03   Q: 20 ORG: 13–DEC–MS

ERYTHROMYCIN 500mg
EXPIRES: 13–DEC–04   **MAY CAUSE DROWSINESS**

DIRECTIONS: Take 1 tablet a day orally four (4) times daily. Finish all medication.

Refill: NONE

DIRECTIONS: Adults and children 2 years of age and older: Clean the affected area. Apply a small amount of this product (an amount equal to the surface area of the tip of a finger) on the area 1 to 3 times daily. May be covered with a sterile bandage. For children under 2 years of age, consult a physician.

What are over-the-counter medicines?

For some medicines you don't need to see a doctor. For a minor problem such as a slight sore throat or a rash, your parents or other adult family members may give you a medicine from the shelf of a pharmacy or supermarket. Medicines adults can buy without prescriptions are called **over-the-counter medicines**, or OTC medicines.

OTC medicines are used for minor problems. They are for short-term use. Cough medicines, laxatives, nose sprays, and some pain relievers are OTC medicines.

Labels on OTC medicines help people use them safely. They tell what health problems the medicine is supposed to treat. The label also gives information about the dose. A medicine's **dose** is the correct amount of the medicine that you should take every time you use it. The label also gives warnings to people who should not take the medicine. The label on aspirin may say "Children or teens should not use this medicine for chicken pox or flu."

OTC medicines must be used carefully. They contain drugs that can be harmful to your health if taken incorrectly. Never take an OTC medicine on your own. Tell a parent or another adult if you do not feel well.

SOCIAL STUDIES CONNECTION

Alternative Medicines

With a Partner
Research medicines from different cultures. You might research Native American medicines or Chinese medicines. How do these medicines treat health problems?

● ●●

How can you use medicines safely?

Medicines can help you only if you use them correctly. That is why you must know how to use and store them safely.

Many people become ill because they don't use medicines correctly. They don't follow the directions on the medicine label. They might take too much of the medicine, or they might take the wrong medicine. They might take medicine too often. Many people stop taking medicine before they should because they start to feel better. This practice can make a health problem worse.

Always use medicines safely. Whenever you take medicine, follow the rules on the Medicine Safety Checklist below.

Myth: If a little medicine is good for you, a lot is even better.

Fact: Taking too much of any medicine could cause illness or death. Scientists who develop medicines do tests to find the best dose. Always follow the directions on *any* medicine.

Medicine Safety Checklist

✓ Take medicines only with the help of an adult you trust.

✓ Follow directions on the medicine label, and use the proper dose.

✓ Do *not* take another person's prescription medicine.

✓ Do *not* buy an OTC medicine with a broken or missing safety seal.

✓ If a medicine makes you ill or has other side effects, tell an adult.

✓ Do *not* take pills with juice or hot drinks. They can stop the medicine from working properly. Use water.

✓ Do *not* crush or break capsules or pills without a doctor's permission.

✓ Store medicines safely and out of the reach of small children.

Activity **Follow the Rules** Study the medicine safety rules listed on these pages. Then list the safety rules you have followed in the past when using medicines. Have you followed all of these rules? If not, how will you change the way you use medicines in the future?

a. An adult should always give medicine to a child. People your age should not take *any* medicine on their own.

b. Keep medicines in the packages they come in. Safety caps help keep small children from harming themselves by taking medicines without the help of a trusted adult.

OPEN
PUSH DOWN & TURN
CLOSE

c. Throw away any medicine that is too old to use. Old medicines can change so that they make you ill. Other medicines no longer work when they get old.

Use Only as Directed

Directions: A
age and over; r
uct on chest an
with a dry, soft
to let the vapors
repeat up to thr
bedtime or as d
under 2 years o

d. Always follow label directions. This includes taking the proper dose and not taking the medicine more often than directed.

LESSON CHECKUP

Check Your Facts

1. What is a prescription medicine?

2. What is an over-the-counter medicine?

3. CRITICAL THINKING Over-the-counter medicine labels have information on the health problem for which the medicine should be used. Prescription medicines do not have such information. Why?

4. CRITICAL THINKING What might happen if medicine is placed in a bottle that has a label for another medicine?

Set Health Goals

5. Review the Medicine Safety Checklist. Which rule do you think is the most important? Why? What can you do to make sure you always follow the rules?

MAIN IDEA
Common household products and OTC medicines can be harmful if they are misused.

WHY LEARN THIS? If you learn about the dangers of common substances, you are unlikely to be harmed by them.

VOCABULARY
• addiction
• expiration date
• caffeine
• inhalants

Common Substances That Can Be Harmful

You probably have heard about the dangers of using illegal drugs like cocaine. But did you know that common substances around your home can also be dangerous?

What is addiction?

Shawna had a habit of drinking a cup of coffee in the morning. During the day she drank cola beverages and took OTC caffeine pills to stay awake. She started to feel nervous all the time. She could not sleep at night. But when she tried to stop drinking the coffee and soft drinks and taking the pills, she got a bad headache and she felt sleepy all the time. Shawna had an addiction.

An **addiction** (uh•DIK•shuhn) is the constant need or craving that makes a person use a drug even when he or she knows it is harmful. People who are addicted to a drug feel ill if they don't use it. It's very hard for them to stop using the drug. The more powerful the drug, the harder it is to break an addiction to it. It's easier to break an addiction to coffee than to cocaine or heroin. The best way to avoid addiction is to never take drugs. Some illegal drugs can get a person addicted after just one use. No one can predict who is likely to develop an addiction.

▶ The world does not look quite right when you take drugs. Drugs distort your senses. They slow coordination. They can make you sleepy or make you see things that are not there. It is impossible to do your best with a mind clouded by drugs.

► OTC medicines can be harmful if they are not used correctly. *Never* take a medicine unless a trusted adult gives it to you. Children should *never* decide on their own to take a medicine.

How can over-the-counter medicines be harmful?

OTC medicines can clear your stuffy nose. They can get rid of pimples. They can take away pain, soothe a sore throat, or stop an itch. But OTC medicines can also harm you if you misuse them.

People can misuse medicines in many ways. In most cases they simply don't read labels and follow directions. For example, medicines can be harmful if you take more than the right dosage. They also can be harmful if you take them more often than you should.

Medicines can be harmful if they are old. When adults buy OTC medicines, they should check the expiration date on the container. The **expiration date** (ek•spuh•RAY•shuhn DAYT) tells you how long it is safe to take the medicine. Medicine should not be used after this date. The safety seal also should be checked. Medicine should not be bought if the seal is broken.

Some people use medicines for purposes other than the intended use. For example, some people drink cough syrup because they like the way it makes them feel. Some people take laxatives to help them stay thin. Such practices often lead to serious health problems.

CONSUMER
FOCUS

Analyze Advertising and Media Messages
Some people misuse OTC medicines to reach what they think is a normal body. Movies and TV shows can give a false idea of what is normal. Look carefully at adults on three or four TV shows. How do they look compared to adults you know? What might happen if all adults tried to look like those on TV? Use the steps for analyzing media messages on page *xv*.

● ● ●

How can caffeine affect the body?

Caffeine (ka•FEEN) is a drug found in coffee, tea, chocolate, and some soft drinks. Caffeine speeds up the heart. It makes most people feel more awake.

Like all drugs, caffeine can change the way you feel, think, and act. Small amounts of caffeine will not harm most people. Many people drink a cup of coffee in the morning to wake up. However, too much caffeine can cause harmful changes in the body.

Large amounts of caffeine really speed up the heart. Caffeine can cause nervousness and prevent sleep. It also can cause headaches and upset stomachs. Like Shawna, described on page 180, people can become addicted to caffeine. Children, especially, should be careful not to take in too much caffeine. If you are thirsty, drink water, milk, fruit juices, or other caffeine-free products.

How can common substances in the home be harmful?

Products like nail polish remover, spray paint, markers, glue, and oven cleaners are safe when used correctly. But they give off poisonous fumes that can be harmful. Some people inhale these fumes to get high. A "high" is a common way of describing the effects people feel when they use drugs. Substances called **inhalants** (in•HAY•luhnts) give off fumes that some people sniff deeply to get high.

Substances used as inhalants contain dangerous poisons. Read their labels. Warnings often state that the products must be used where there is fresh air. Inhalants should be stored in a safe place, away from young children and food.

◀ Using inhalants such as correction fluid and marker pens can ruin your health or even kill you.

SNIFFING CORRECTION FLUID CAN STOP YOUR HEART.

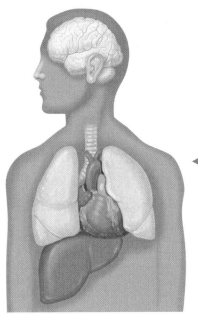

◄ Inhalants affect many parts of the body.

Tracking Inhalants

Identify the body systems that inhalants affect. Use the illustration of the human body on the left and the body systems shown on pages 1 to 15 to help you.

• • •

Immediate effects of inhalants include lack of coordination, tiredness, headache, nausea, confusion, and memory loss. People who use inhalants can become violent. Inhalants also can kill. Some inhalant users have died immediately from breathing in these poisons.

People who use inhalants over a long period of time can ruin their health. Inhalants can damage the skin, lungs, kidneys, and liver. Inhalants also can cause serious brain damage.

It is easy to become addicted to inhalants. Many inhalant users become so used to sniffing these poisons that they need more and more to get high. As they inhale larger amounts of the poisons, they increase their risk of serious illness or death.

LESSON CHECKUP

Check Your Facts

❶ What is addiction?

❷ Can over-the-counter medicines be harmful? Explain.

❸ Why is it important to know the effects of caffeine on the body?

❹ CRITICAL THINKING How can reading the labels on products used as inhalants protect people from harm?

Set Health Goals

❺ How many foods that contain caffeine do you eat or drink each day? Write down what you might do to reduce the amount of caffeine you take in each day.

MAIN IDEA
Marijuana and cocaine are illegal drugs that can harm the body and lead to addiction.

WHY LEARN THIS? Learning the dangers of marijuana and cocaine will make it easier for you to refuse to use them.

VOCABULARY
• illegal drug
• drug user
• marijuana
• drug dependence
• cocaine

Marijuana and Cocaine

Some drugs are so harmful that they are illegal (il•LEE•guhl). An **illegal drug** is a drug that is not a medicine and that is against the law to sell, buy, have, or use. A **drug user** is someone who uses illegal drugs. Drug users are harming their health and breaking the law. They often end up in jail.

▲ 1. Marijuana comes from this tall, leafy plant. It is illegal to grow marijuana in the United States.

▼ 2. Law enforcement officers find marijuana that is illegally grown and shipped on trucks and ships. They destroy the marijuana and arrest people who transport it.

What is marijuana?

Marijuana (mair•uh•WAH•nuh) is an illegal drug made from the hemp plant. It is sometimes called grass or pot. Some marijuana users roll loose marijuana into cigarettes called joints. Drug users also smoke marijuana in pipes or mix it into foods and eat it.

Hashish is another illegal drug made from the hemp plant. It is stronger than marijuana.

It is illegal to buy, sell, or use marijuana or hashish. It is even illegal to have some in your pocket. Different states have different marijuana laws. Most states impose a fine and time in jail for buying, selling, or using marijuana.

At one time leading drug experts did not think that marijuana was dangerous. However, scientists have gathered a lot of evidence that shows marijuana is indeed harmful to your health. Marijuana contains more than 400 substances, including THC. THC is a powerful drug that affects the brain.

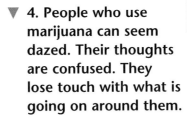

▼ 4. People who use marijuana can seem dazed. Their thoughts are confused. They lose touch with what is going on around them.

▲ 5. Most people do not use marijuana. But some are foolish enough to do so. Imagine the embarrassment of being arrested in front of the whole school!

▲ 3. Drug dealers sell marijuana illegally. If you are caught buying marijuana or if you just have it in your pocket, you can be arrested.

The effects of all of the substances in marijuana are not known. However, one ingredient is known to cause cancer. Marijuana smoke has 70 percent more of this ingredient than tobacco smoke does. There is more tar in marijuana than in cigarettes. Tar also is known to cause cancer. Marijuana users inhale deeply and hold the smoke in the lungs for as long as possible. It has been shown that someone who smokes five joints a week can take in as many cancer-causing chemicals as someone who smokes a pack of cigarettes a day. The other substances in marijuana may have other, as yet unknown, harmful effects on the body.

SOCIAL STUDIES CONNECTION

Looking Back at Hemp

On Your Own A type of hemp, called industrial hemp, is grown for nondrug use. People use the strong fibers of this plant to make rope. Research other ways industrial hemp is used.

● ●●

▲ The dried leaves and flowers of marijuana may be rolled into cigarettes called joints.

What are the short-term and long-term effects of marijuana use?

When someone smokes marijuana, many things happen to the body right away. Within a few minutes users often start to feel high. Their hearts start to beat very fast. Their mouths feel dry. They lose coordination and may feel dizzy. Their eyes may look red. People may also start to feel hungry after using marijuana. Some new users of marijuana have bad reactions to the drug. They may become nervous or think someone is after them.

THC, a drug in marijuana, affects nerve cells in the part of the brain that forms memories. That's why marijuana users find it hard to remember things that happen while they are high—even things that have just happened. They find it hard to pay attention to what is going on around them. THC also changes the way the senses work. Things may look or sound distorted. Time may seem to move very slowly.

How marijuana harms the brain:
- It makes it hard to learn.
- It makes it hard to remember things.
- It causes confusion.
- It makes it hard to judge time and distance.

How marijuana harms the heart:
- It makes the heart work harder than it should.

How marijuana harms the lungs:
- It damages the inside tissues.
- It may cause cancer.

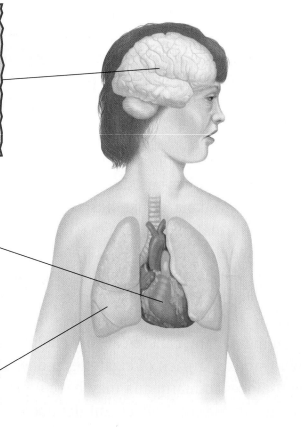

Heavy or long-term marijuana use causes serious problems. You already know that marijuana use affects the lungs. It also causes problems with the immune system, which protects the body from disease. Long-term marijuana use weakens the immune system, making it hard for the body to fight infections. Marijuana users tend to have more colds and other health problems than nonusers. Long-term marijuana use also can prevent the reproductive systems of young people from developing correctly.

Heavy marijuana use can lead to dependence on the drug. **Drug dependence** is the need to take a drug just to feel normal. When marijuana users try to stop using the drug, they might start shaking or have trouble sleeping. Each year thousands of people need help to stop using marijuana.

Tracking Marijuana

The diagram on page 186 shows some of the body organs harmed by marijuana smoke. Locate these organs on pages 1 to 15 of The Amazing Human Body. To which system does each organ belong?

How can cocaine harm the body?

Cocaine (koh•KAYN) is a powerful drug made from the leaves of the coca plant. Cocaine is often used as a white powder. Drug users sniff or snort it through the nose. When drug users sniff powdered cocaine, it reaches the brain in three to five minutes. Cocaine gives the users a burst of energy and increases the amount of chemicals in the brain that cause feelings of pleasure and self-confidence. But the feelings last for only five to forty minutes.

Cocaine harms the body. It forces the heart to beat faster. Users can find it hard to breathe. They can have severe chest pain. Large doses of cocaine can cause seizures or death from heart failure. Cocaine can also make blood pressure rise so high that blood vessels burst in the brain.

Crack is a solid rock form of cocaine. It is smoked rather than snorted. It produces the same effects as cocaine, but the body absorbs it faster. Crack is believed to be one of the most addictive illegal drugs in use.

▲ Cocaine is sold as a white powder. Crack, a powerful form of cocaine, is sold as lumps called rocks.

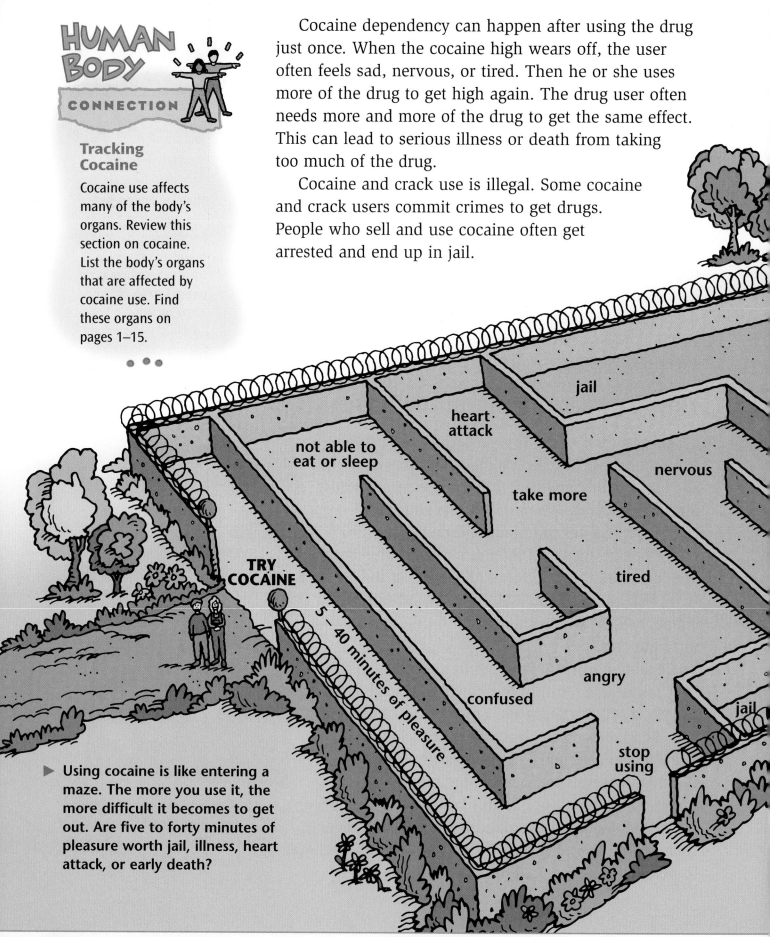

HUMAN BODY CONNECTION

Tracking Cocaine

Cocaine use affects many of the body's organs. Review this section on cocaine. List the body's organs that are affected by cocaine use. Find these organs on pages 1–15.

Cocaine dependency can happen after using the drug just once. When the cocaine high wears off, the user often feels sad, nervous, or tired. Then he or she uses more of the drug to get high again. The drug user often needs more and more of the drug to get the same effect. This can lead to serious illness or death from taking too much of the drug.

Cocaine and crack use is illegal. Some cocaine and crack users commit crimes to get drugs. People who sell and use cocaine often get arrested and end up in jail.

jail

heart attack

not able to eat or sleep

nervous

take more

tired

TRY COCAINE

5 – 40 minutes of pleasure

angry

confused

jail

stop using

▶ Using cocaine is like entering a maze. The more you use it, the more difficult it becomes to get out. Are five to forty minutes of pleasure worth jail, illness, heart attack, or early death?

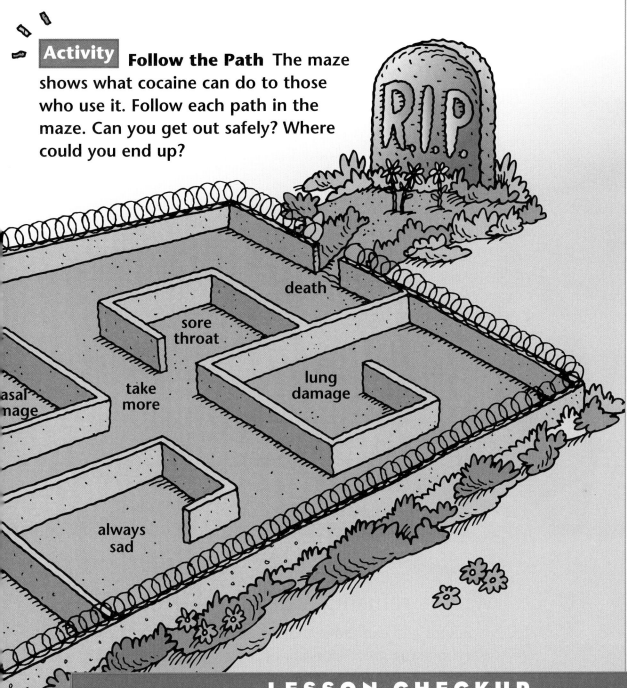

Activity **Follow the Path** The maze shows what cocaine can do to those who use it. Follow each path in the maze. Can you get out safely? Where could you end up?

death

sore throat

lung damage

asal nage

take more

always sad

LESSON CHECKUP

Check Your Facts

1 What is marijuana, and what are its effects on the body?

2 CRITICAL THINKING Why would using marijuana make it hard to do well in school?

3 What is cocaine, and what are its effects on the body?

4 How could the use of cocaine lead to addiction?

Use Life Skills

5 REFUSE Imagine that you have an older friend who offers you marijuana. How could you use refusal skills to help you say *no*?

Refusing to Use Drugs

MAIN IDEA
Knowing the facts about drugs makes it easy to say *no*.

WHY LEARN THIS? You can learn how to refuse drugs.

VOCABULARY
• peer pressure
• self-respect

Illegal drugs can make you ill. They can even kill you. If you use drugs, you are gambling with your health and your life. When you know the facts about drugs, it is easy to say *no* to drug use.

RESPECT YOURSELF

I like myself just the way I am.

KNOW THE FACTS

I don't think people would use drugs if they knew what could happen to them.

Why is refusing a healthful decision?

Before you can make a decision, you need facts. When making a decision about drugs, you need to know the health problems they cause. Think about what you have learned about drugs. You already know many of the reasons it is smart to stay away from drugs.

When you make a decision to refuse drugs, stick to your decision. Only you can decide what is right for you. Do not give in to peer pressure. **Peer pressure** is the longing to follow the crowd and do what others are doing. Others may try to tell you that using drugs is cool. Is putting your health at risk a cool thing to do? Remember, most people do not use drugs.

HAVE GOALS

I don't want anything to stop me from doing what I want to do with my life.

PURSUE YOUR INTERESTS

My friends and I are really into music.

STAY AWAY FROM DANGEROUS SITUATIONS

I've got better things to do.

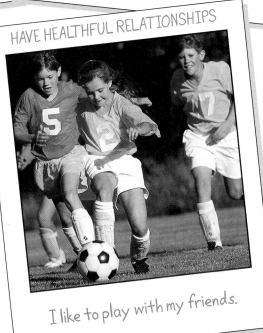

HAVE HEALTHFUL RELATIONSHIPS

I like to play with my friends.

When you refuse drugs, you are making a healthful, positive decision. You are building **self-respect**, the good feeling you have about yourself when you like yourself and are proud of what you do. Refusing drugs is one of the most healthful decisions you can make. It allows you to keep your body safe from harm and your mind clear. It helps you obey the law and stay out of trouble. You can then pursue your interests and achieve your goals.

JOURNAL

The photos here show many good reasons to refuse drugs. In your Health Journal, list your own reasons for refusing drugs. Remember, your journal is private and need not be shared with others.

How can you say *no* to drugs?

Are you ever tempted to try drugs? If so, first think about what might happen. If you use drugs, you will have to deal with the harm drugs can do to your body. You also will have to deal with the problems you could cause for your family and your friends. If you are caught, you will have to deal with the punishment.

Remember that it is *your* responsibility to keep yourself healthy and safe. Other people can give you reasons to avoid drugs, but you are the only person who can make the decision to say *no* to drugs and stick to that decision. If you want to live a long life, have fun, and reach your goals, stay away from drugs.

▶ This boy has thought about how he will say *no* to drugs. How will you say *no*?

What will you say if someone tries to get you to use drugs? Having a plan can help you say *no* with more confidence.

Getting involved with other activities you enjoy also will help you find friends who don't use drugs. You could join a sports team or a club. You could get involved in school plays or musical groups. Or you could work on art. What kinds of activities do you enjoy?

Organizations in your community offer activities for children. Check out a community center, a YMCA, or a religious center. Find ways to volunteer your time to help others.

If you have a problem, don't turn to drugs to get away from it. The problem will still be there when the drugs wear off. Talk to a trusted adult about your problem. At home, talk to your parents or guardians, grandparents, or an older brother or sister. At school, talk to a teacher or counselor. You also can talk to a school nurse or coach whom you trust.

People in your community can help too. Set up a time to speak to a trusted adult such as a doctor, a member of the clergy, or an adult family friend. Your community might have a drug counseling and treatment center. People there can talk to you about your problem and help you refuse drugs.

Remember that if you have a problem, you should not face it alone. And you should not turn to drugs. Many people can help you.

MUSIC CONNECTION

Check Out Lyrics

On Your Own
Listen to some popular music. Do any lyrics refer to drugs? Give examples. Rewrite any lyrics that send out the wrong messages about drug use.

LESSON CHECKUP

Check Your Facts

❶ List two reasons why refusing to use drugs is a healthful decision.

❷ List three healthful alternatives to drug use.

❸ CRITICAL THINKING How can knowing the harmful effects of drugs help you say *no*?

❹ CRITICAL THINKING Why is it important to talk to a trusted adult to get help in refusing drugs?

Use Life Skills

❺ REFUSE With a friend, practice ways of saying *no* to someone who offers you drugs.

REFUSE
OTC Medicines

Sometimes people think over-the-counter medicines are safer than prescription drugs. They might take more of these medicines than they should. They might take medicines they don't need. Learn to refuse medicines you don't need.

Learn This Skill

Lucy and Sofia are talking about finding time to study for a big math test. Lucy says her brother gave her some white pills that help her stay awake. She offers one to Sofia.

1. Say *no* and say why not.

"No, thanks," Sofia says. "My parents say not to take any kind of medicine unless they give it to me."
"My brother bought these at the drugstore," Lucy replies. "It's no big deal!"

2. Remember a consequence, and keep saying *no*.

"You might get sick if you take something you don't need," Sofia says.
"These little white pills won't hurt me," Lucy answers.

3. Suggest something else to do.

"Why don't you just go to bed earlier?" Sofia asks.
"Take one," Lucy says. "You'll thank me when you get an *A* on the math test!"

4. Repeat *no* and walk away.

"No, I don't need pills to get an *A*. I'll see you later," Sofia says as she walks away.

Practice This Skill

Use this summary as you solve the problems below.

Steps for Refusing

1. Say *no* and say why not.
2. Remember a consequence and keep saying *no*.
3. Suggest something else to do.
4. Repeat *no* and walk away.

A. Brett shows K.J. a bag of red pills he got from his brother. Brett says they are supposed to make you feel good and offers one to K.J. Help K.J. refuse.

B. Erin and Rosita find a small container with white powder in it. Erin suggests they take a small taste to see if they can tell what it is. How can Rosita use refusal skills to avoid tasting the powder?

MAIN IDEA
It's important to know the warning signs of a drug use problem and where to go for help.

WHY LEARN THIS? You can use what you learn to get help for yourself, family members, or friends who might need it.

VOCABULARY
• recovery

How Drug Users Can Get Help

Is someone you know using drugs? If so, he or she needs help. Learn to spot the warning signs of drug use. Once someone admits to having a drug problem, he or she can get help from many places.

What are the warning signs?

Matt is worried about his fifteen-year-old cousin Tim. They used to be very close. They did things together all the time. They went to the movies, to the park, and to baseball games. Now Tim has changed.

He is quieter than he used to be. He stays away from home a lot. When he does come home, he avoids the family. He often says that he is not hungry, and he does not eat with the rest of the family. He heads straight for his room and stays there most of the time with the door closed.

Tim used to be a good student. Now he skips school a lot. He says he doesn't feel well. Sometimes he goes out as if he's heading to school, but he never gets there.

Tim also used to be good at sports. He played on the basketball team. His basketball game has suffered too. When he plays, he misses shots he used to be able to make easily. He was one of the team's stars, but now he spends most of his time on the bench. He misses practice a lot, but he doesn't seem to care. The coach says that if his behavior does not improve, he'll be off the team.

Tim looks nervous and tired all the time. His eyes are red. He doesn't seem to care how he looks. Often his clothes aren't clean and his hair looks as if he didn't even comb it when he got out of bed.

Not only that, he doesn't want to be with Matt anymore. In fact, Tim seems to get mad at Matt for no reason at all. He yells at Matt for the slightest reason and ends up telling him to just go away.

Tim is showing many of the warning signs of someone who might have a drug problem. He probably won't admit his problem—at least not right away. But there are ways Matt can get help for Tim.

▼ Know the warning signs of drug abuse. Is someone you know suddenly nervous and secretive all the time? Does he or she neglect his or her health and appearance? Is he or she missing school or work? Does his or her mood change from one minute to the next, as shown here? He or she might be using drugs.

When does someone need help?

Answers to the following questions can help you decide if you or anyone you know needs help.

- Do you have friends who use drugs?
- Have your friends tried to get you to use drugs?
- Have you used drugs just for fun?
- Have you ever taken OTC drugs just to improve your mood?

If you can say *yes* to one or more of these questions, you might need to find help for yourself or for someone else.

You might think that a friend's or family member's drug problem is not your business. You also might think that you will hurt the person if you tell others. These ideas are not true. Taking drugs is harmful. You are doing the right thing if you try to help the person stop using drugs.

If you think you need help, or if a friend or a family member needs help, talk to your parents or guardians first about what you are feeling. If your parent or guardian needs help, speak to another adult you trust.

◀ **Does a friend suddenly seem distant and sad? Has he or she stopped taking part in activities with you and his or her other friends? Your friend might need help with a drug problem.**

Where can people get help?

There are many people in your family, school, and community to talk to about a drug problem—yours or someone else's. Don't be afraid to ask for help.

Many organizations also can help with **recovery**, the process a user goes through to stop taking drugs. You can find the names of these organizations at your school or community library. The librarian can help you find their names and addresses.

LIFE SKILLS
FOCUS

Make Decisions

Chad is worried about his older sister. She is always taking medicine even though she's not ill. Chad knows he should talk to someone about his sister. How could he use decision-making steps to decide whom to talk to? Use the steps for making decisions shown on page ix.

doctor

parents

◀ You can turn to many people for help with a drug problem.

therapist

guidance counselor

LESSON CHECKUP

Check Your Facts

❶ List three warning signs of drug use.

❷ What should you do if you think a friend has a drug problem?

❸ CRITICAL THINKING Why might missing more school than usual and getting lower grades be warning signs of a drug problem?

❹ CRITICAL THINKING Why might you know that your friend needs help before he or she knows it?

Use Life Skills

❺ COMMUNICATE Imagine that you have a friend who has a drug problem. What could you say to make him or her want to get help?

199

USE VOCABULARY

addiction (p. 180)
caffeine (p. 182)
cocaine (p. 187)
dose (p. 177)
drug (p. 174)
drug dependence (p. 187)

drug user (p. 184)
expiration date (p. 181)
illegal drug (p. 184)
inhalants (p. 182)
marijuana (p. 184)
medicine (p. 174)

over-the-counter
  medicines (p. 177)
peer pressure
  (p. 190)
pharmacists (p. 175)
prescription (p. 176)

prescription
  medicines (p. 176)
recovery (p. 199)
self-respect (p. 191)
side effects (p. 175)

Use the terms above to complete the sentences. Page numbers in ( ) tell you where to look in the chapter if you need help.

1. Unwanted changes in the body caused by a medicine are _____.

2. A drug in coffee that speeds up the body's systems is _____.

3. The process a user goes through to stop taking drugs is _____.

4. A _____ is someone who uses illegal drugs.

5. A substance other than food that changes the way the body works is a _____.

6. A powerful drug made from the leaves of the coca plant is _____.

7. The good feeling you have about yourself when you like yourself is called _____.

8. Medicines that an adult can buy without a prescription are _____.

9. A _____ is the correct amount of medicine that should be taken with each use.

10. The constant need or craving that makes people use a drug even when they know it is harmful is _____.

11. An illegal drug made from the hemp plant is _____.

12. _____ are substances that give off fumes people sometimes sniff to get high.

13. A drug that is against the law to sell, buy, have, or use is an _____.

14. The push to follow the crowd and do what other kids are doing is _____.

15. Medicines that an adult can buy only with a doctor's order are _____.

16. _____ are people trained to prepare medicines.

17. The _____ is the last date a medicine can be used safely.

18. A drug used to treat or cure a health problem is a _____.

19. The need to take a drug just to feel normal is _____.

20. A _____ is a doctor's order for a medicine.

CHECK YOUR FACTS

Page numbers in ( ) tell you where to look in the chapter if you need help.

21. What is a medicine? (p. 174)

22. Study the OTC medicines in the photo below. List three safety rules you should follow when taking such medicines. (p. 178)

23. List three beverages that contain caffeine. (p. 182)

24. List three illegal drugs. (pp. 184, 187)

25. Name two people you can talk to about a problem. (p. 193)

26. How can you find the names of drug counseling and treatment organizations? (p. 199)

THINK CRITICALLY

27. Why aren't all medicines over-the-counter medicines?

28. Why is it important to know the warning signs of drug use?

APPLY LIFE SKILLS

29. **Make Decisions** You have just returned from a long hike. Your legs are tired and your feet hurt. You can ask your parents for medicine to make you feel better, or you can try something that does not require medicine. What do you decide? Explain your decision.

30. **Refuse** Someone offers to sell you marijuana. How would you refuse?

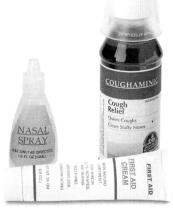

Promote Health Home and Community

1. Discuss with family members the information and safety rules you have learned about taking medicines. Make a medicine safety checklist like the one shown on page 178 to post near where medicines are stored.
2. Draw a poster that tells people to say *no* to drugs. Display it in class.

Activities

Magazine Search

With a Team • Look at pictures and ads in magazines to see how they show medicines. Do the ads and pictures encourage people to use medicines? Do the ads include warnings about how medicines can be misused? Give your opinion of the way the medicines are shown. Share the pictures and ads, along with your opinions of them, with your class.

Eye on Inhalants

With a Partner • If you don't think inhalants are dangerous, read the labels. Look at the labels of several products used as inhalants such as markers, glue, spray paint, nail polish remover, and oven cleaner. Make a list of the warnings from each label.

SNIFFING CORRECTION FLUID CAN STOP YOUR HEART.

What's the Story?

On Your Own • Interview a person in your community who works with drug users. Ask the person to tell you about the problems drugs cause for others. You might talk to a police officer, a doctor, a nurse, or a counselor. Take notes and share the stories you hear with your class.

Medicine Hunt

At Home • Medicines come in many different forms, including pills, liquids, sprays, and creams. With an adult family member, look for different forms of medicine in your home. List the types you find. What is each used for?

Multiple Choice

Choose the letter of the correct answer.

1. A _____ is a drug that treats or cures a health problem.
   a. dose
   b. recovery
   c. medicine
   d. pharmacy

2. Inhalants are common substances with poisonous _____.
   a. coverings
   b. fumes
   c. rays
   d. side effects

3. _____ is a powerful substance in marijuana that affects the brain.
   a. THC
   b. Cocaine
   c. Nitrogen
   d. TLC

4. People who have self-respect _____ themselves.
   a. hurt
   b. hate
   c. like
   d. teach

5. People who have a constant need for a drug have an _____.
   a. attack
   b. aversion
   c. apprehension
   d. addiction

Modified True or False

Write _true_ or _false_. If a sentence is false, replace the underlined term to make the sentence true.

6. <u>All</u> medicines are drugs.

7. OTC medicines are for <u>short-term</u> use.

8. Caffeine <u>slows down</u> the heart.

9. Inhalants include <u>glue</u>, spray paint, and markers.

10. Marijuana and cocaine are <u>legal</u> drugs.

11. Cocaine users easily can become <u>addicted</u>.

12. <u>Peer pressure</u> is the longing to follow what other kids are doing.

13. You can talk to a <u>parent</u> if you have a problem.

14. People who suddenly <u>love</u> their appearance might be using drugs.

15. People who know the <u>warning signs</u> of drug use can help others who have a problem.

Short Answer

Write a complete sentence to answer each question.

16. Why is it important to know a medicine's side effects?

17. Why is it necessary to read medicine labels?

18. Why does coffee give people an extra boost when they drink it?

19. Why is it dangerous to sniff inhalants?

20. How does the THC in marijuana affect the brain?

21. What harmful effects does cocaine have on the body?

22. Someone tells you that using drugs is cool and that everyone is doing it. What would you say to that person?

23. Why is it important to know where to find help for someone with a drug problem?

Writing in Health

Write paragraphs to answer each item.

24. How can over-the-counter medicines sometimes be dangerous?

25. Some drugs are illegal to have, buy, or use. Why?

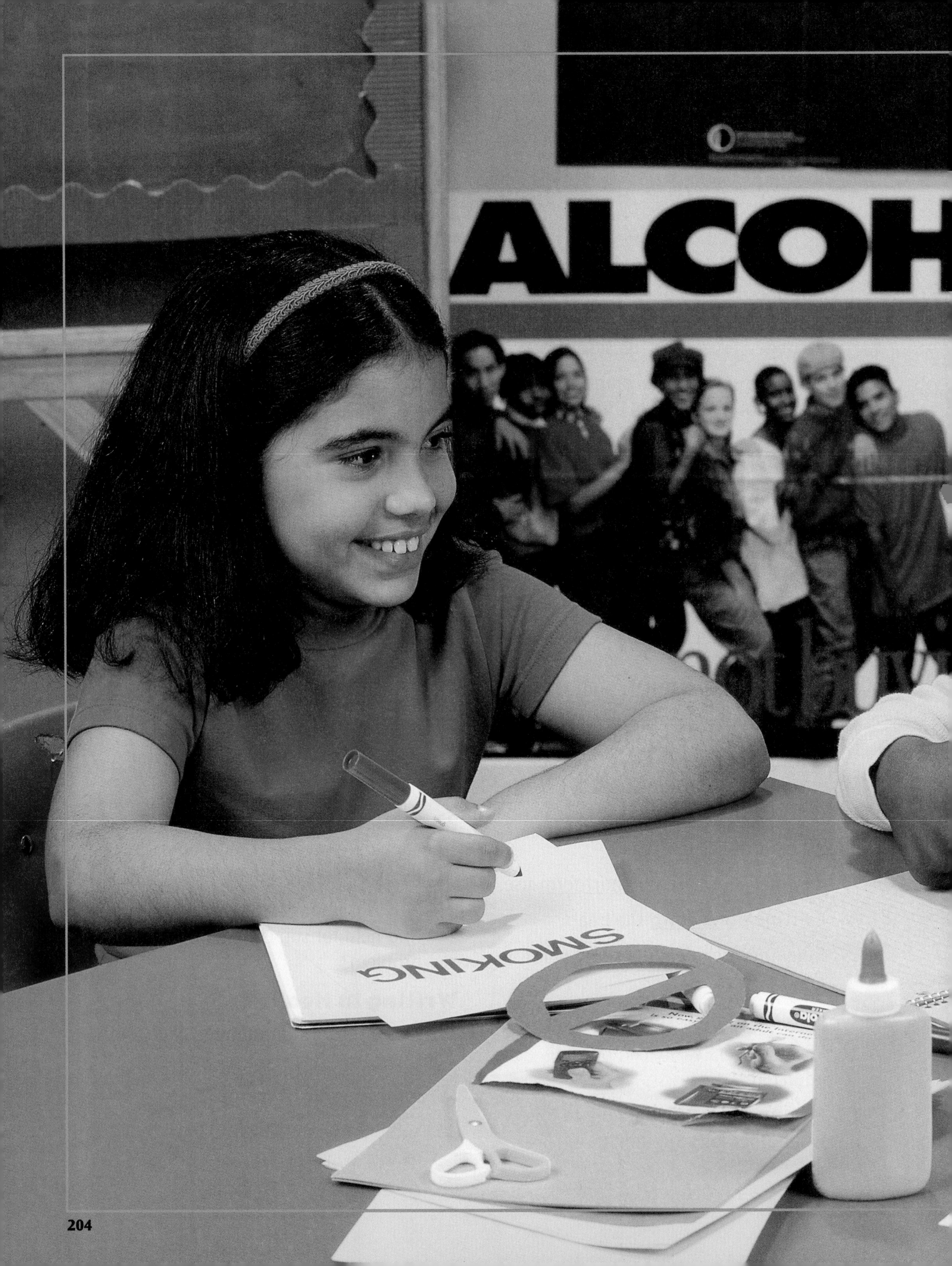
ALCOH
SMOKING

Harmful Effects of Tobacco and Alcohol

Project

TRUTHFUL AD SCRAPBOOK

Gather several different ads for alcohol and tobacco products. What is the stated message in each ad? What else do the ads suggest? Rewrite each ad to present the facts about alcohol and tobacco, using what you learn in this chapter. Put the old ads and new ads together in a scrapbook.

For other activities, visit the Harcourt Learning Site. www.harcourtschool.com

MAIN IDEA
Tobacco products contain many substances that harm the body.

WHY LEARN THIS?
Understanding that tobacco is a harmful drug can help you refuse to use it.

VOCABULARY
• tobacco
• nicotine
• tar
• environmental tobacco smoke (ETS)

How Tobacco Harms Body Systems

Would you put garbage into a beautiful clear pond? What would you do if you found someone else pouring garbage into it? Breathing smoke into your lungs is like polluting a clear pond. When people smoke, they poison both themselves and others.

What is tobacco?

A tobacco plant is about as tall as an adult human and has big green leaves. The shredded brown material inside a cigarette, called **tobacco**, is made from the dried leaves of this plant.

When people light cigarettes, they breathe tobacco smoke into their lungs. Another kind of tobacco—chewing tobacco—comes in pouches. People who use chewing tobacco put small wads of it into their mouths.

Snuff is another tobacco product. People put a pinch of snuff in their mouths along the gums. This is called *dipping*.

◀ Unlike tobacco ads, which often glamorize smoking, these posters tell the truth about cigarettes.

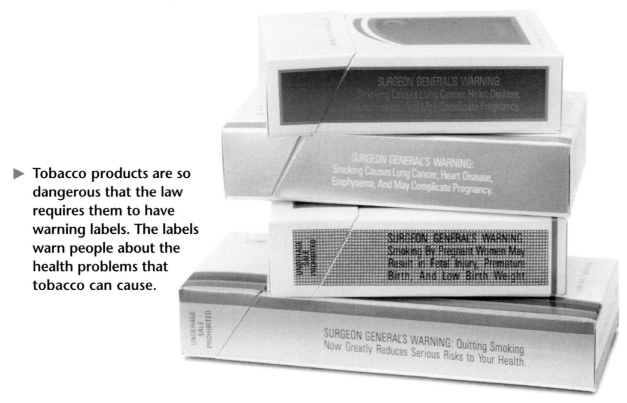

▶ Tobacco products are so dangerous that the law requires them to have warning labels. The labels warn people about the health problems that tobacco can cause.

All forms of tobacco contain a chemical called nicotine. **Nicotine** (NIH•kuh•teen) is a highly addictive substance that speeds up the nervous system. Being addicted to nicotine means that it is hard to stop using it. Tobacco users find it very hard to be without nicotine.

Nicotine is also a powerful poison. Some farmers have sprayed their crops with nicotine. The nicotine kills insects that harm the crops. Drinking just a tablespoonful of pure nicotine can kill a person.

Tobacco smoke also contains many other harmful substances. In fact, tobacco smoke contains more than 4,000 different substances. More than 40 of those substances are known to cause cancer. You learned in Chapter 5 that cancer is a disease in which clumps of deadly cells grow. These clumps, called *tumors*, harm the normal cells around them. Cancer often causes death.

Another dangerous substance in tobacco smoke is tar. **Tar** is a dark, sticky material that coats the lungs and air passages of smokers. Tar buildup makes it hard for a smoker to breathe.

The people who make laws know about the dangers of using tobacco. By making it against the law for young people to use or buy tobacco, they try to protect young people from these dangers.

Why do some people use tobacco?

Most adults who use tobacco started when they were young. They may have tried tobacco because they were curious about its effects. Or they may have started smoking because friends urged them to try it. Other people may have tried chewing tobacco because they saw their favorite baseball player using it.

Some young people think that using tobacco will make them look grown up. Instead, smoking makes a smoker's body and clothing smell bad. All the tars and poisons make a smoker's hair sticky. Chemicals from smoking and chewing tobacco cause bad breath and yellow teeth. Some cigarettes and all chewing tobacco and snuff contain sugars that can lead to tooth decay.

▶ Young people who see adults smoking may want to do the same thing.

Many young people see adults around them using tobacco. They see people using it on television or in movies. Some young people think that using tobacco is a way to act grown up. But they don't know something important—most adult tobacco users wish they didn't smoke or use chewing tobacco or snuff! Many want to quit but can't.

She has yellow teeth.

Her hair smells like smoke.

She has bad breath.

Her clothes stink.

"Smoking is gross!"

Smoking stinks!

◀ This woman can't smell the truth about cigarette smoke.

Ask any adult tobacco user how he or she started using this drug. Most will tell you a similar story. They will say that people who use tobacco for the first time usually think they can quit any time. They think they can try smoking or chewing tobacco just for a short while. They may plan to smoke only when they are with friends or to chew tobacco or dip snuff only when they play sports. They never consider that they might not be able to stop easily.

Most people cough the first time they smoke a cigarette. They might get dizzy or have an upset stomach or shortness of breath. These feelings are warning signs that cigarette smoke is poisoning their bodies. Their bodies are telling them not to smoke.

Some first-time users will stop smoking, but many will try to smoke again and again. After a while the body gets used to the smoke, and the smoker begins to smoke more often. In a short time quitting becomes hard for the smoker. The person begins to crave the nicotine in cigarettes. The smoker may get nervous or depressed when he or she doesn't smoke. The smoker has little control over his or her use of tobacco. He or she has become addicted to nicotine.

How is tobacco harmful to body systems?

Smoking is very dangerous to a person's health. Over time a smoker is much more likely than a nonsmoker to develop cancer and other diseases.

Cancers caused by using tobacco include lung cancer and mouth cancer. Lung cancer grows in a smoker's lungs. It eventually blocks the lungs' air passages and can cause death. Mouth cancer occurs most often in people who use chewing tobacco or snuff. To treat it, doctors often must cut away part of the patient's face, lips, or tongue to remove the cancer. Some cancers of the mouth can't be treated and can lead to death.

HUMAN BODY CONNECTION

The Heart and Lung Connection

Look at the circulatory and respiratory systems on pages 10–13. Trace how nicotine from the lungs gets into the bloodstream to affect blood vessels, the brain, and the heart.

Smoking can ruin your game!

Nicotine changes the brain. The body begins to crave tobacco. Quitting tobacco becomes hard.

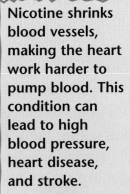

Nicotine shrinks blood vessels, making the heart work harder to pump blood. This condition can lead to high blood pressure, heart disease, and stroke.

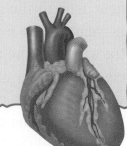

Tar coats the lungs and air passages, leading to coughs and respiratory diseases. Lung cancer or lung disease can develop. Breathing can become difficult—or impossible!

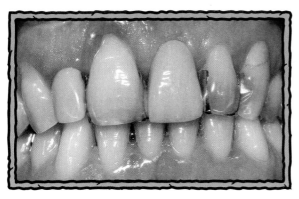

◄ **Using tobacco can ruin a smile. Nicotine in tobacco leaves dark stains on teeth and harms gums.**

Other diseases affect smokers' lungs, too. Smokers get more coughs, colds, and sore throats than nonsmokers do. Smokers are also more likely to have bronchitis (brahn•KY•tuhs) and emphysema (emp•fuh•ZEE•muh) because of tar damage in their lungs. Both of these diseases limit a person's ability to breathe, and both can kill.

Tobacco users are also much more likely to have heart disease. Nicotine makes the heart work harder and faster than usual because the gases in cigarette smoke take the place of oxygen in the blood. All the cells in your body need oxygen to live. When tobacco smoke lowers oxygen in the body, the heart must work harder to get oxygen to all the body's cells. High blood pressure and heart disease can result when the heart has to work too hard. Heart disease kills many smokers.

Environmental tobacco smoke can cause the same diseases in nonsmokers. **Environmental tobacco smoke (ETS)** comes from burning cigarettes, pipes, or cigars and from smoke that is breathed out by smokers. Children who live with smokers get more infections—including coughs, colds, sore throats, bronchitis, and asthma—than do children in smoke-free homes.

ART CONNECTION

Make a Poster

On Your Own Make a poster that encourages young people not to use tobacco. Draw pictures that show how cigarettes, chewing tobacco, and snuff can harm a person's health.

LESSON CHECKUP

Check Your Facts

1 Give two reasons why nicotine is dangerous.

2 Many people who are addicted to tobacco try to quit. How might they feel at first without tobacco?

3 CRITICAL THINKING Why would nonsmokers want to limit the places where people can smoke?

4 Name two diseases that can happen to people who use chewing tobacco or snuff.

Use Life Skills

5 COMMUNICATE Write about a physical activity you enjoy. How would smoking affect your ability to do this activity?

MAIN IDEA Alcohol is an addictive drug that can harm the body and mind.

WHY LEARN THIS? Knowing the dangers of alcohol can help you refuse to use it.

VOCABULARY
- alcohol
- blood alcohol level (BAL)
- cirrhosis
- intoxicated
- alcoholism
- alcoholic

How Alcohol Harms Body Systems

Do you know the difference between legal and illegal drugs? Legal drugs can be bought in stores. But it is against the law to buy, sell, or use illegal drugs. Some drugs are legal for adults to use but illegal for young people. Alcohol is a drug that is legal for adults to use, if they use it responsibly.

What is alcohol?

Alcohol is a drug found in drinks such as beer and wine and in liquors such as vodka, gin, rum, and brandy. A single serving of most types of alcoholic drinks contains the same amount of alcohol. One 12-ounce bottle of beer has about the same amount of alcohol as 5 ounces of wine or an ounce and a half of liquor.

The more a person drinks, the higher the person's blood alcohol level will be. **Blood alcohol level (BAL)** is the amount of alcohol in a person's blood. For example, a person who drinks two beers will have a blood alcohol level of 0.04 and may have trouble remembering things.

Alcohol changes the way a person feels, acts, and thinks. It also changes the way the body works. People

*These effects are based on adults who weigh about 150 pounds (about 68 kg). Young people or lighter-weight people might show these effects with fewer drinks.

HOW ALCOHOL AFFECTS THE BODY*

Number of Beers	BAL	Effect on a Person's Body
1 beer mug	0.015	reduced concentration, reflexes slowed
2 beer mugs	0.04	short-term memory loss
4 beer mugs	0.1	seven times more likely to have a car crash if driving
12 beer mugs	0.3	vomiting/unconsciousness

may find it hard to walk or speak after drinking alcohol. Size and age can affect how the body responds to alcohol. After drinking the same amount of alcohol, a person who is small will have a higher BAL than will someone who is large. Young people often feel the effects of alcohol more intensely than do older people.

Why do some people use alcohol?

Some adults drink alcohol as part of religious ceremonies, cultural events, or celebrations. For example, some people drink champagne at weddings. Others drink small amounts of wine in church as part of a ceremony.

Some adults have small amounts of wine or beer with meals or at parties. Most adults who drink in these instances do not have problems with alcohol. Alcohol does not interfere with their work or family life.

But some people drink too much alcohol, or drink it too often. They may drink to relax or to hide feelings of loneliness, nervousness, or depression. They may become addicted to alcohol. They crave alcohol and need it more and more often.

Some young people begin using alcohol because they see adults using it. They are curious about its effects. They think drinking alcohol will make them seem grown up. Many young people think drinking alcohol will increase their fun. Other young people may try alcohol because their friends pressure them to try it. They want to feel part of a group.

Activity **Evaluate a Role Model** Notice how the younger sister has imitated her older sister. Suppose the younger sister has seen her older sister drinking a beer. What choice might the younger sister make in picture 3?

SOCIAL STUDIES
CONNECTION

Historic Beverages

With a Partner When Europeans first came to North America, people did not commonly drink water. Find out what beverages they drank instead. Were any of these beverages alcoholic? How were these beverages made?

● ● ●

▼ Driving after drinking alcohol is dangerous. So is riding with a driver who has been drinking. Alcohol affects many skills that are needed to drive safely.

How can alcohol harm body systems?

The food a person eats is slowly digested into nutrients that are small enough to enter the bloodstream. The blood then delivers these nutrients to all parts of the body. Alcohol does not need to be digested. Instead, it goes directly into the bloodstream from the stomach and small intestine. The blood then quickly carries alcohol to the brain.

Alcohol slows down the brain. Because the brain controls the body's functions, alcohol can have many immediate effects, including

- difficulty walking steadily
- loss of memory
- decreased ability to think clearly and make decisions
- blurred vision
- slurred speech
- dizziness

Alcohol changes the way a person feels, too. After one drink an average-size adult might feel relaxed. After several drinks the person might feel ill, sleepy, angry, or depressed.

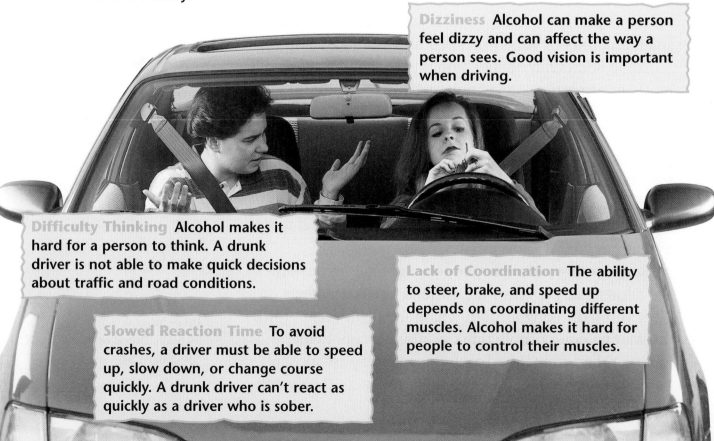

Dizziness Alcohol can make a person feel dizzy and can affect the way a person sees. Good vision is important when driving.

Difficulty Thinking Alcohol makes it hard for a person to think. A drunk driver is not able to make quick decisions about traffic and road conditions.

Lack of Coordination The ability to steer, brake, and speed up depends on coordinating different muscles. Alcohol makes it hard for people to control their muscles.

Slowed Reaction Time To avoid crashes, a driver must be able to speed up, slow down, or change course quickly. A drunk driver can't react as quickly as a driver who is sober.

Alcohol in the Body

Nervous System Nerves carry messages more slowly between the brain and the rest of the body, slowing reaction time.

Brain Heavy drinking can damage the parts of the brain linked to memory. Over time some short-term effects of alcohol—poor vision and loss of coordination—become permanent.

Liver Poisons in alcohol collect in the liver, scarring the liver and making it hard for the liver to clean the blood. Over time the liver may stop working.

Heart Alcohol makes the heart beat faster, raising blood pressure. Heavy drinking can cause hypertension, a condition of constant high blood pressure.

Pancreas The pancreas makes important chemicals that help the body work. Alcohol can harm the pancreas, causing severe pain and vomiting.

Stomach Alcohol causes the stomach to secrete digestive juices. These juices irritate the stomach when there is no food present. Small holes, called ulcers, may form in the stomach lining.

Long-time overuse of alcohol can damage the brain permanently. Alcohol affects the way a person thinks and makes decisions and can affect memory. Long-term heavy drinking affects the nervous system and can cause stomach cancer. Drinking too much alcohol also contributes to heart disease.

Other organs of the body, especially the liver, can be damaged by heavy drinking. The liver cleans the blood of poisons, such as alcohol. It also stores some nutrients the body needs. Alcohol can cause the liver to work too hard. **Cirrhosis** (suh•ROH•suhs) is a liver disease that results from drinking too much alcohol. The liver can become so damaged that it won't work anymore. The drinker can die.

Many heavy drinkers do not eat well. Alcohol makes it hard for the body to absorb nutrients from food. A heavy drinker may suffer from malnutrition because the body doesn't get all the nutrients it needs.

HUMAN BODY CONNECTION

Identify Body Systems

Identify all body systems that are affected by drinking alcohol. Refer to the diagrams shown here and the ones on pages 1–15 of The Amazing Human Body.

▲ Alcohol is a safety problem as well as a health problem. About four of every ten fatal car crashes are related to alcohol use.

How does problem drinking affect people?

A problem drinker is often intoxicated from drinking too much alcohol. Being **intoxicated** (in•TAHK•suh•kay•tuhd) means being strongly affected by alcohol. Intoxicated people behave differently than they would if they were not drinking. They have trouble thinking and making good decisions. They may say things that make others angry. They lose friends.

Problem drinkers may get into serious situations that hurt themselves and others. They cause car crashes that may harm or kill themselves and other people. Sometimes problem drinkers fall asleep when smoking cigarettes, resulting in fires that can harm themselves and others.

Problem drinkers often miss work or do a poor job. As a result, they may have trouble keeping a job. Young drinkers can't concentrate on schoolwork and often miss school. As they lose interest in their classes, their grades fall.

Activity **Examine a Drinker's Problems** Like a chain of dominoes, drinking can start small and spread to affect all parts of an alcoholic's life. Write a story that describes how a family might react to a family member's drinking.

Problem drinkers often are addicted to alcohol. They cannot stop drinking without help. They have a disease called **alcoholism** (AL•kuh•haw•lih•zuhm). A person who has this disease is called an **alcoholic** (al•kuh•HAW•lik).

The families of alcoholics often suffer. People who are intoxicated can't think about the needs of others—not even family members. Alcohol makes some people verbally and physically abusive. Some intoxicated people become violent and destroy property. They may hurt others or be arrested by the police. Their behavior can change from day to day.

LESSON CHECKUP

Check Your Facts

❶ Name three types of drinks that contain alcohol.

❷ CRITICAL THINKING Why does alcohol affect so many skills that are needed to drive safely?

❸ You know that alcohol damages several body systems. What are some other reasons that drinking alcohol can be a problem?

❹ Why is it a bad idea for anyone who has been drinking to drive?

Set Health Goals

❺ List five things you enjoy doing that require good vision, memory, coordination, speed, balance, or speaking skills. What would happen if a person tried to do these things while drinking alcohol? Explain your answer.

MAIN IDEA
Knowing the facts about alcohol and tobacco can help prepare you to refuse them.

WHY LEARN THIS? Saying *no* to alcohol and tobacco can help keep you safe and healthy.

VOCABULARY
• peer pressure

Saying *No* to Alcohol and Tobacco

Some young people think using alcohol and tobacco shows that they are grown up. But most adults choose not to use tobacco. Many adults use alcohol rarely, if ever. You should know how to refuse to use these drugs because they can be harmful to your health and well-being.

How can you prepare to say *no*?

Someday, someone may offer you alcohol or tobacco. You learned earlier in this chapter about the harmful effects of these products. For many people, knowing about these harmful effects is enough to make them choose to say *no*.

But what if someone tells you that everyone else uses alcohol and tobacco? You might feel pressured to do something you don't want to do. Knowing several reasons why people don't use these drugs can help you prepare to say *no*.

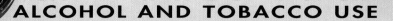

ALCOHOL AND TOBACCO USE

If You Say *Yes*	If You Say *No*
You may develop lung or liver disease.	Your organs are more likely to be healthy.
Your breath, clothing, and hair will smell bad.	You are more likely to be alert and in control.
You are more likely to be in a car crash or a fire.	Your body is more likely to be healthy, and you will have more energy.
You may have problems at home or at school.	You will have a better chance to do your best.

Many people simply don't like the way alcohol or tobacco tastes or smells. Other people are allergic to alcohol or tobacco. Drinking or using tobacco makes them physically uncomfortable or ill. Still others find that alcohol makes them feel nervous, sad, or out of control. They have more fun and feel better without these drugs.

Some families have rules that don't allow family members to drink alcohol or use tobacco. Others may practice a religion that doesn't allow them to use these drugs. Still others want to spend their money wisely. They don't want to use it to buy things that ruin their health.

Finally, it's against the law for people under age twenty-one to buy or use alcohol. Although local laws vary, in most places people under the age of eighteen cannot buy tobacco products. People who offer these drugs to you are breaking the law. They are inviting you to break the law, too.

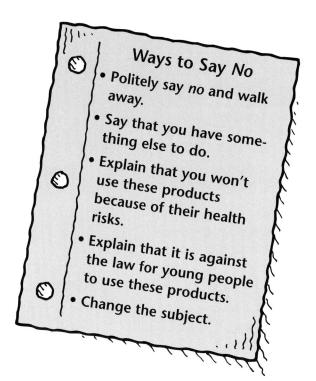

Ways to Say No
- Politely say no and walk away.
- Say that you have something else to do.
- Explain that you won't use these products because of their health risks.
- Explain that it is against the law for young people to use these products.
- Change the subject.

How can you deal with peer pressure?

Think about ways to refuse alcohol and tobacco products. Practice saying *no* so that you will know what to do when someone offers you tobacco or alcohol.

The best way to say *no* to alcohol and tobacco is to avoid situations where there is peer pressure to use them. **Peer pressure** means being influenced by friends to do something. Young people often find it difficult not to give in to peer pressure.

You can avoid peer pressure by staying away from people who use alcohol and tobacco. Don't go to places where alcohol is being served to young people. Make friends with people who share your decision not to use these drugs. Most important, feel good about yourself. You have the right to do what you think is best for your health and safety.

LIFE SKILLS FOCUS

Refuse

Lorna loves to play basketball. Lately her friends have been pressuring her to smoke cigarettes. Tell how smoking might affect Lorna's ability to play basketball. List the ways she can refuse to use tobacco. Use the steps shown on page *xi*.

● ● ●

CONSUMER FOCUS

Analyze Advertising and Media Messages
Take notes about TV or magazine ads for alcohol or tobacco. How do the ads try to make tobacco and alcohol use seem glamorous? Use the steps for Analyzing Advertising and Media Messages on page *xv* in the front of this book.

What should you know about advertisements for alcohol and tobacco?

Companies that make alcoholic beverages and tobacco products use advertisements to send messages. They want you to think that people who use alcohol and tobacco have lots of fun. The people in the ads are young and beautiful. They wear stylish clothes and drive expensive cars. Advertisers want young people to think that using alcohol and tobacco is glamorous, fun, and healthful.

Beer makers use TV commercials to advertise their products during sporting events. They hope you will see their commercials and think that their beer is fun and exciting.

▶ Tobacco ads often present a glamorous picture of smoking. The made-up names on these cigarettes tell the real facts about smoking.

Activity **Put Truth into Advertising**
Alcoholic beverages often have trendy
names to get people to use the products.
Use what you know about the effects of
alcohol to make up a truthful brand name
for this product.

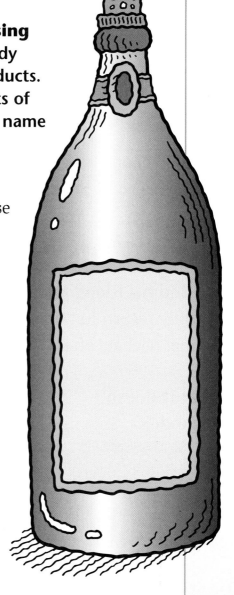

Cigarette companies are not allowed to advertise
on television. But you can still see the names of
their products on TV. They sponsor sporting and
cultural events and use signs and billboards to
advertise. Quite often you'll see the names or
pictures of cigarette products in the background.

Look at ads for alcohol or tobacco on
billboards, in magazines, or on television. Think
about what really happens to people who use
alcohol or tobacco—they aren't healthy, they
don't have much fun, and they smell bad. They
may have a hard time keeping jobs or keeping
their families together. They waste money on
these drugs.

Ads for alcohol and tobacco never show
how hard it is for a person to quit using these
products. They never show how much money
has been wasted or the ways in which people
become ill or die from using these products.

LESSON CHECKUP

Check Your Facts

❶ List three reasons for refusing to use
tobacco and alcohol.

❷ How can your choice of friends affect
your health and safety?

❸ CRITICAL THINKING Tobacco ads often
appear on the walls of places where
sporting events take place. Why does this
seem wrong?

❹ List four ways to say *no* to alcohol and
tobacco.

Use Life Skills

❺ COMMUNICATE Create an honest
billboard ad for an alcohol or tobacco
product. Using pictures and words, show
or tell what really happens to people who
use the product.

REFUSE TO USE
Alcohol and Tobacco

Someday someone may offer you alcohol or tobacco. Knowing how to say *no* can help you make a healthful choice.

Learn This Skill

Davon and his friend Michael are thirsty after playing soccer. When they return to Michael's house, Michael's parents are not home. Michael offers Davon a beer. How can Davon refuse?

Say that it doesn't taste good.

"Hey, let's have a beer," Michael says. "That stuff tastes awful," Davon says.

Say that it's against the law.

"All the kids are drinking it at parties," Michael insists.
"I don't want to get in trouble," says Davon. "It's against the law for kids to drink."

Suggest something else to do.

"Just try a sip," Michael says.
"I'm really thirsty. I'd rather have a glass of water," Davon suggests.

Say *no* and walk away.

"I don't want any. I really should be going," Davon says as he walks away.

Practice This Skill

Use this summary as you solve the problems below.

> ### Ways to Refuse
>
> - Say that it doesn't taste good.
> - Say that it's against the law.
> - Suggest something else to do.
> - Say *no* and walk away.

A. A boy offers Cecilia and Mattie cigarettes as they are walking home from school. How can Cecilia and Mattie refuse?

B. Jeff's older sister offers him a glass of wine when their parents are away. How can Jeff refuse?

How Alcoholics and Tobacco Users Get Help

MAIN IDEA
Knowing the warning signs that a person needs help and knowing where to get help can start a user on the road to recovery.

WHY LEARN THIS? Knowing about sources of help for users of alcohol and tobacco may allow you to help yourself and others.

When does someone need help?

Have you ever been afraid to ask someone for help? People who have a problem with alcohol or tobacco need help. It's hard for a person who is addicted to alcohol or tobacco to stop using the drug. The person may be afraid to ask for help.

If you are worried about someone you know who uses alcohol or tobacco, there are some warning signs that you should know. These signs can help you decide whether an alcohol or tobacco user needs help.

Problem Drinkers People who are problem drinkers often don't take good care of themselves. They might not wash their hair or clothing. Sometimes they don't get enough rest or eat a healthful diet. Alcohol users who don't care for themselves need help.

◀ John is worried about his brother's behavior. He thinks his brother needs help. What advice would you give John?

Someone who misses school or work because of drinking has a problem. Alcoholics might not go to school or work because they are too intoxicated or too ill. Some people with alcohol problems don't go to work or school because they don't care about their jobs or schoolwork anymore. These people need help.

Alcohol users might have trouble controlling their moods. Alcohol causes some people to become very angry. Others might become sad about small problems. They may also say and do things that hurt others. Some alcohol users may have trouble doing things they are normally expected to do. Young people may forget to do schoolwork or household chores. Adults may forget to pay the bills. These people also need help.

Tobacco Users Tobacco users who get nervous when they don't smoke or chew tobacco probably need help. People who hide tobacco use feel uneasy about what they are doing. So do those who lie about smoking or chewing tobacco. These signs show that the person needs help to quit using tobacco.

People who drink alcohol or use tobacco aren't the only ones who need help. A young person who has friends or family who use too much alcohol or tobacco may need help. This person might need help dealing with the worry and hurt that result from another's drinking or smoking problem.

JOURNAL

In your journal, write a dialogue between yourself and someone who has a drinking problem. What would you say to let this person know that help is available to overcome the problem?

▶ John decides to talk to his parents about his brother's alcohol problem. Whom would you talk to if someone in your family had a problem with alcohol or tobacco?

How can a person get help?

If you're worried about someone's alcohol or tobacco use, where can you go for help? Talk to an adult you trust, such as a parent, adult relative, or family friend. You could also talk to a teacher, counselor, school nurse, family doctor, or religious leader. Telling someone else about the problem might help you feel better.

► This young adult's family is talking to him about his drinking problem. They want him to get help.

Communicate

Curt's mother is an alcoholic. Sometimes when his mother is drunk she yells at Curt, and Curt feels hurt. Name some trusted adults Curt could talk to. What could Curt say to these adults? Use the steps for communicating shown on page *xii*.

● ● ●

Don't worry that telling someone will hurt the person with the alcohol or tobacco problem. The adult you talk to may be able to find help for the drug user.

There are other places you can go to for help. Many communities have programs that help people stop using alcohol and tobacco. You might find these programs at a hospital, clinic, or community mental health agency.

Some national programs help alcohol and tobacco users. Alcoholics Anonymous (AA), Rational Recovery (RR), and Al-Anon help alcoholics and their families. In addition, each year the American Cancer Society sponsors the Great American Smokeout. On this day in November, smokers are asked to stop smoking for the entire day. If users can quit for one day, perhaps they can quit for good. There are also some products that can help tobacco users overcome their addiction. Nicotine gums and patches can help people slowly reduce their dependence on nicotine.

Career

Alcohol Treatment Counselor

What They Do

Counselors work in hospitals, treatment centers, government agencies, and private practices. They study an individual's problem, counsel individuals and groups, and design treatment programs for people with alcohol problems.

Education and Training

Most counselors have college degrees. Employers look for people who have been through at least a two-year counselor-in-training program. People entering training programs must have good counseling skills. They need to know a lot about alcohol and problem drinkers. They can help people who want to overcome their addiction.

▼ A trained counselor can help this young man and his family deal with the problems alcohol is causing in their lives.

LESSON CHECKUP

Check Your Facts

1. Why is it important for someone who has a problem with alcohol or tobacco to get help?

2. CRITICAL THINKING Why might someone who doesn't use alcohol or tobacco need help dealing with problems caused by these drugs?

3. What are three signs that a person is having a problem with alcohol?

Set Health Goals

4. List three adults you might turn to if someone you knew had a problem with alcohol or tobacco.

USE VOCABULARY

alcohol (p. 212)
alcoholic (p. 217)
alcoholism (p. 217)
blood alcohol level (BAL) (p. 212)

cirrhosis (p. 215)
environmental tobacco smoke (ETS) (p. 211)
intoxicated (p. 216)

nicotine (p. 207)
peer pressure (p. 219)
tar (p. 207)
tobacco (p. 206)

Use the terms above to complete the sentences. Page numbers in ( ) tell you where to look in the chapter if you need help.

1. People who drink so much alcohol that it strongly affects their ability to function are ____.

2. An ____ is someone who is addicted to alcohol.

3. Children who breathe a lot of ____ get more coughs, colds, and sore throats than children who live in smoke-free homes do.

4. The shredded brown substance inside a cigarette is ____.

5. When other young people influence you to do something, they are using ____.

6. ____ is a poisonous substance that causes people to become addicted to tobacco.

7. A sticky substance called ____ coats a smoker's lungs and makes breathing difficult.

8. If someone is addicted to alcohol, that person suffers from a disease called ____.

9. A small person will have a higher ____ than a larger person does if they both drink the same amount of alcohol.

10. ____ is a disease of the liver that results from drinking too much alcohol.

11. ____ is a drug found in beer, wine, and liquor.

CHECK YOUR FACTS

Page numbers in ( ) tell you where to look in the chapter if you need help.

12. List three types of tobacco products. (p. 206)

13. Use the chart below to find out how a blood alcohol level of 0.1 affects a person's ability to drive. (p. 212)

HOW ALCOHOL AFFECTS THE BODY*		
Number of Beers	BAL	Effect on a Person's Body
1 beer mug	0.015	reduced concentration, reflexes slowed
2 beer mugs	0.04	short-term memory loss
4 beer mugs	0.1	seven times more likely to have a car crash if driving
12 beer mugs	0.3	vomiting/unconsciousness

14. Why do laws put limits on how and where alcohol and tobacco products can be advertised? (p. 220)

15. What should you do if you know someone who hides alcohol or tobacco and lies about using it? (p. 226)

16. If smoking is so dangerous, why do so many adults do it?

17. What do you think is the best reason for not using alcohol or tobacco?

18. Study the warning labels shown below. Similar warnings appear on alcoholic beverages. Make up your own warning label for a tobacco or alcohol product. How would this warning help people refuse to use the product?

19. **Refuse** You're visiting a new friend. While you're there, your friend's father watches a football game and drinks beer. At the end of the game, the father offers to drive you home. You see four empty beer cans next to the sofa. What would you do?

20. **Refuse** Some older students you admire start talking to you after school one day. You're really excited to have their attention. Then one of them offers you a cigarette. What should you do?

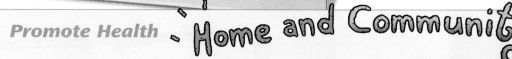

Promote Health - Home and Community -

1. Talk to your classmates about ways to say *no* to tobacco and alcohol. Make posters that show your ideas. Display the posters in your school cafeteria where other students will see them.

2. Get information about alcohol-related car crashes and deaths in your community or state. You might get information from the police department or on the Internet. Make a chart showing the total number of car crashes and how many of them were related to alcohol use.

Activities

Read a Book

On Your Own • Find a book about someone who overcame a problem with tobacco or alcohol. How did the person get into trouble with this drug? Why did he or she want to stop? What did the person do to get help? Write a short report about the book you read.

Places for Help

At Home • Make a list of people and places someone could go to for help if that person had a problem with alcohol or tobacco. Include trusted adults as well as organizations, community agencies, businesses, and government programs offering services that could help.

Rule Posters

On Your Own • Find out school rules about using alcohol and tobacco. Make a poster for each rule. Display your posters.

Body Atlas

With a Team • Decorate a bulletin board with a full-size picture of the human body, showing organs that are affected by alcohol and tobacco. Color the organs that are affected by tobacco one color. Use another color to show those organs affected by alcohol. Use a third color to show those affected by both.

Multiple Choice

Choose the letter of the correct answer.

1. A sticky substance in tobacco smoke that coats a smoker's lungs is _____.
   a. tar
   b. carbon dioxide
   c. tumors
   d. nicotine

2. Gases in cigarette smoke take the place of _____ in the blood.
   a. nicotine
   b. nitrogen
   c. carbon monoxide
   d. oxygen

3. A 12-ounce bottle of beer has _____ alcohol as 5 ounces of wine.
   a. twice as much
   b. as much
   c. half as much
   d. not as much

4. Which of the following choices is a good way to avoid peer pressure?
   a. feel good about yourself
   b. go to parties that have alcohol
   c. don't practice refusal skills
   d. choose friends who use drugs

5. Which group could help someone quit smoking?
   a. AA
   b. Al-Anon
   c. Rational Recovery
   d. American Cancer Society

Modified True or False

Write *true* or *false*. If a sentence is false, replace the underlined term to make the sentence true.

6. Cigarettes and other tobacco products contain <u>nicotine</u>.

7. Once people start using tobacco, it's hard to quit because they become <u>intoxicated</u>.

8. People who use tobacco risk getting lung disease and <u>heart</u> disease.

9. Alcohol affects so many things a person does because it goes right to the <u>heart</u>.

10. The more a person drinks, the higher his or her <u>brain-alcohol level</u>.

11. Feeling good about yourself can give you the confidence to avoid being influenced by <u>peer pressure</u>.

12. If someone's alcohol or tobacco use worries you, you should <u>mind your own business</u>.

Short Answer

Write a complete sentence to answer each question.

13. Why is smoking a bad idea for someone who wants to be a good athlete?

14. Why do children who live with smokers have more colds, sore throats, coughs, and asthma than other children do?

15. What kinds of problems might an alcoholic have?

16. What can help you resist pressure to use alcohol or tobacco?

17. Why is it useful to know the warning signs of a person who has a problem with tobacco or alcohol?

18. Where can you find programs that help people overcome problems with alcohol or tobacco?

Writing in Health

Write paragraphs to answer each item.

19. Describe how using alcohol or tobacco makes life less fun.

20. Write a paragraph comforting a friend who has been teased or mocked for refusing to use alcohol or tobacco.

Staying Safe

MAKE A SAFETY MANUAL

Work with a partner to make a manual that includes information about safety, first aid, and emergency plans. You might want to use a Red Cross first-aid manual as a model. Add to your manual as you learn new things in this chapter.

For other activities, visit the Harcourt Learning Site.
www.harcourtschool.com

Responding to Emergencies and Giving First Aid

If you or another person got hurt, would you know what to do? Injuries usually happen without much warning. Often people get hurt when they don't follow safety rules. If someone gets hurt, you may be able to help.

What actions can you take in an emergency?

An **emergency** (ih•MER•juhnt•see) is a situation in which help is needed right away. A fire is an emergency. Someone drowning is an emergency. Often in emergencies people are injured. These are some different kinds of emergencies.

- severe burns
- stopped breathing
- stopped heartbeat
- drowning
- poisoning
- broken bone
- severe bleeding
- fire

In an emergency you must act quickly. You must also stay calm so you can make good decisions. The first thing to do is to call for help. If possible, tell an adult such as a parent, teacher, or neighbor. If you can't find an adult, dial 911 or another emergency phone number.

To help you act quickly in an emergency, make a list of emergency phone numbers, and post the list near your telephone. You can find the emergency numbers for your area in your local phone book. They are usually printed on the first page. Include these numbers on your list:

- fire department
- police
- poison control center
- hospital
- doctor
- dentist

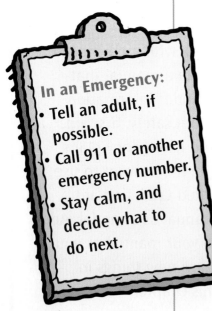

In an Emergency:
- Tell an adult, if possible.
- Call 911 or another emergency number.
- Stay calm, and decide what to do next.

In many cities you can dial 911 in an emergency. If your city has 911 service, you don't need to call the doctor, hospital, fire department, or police. You call 911. The 911 operator will send the right kind of help to you and will tell you what to do next.

When you call the emergency operator, stay calm and speak slowly and clearly. Try to answer the operator's questions as completely as possible. Don't hang up until you are told to do so. Read the note below to find out what information you need to give the operator.

Communicate

Rena is practicing giving information to an emergency operator. She knows that she needs to speak clearly. What else does Rena need to do? Use the steps for communicating shown on page *xii*.

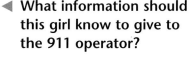

Dialing for Help

The operator will need to know

- your name.
- the phone number you are calling from.
- what the problem is.
- the address where you are.
- a family member's name and phone number.

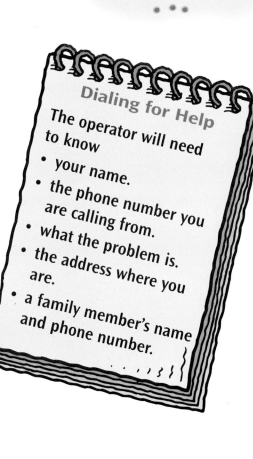

◄ **What information should this girl know to give to the 911 operator?**

How can you help someone who is hurt?

When someone has been injured, you sometimes need to give first aid while you wait for help to arrive. This immediate treatment of an injury is called **first aid**. Always remember to wash your hands before giving first aid to yourself or others.

One common injury that you probably have had is a wound. A **wound** (WOOND) is a cut or break in the skin. The first thing you should do to treat a wound is stop the bleeding. It is important not to touch another person's blood, so don't use your bare hand. Use a clean folded cloth, and press down hard on top of the wound. If you don't have a clean cloth, put the injured person's hand on the wound. Place your hand on top of his or her hand, and press down hard until the bleeding stops. Do not touch blood unless you are wearing gloves.

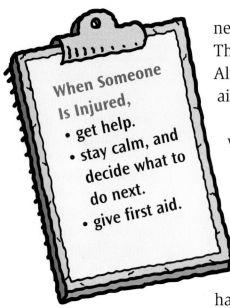

When Someone
Is Injured,
• get help.
• stay calm, and decide what to do next.
• give first aid.

FIRST AID FOR MINOR INJURIES

Injury	First Aid
Small Cuts and Scrapes	Stop the bleeding. Wash the cut or scrape with soap and water. Dry the wound. You may apply antibiotic ointment or cream to kill germs. Put on a clean, dry bandage. Change the bandage every day. Change it more often if it gets wet or dirty.
Blisters	Do not open or pop the blister. Clean the area around the blister with soap and water. Dry the area. Put a clean bandage over it.
Mild Burns	Use a lot of cold water to cool the burned area. Do not use ice or ice water. Carefully dry the area. Place a clean bandage loosely over the burn. Don't break burn blisters. Don't use ointments on burns.

◄ The chart shows first-aid steps for minor injuries.

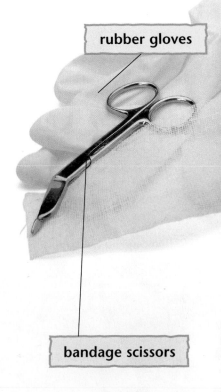

rubber gloves

bandage scissors

One way to prepare for an emergency is to put together a first-aid kit. A first-aid kit contains the supplies you need for treating injuries. A first-aid kit should be kept where it can be found quickly. It is helpful to have a first-aid kit in your home and another in your family's car or truck. You should also take a first-aid kit when you hike or camp.

▼ The picture shows some supplies to include in a first-aid kit. How might each item be used to treat injuries?

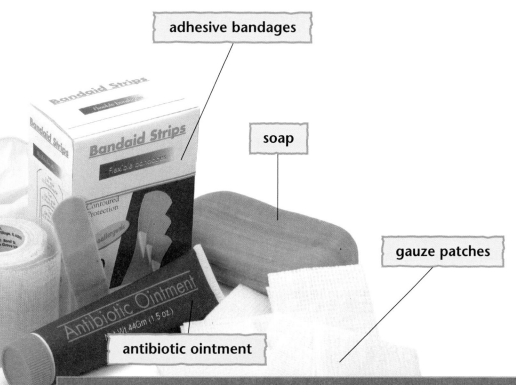

adhesive bandages

soap

gauze patches

antibiotic ointment

LESSON CHECKUP

Check Your Facts

❶ What emergency phone numbers should you keep by your phone?

❷ What is the first action to take in an emergency?

❸ CRITICAL THINKING If someone in your home broke a bone, what information would you give the 911 operator?

❹ CRITICAL THINKING If your friend scraped her knee at your house, what first-aid supplies could you use to treat her wound?

Set Health Goals

❺ Take steps to make your home a safer place. Help your family gather supplies to put in a first-aid kit and decide where to keep the kit in your home.

Staying Safe at Home and While Camping

Injuries can happen anywhere, but many take place at home. Often they happen to children. **Injury prevention** (INJ•ree prih•VENT•shuhn) means keeping injuries from happening. One way you can prevent injuries is by practicing safety measures. **Safety measures** are actions you take to stay safe. **Hazards** (HA•zerdz) are conditions that are not safe. Another way to prevent injuries is to get rid of or stay away from hazards.

What can you do to prevent injuries at home?

Safety Measures to Prevent Electric Shock
Electricity is a hazard when it's not used safely.

• If there are young children in your family, make sure electrical outlets are covered so children can't stick things into them.

• Don't use electrical appliances near water.

• Never insert metal objects into electrical appliances.

DO use a handrail when going up and down stairs.

DON'T place candles, space heaters, or night lights near curtains.

DON'T leave matches or lighters where children can reach them.

DON'T pile papers and magazines on the floor.

Safety Measures to Prevent Falls Falls are the most common cause of home injuries. People fall in bathtubs, out of windows, and out of beds. Some people fall off of furniture or stacked objects that they have climbed or stood on to reach high places. Stairs are the most dangerous places for falls. Floors also can be dangerous when they are wet or slippery. Here are some ways to prevent falls.

- Use enough light when walking at night.
- Be careful when walking on slippery or wet surfaces.
- Use a rubber mat in the bathtub.
- Take one step at a time going up or down stairs.
- Always pick up after yourself so people won't trip over your things.
- Anchor area rugs with foam or tape.

Safety Measures to Prevent Fires Heat, flame, and electricity can cause fires.

- Don't use an electrical appliance until an adult shows you the proper way to use it.
- Keep one or more fire extinguishers in the house and garage, and know how to use them.
- Install smoke detectors in each room.

 **Activity** **Recognize Hazards** The labels point out some of the hazards in this room. The picture also shows some of the proper safety measures that have been taken. In what other ways is the room safe and not safe?

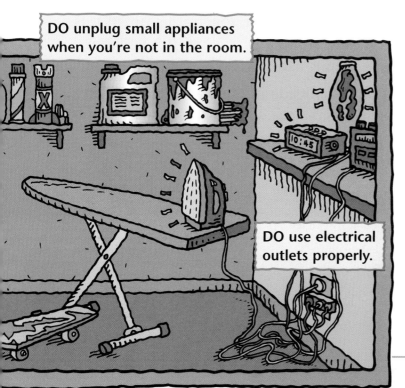

DO unplug small appliances when you're not in the room.

DO use electrical outlets properly.

What can you do to stay safe in a fire?

A fire at home can cause the loss of the building and everything in it. It can also cause the loss of lives. Knowing and practicing fire safety can help prevent fires. It can also help you stay safe if a fire happens.

A large number of fires start from lit cigarettes. People who smoke need to be extra careful. They should never smoke in bed. Space heaters also cause many fires. Matches, space heaters, and candles should be used only by adults.

Your family needs a plan for escaping from your home in case of a fire. Everyone should know two ways to escape from each room. One way to escape is to go out a window. Someone should make sure all the windows in your home can be opened. Your family should also identify a place to meet outside your home after escaping. For more information about a family emergency plan, see pages 326–327.

Here's what to do if a fire happens.

- Get low, and crawl on the floor. The air is safest down low. Hold a cloth over your nose and mouth. Follow one of your escape routes. If your way is blocked by fire, crawl to a different exit. Yell "Fire!" loudly to warn others.

- If you come to a closed door, touch it lightly. If it is cool, open it, and continue crawling. If it is warm or hot, leave it shut. Use a different exit.

- Meet your family outside in the place you decided on. Then make sure someone uses a neighbor's phone to call for help.

▼ **A lit cigarette caused this fire.**

▼ **If your clothes catch on fire:**

1. Stop

2. Drop

Roll slowly!

3. Roll

What can you do to prevent poisoning?

A poison can cause injury or death. Poisons can enter the body through the nose, mouth, or skin. Most people use glue, paint, and cleaning products in their homes. These products are usually safe when used properly, but they can be poisonous if they are swallowed or breathed in deeply. Medicines are useful in prescribed doses, but they can be poisonous when someone takes too much or takes someone else's medicine. Some plants are poisonous if they are eaten. Extra care should be taken to keep all poisonous substances out of the reach of young children.

The Respiratory System
Look at the respiratory system on pages 12 and 13 of The Amazing Human Body. Identify the organs that could be harmed if household products like the ones shown here aren't used properly.

◀ How can these products be poisonous?

HOUSEHOLD POISONS

Product	How It Is Used	Signs of Poisoning
Lighter Fluid	to light charcoal in outdoor grills	Burns on skin or in eyes, mouth, throat, or stomach; coughing; coma (deep unconsciousness)
Paint	to coat, protect, and decorate walls, furniture, and other things	Soreness of eyes, nose, and throat; headaches; dizziness; difficulty breathing; coma
Bleach	to take stains out of clothes and make them whiter or brighter	Burning pain or soreness of skin and eyes; coughing; burns to mouth, throat, and stomach
Furniture Polish	to shine and polish wooden furniture	Coughing; sleepiness
Insecticide	to kill insects	Headache, body secretions (oozing fluids), vomiting, diarrhea, convulsions (powerful tightening of muscles)
Cough Medicine	to help stop coughing	Hyperactivity (unable to be still), convulsions, coma

What can you do to stay safe while you are home alone?

Sometimes you have to spend time alone at home. To be safe, it is important to have a *routine,* or certain things you do every day. Here are some safe things to do.

- Always keep your key in the same place, such as around your neck or fastened on the inside of your backpack. If you wear your key around your neck, keep it inside your shirt so that it is out of sight. This will keep others from knowing you are going to be home alone.

- Check in with an adult family member as soon as you arrive at home. Have a list of other family members' or neighbors' phone numbers. Call an adult if anything unusual happens.

- Keep all doors locked. Don't open the door for anyone you don't know. If someone comes to your door to deliver a package, you do not have to open the door to take the package. He or she can leave the package outside the door. It is safest not to answer the door at all.

- If someone calls, it is safest to let an answering machine take a message. You can hear who is calling before you answer the phone. If you must answer the phone and someone asks for an adult in your family, say "She (or he) can't come to the phone right now. Would you like to leave a message?" If the person asks more questions or if you feel uncomfortable, hang up. Call a trusted adult and tell him or her about the call. It is always safest not to answer the phone at all.

- Do not let anyone know you are home alone. If a person on the phone or at the door threatens you or makes you uncomfortable, call a family member or neighbor right away.

Lock your doors

◀ **What safety rule does this picture show?**

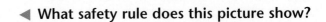

What can you do to stay safe while camping?

Prepare for the weather. Wear sunscreen rated SPF 15 or higher whenever you are outdoors. In cool weather, dress in layers and have rain gear on hand.

Prepare for insects. Many outdoor areas have mosquitoes, fleas, ticks, bees, and other insects. Use an insect repellent, and keep your skin covered by clothing if necessary. Be sure to bring first-aid supplies.

Stay away from animals. Do not go up to a wild animal, even a young one. Its mother is probably nearby and might attack you to protect her baby. Many wild animals bite when they are cornered or afraid.

Keep your food safe. Use a cooler for food that can spoil. Remember, the smell of food attracts animals. Store all food in tightly sealed containers, and never leave unwrapped food outside.

Have a safe campfire. An adult should always be with you when a campfire is burning. The campfire should be built inside a fire ring. Keep a bucket full of water nearby. Douse your campfire with water to put it out.

Avoid poisonous plants. If you touch poison ivy, poison oak, or poison sumac, you may get a rash. Wash well with dishwashing soap to remove the plant oil to which you may be allergic. If your skin begins to itch, cover the rash with calamine lotion or a mixture of baking soda and water.

▼ "Leaves of three—let them be." Poison ivy and other poisonous plants have leaves that grow in groups of three. Poison ivy can cause skin redness, swelling, blisters, and itching.

LESSON CHECKUP

Check Your Facts

❶ What is the most common cause of home injuries?

❷ CRITICAL THINKING Why do you need to know two ways to escape from each room if there is a fire at home?

❸ Name two places where a child who will be home alone after school could keep his or her key during the day.

❹ CRITICAL THINKING What should you do if you see a wild animal in the woods?

Use Life Skills

❺ MAKE DECISIONS Suppose you woke up one night and heard the smoke alarm beeping. Write what you would do.

Staying Safe Outdoors

MAIN IDEA
Wearing proper safety gear and practicing safety measures help prevent injuries while you play sports and games outdoors.

WHY LEARN THIS? What you learn can help keep you from getting hurt while outdoors.

VOCABULARY
• safety gear
• lightning

Rhonda and César are skating. Rhonda wears a helmet, wrist guards, and knee and elbow pads. César doesn't think he needs to wear these items. What César doesn't know is that he can be injured painfully if he falls while skating. Wearing safety gear and practicing safe habits can help protect you when playing outdoors.

What safety gear should you wear while playing sports?

To be safe when you play most sports, you need to wear safety gear. **Safety gear** is clothing or equipment worn to prevent injury. The shin guards you wear while playing soccer shield your legs from kicks. A padded glove protects your hand when you catch a baseball.

Many sports involve the risk of falling or running into other players or equipment. Any of these actions can cause mouth, tooth, or jaw injuries. Wearing a mouth guard helps protect you against these injuries. Dentists recommend wearing mouth guards in gymnastics, basketball, hockey, football, skating, skateboarding, volleyball, surfing, soccer, and skiing.

Helmets are important safety gear for many sports, too. Helmets help protect your head from injuries. If you are wearing a bicycle helmet when you fall off your bicycle or scooter, for example, you will be much less likely to get hurt. In fact, some states and cities have laws that require you to wear a helmet when bicycling.

◄ **What safety gear are these children wearing? What is the purpose of each piece of safety gear?**

244

For skateboarding and in-line skating, you need a helmet and wrist guards. Wrist injuries are the most common injuries in skating sports. You also need elbow and knee pads.

The shoes you wear can help protect you while you play. Not all sports shoes are the same. Each sport has a shoe with special features just for that sport. Cleats or spikes help keep players from slipping on grass fields. Running shoes often have pads in the heel, toe, and middle of the sole to protect these parts of the feet as they hit the ground. Tennis shoes have added support on the sides because players move from side to side. Basketball shoes often have high tops to help hold ankles straight. If you play a sport for five hours or more each week, you should replace your sports shoes every six months. When the cushioning becomes thin and the side materials stretch, the shoes no longer protect your feet.

ART CONNECTION

Buy This Equipment

With a Partner Design a magazine advertisement or billboard that promotes a certain sports shoe or piece of protective equipment. Make sure that the ad points out all of the equipment's safety features.

● ● ●

▼ How does the sole design of each of these shoes help players of each sport?

Shoes for Sports

◄ basketball

◄ soccer

◄ running

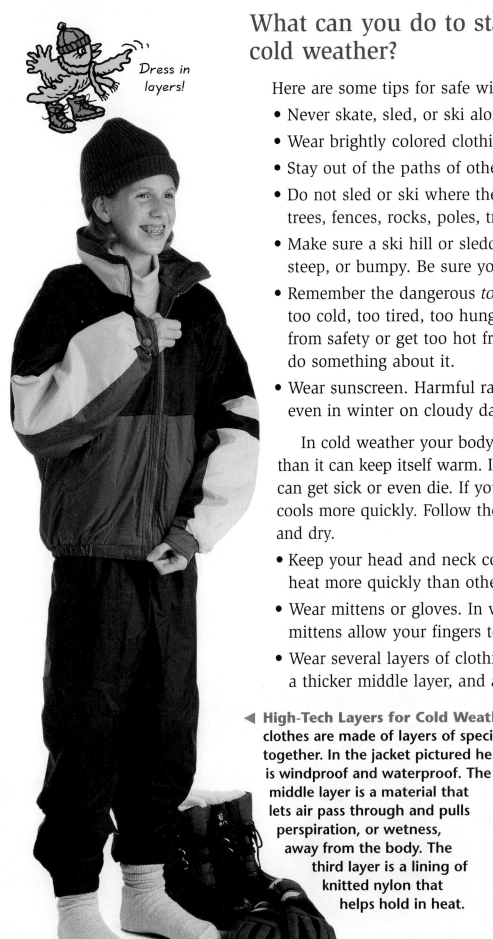

Dress in layers!

What can you do to stay safe in cold weather?

Here are some tips for safe winter play.

- Never skate, sled, or ski alone or after dark.
- Wear brightly colored clothing so you can be seen.
- Stay out of the paths of others.
- Do not sled or ski where there are hazards such as trees, fences, rocks, poles, traffic, or roads.
- Make sure a ski hill or sledding hill is not icy, too steep, or bumpy. Be sure you can stop safely.
- Remember the dangerous *too*s. If you feel too wet, too cold, too tired, too hungry or thirsty, too far from safety or get too hot from the sun, STOP and do something about it.
- Wear sunscreen. Harmful rays can reach the skin even in winter on cloudy days.

In cold weather your body can lose heat faster than it can keep itself warm. If you get too cold, you can get sick or even die. If you get wet, your body cools more quickly. Follow these tips for staying warm and dry.

- Keep your head and neck covered. These parts lose heat more quickly than other parts of your body.
- Wear mittens or gloves. In very cold weather mittens allow your fingers to warm each other.
- Wear several layers of clothing. Include a base layer, a thicker middle layer, and a waterproof jacket.

◀ **High-Tech Layers for Cold Weather** Some cold-weather clothes are made of layers of special fabrics sandwiched together. In the jacket pictured here, the outer layer is windproof and waterproof. The middle layer is a material that lets air pass through and pulls perspiration, or wetness, away from the body. The third layer is a lining of knitted nylon that helps hold in heat.

What should you do to stay safe during a thunderstorm?

Thunderstorms are the most frequent kind of dangerous storm. The danger comes from lightning. **Lightning** is an electrical flash in the sky. It carries a strong current of electricity that can injure or kill people, cause fires, and damage property. Here are some tips for staying safe during a thunderstorm.

- Go inside a house or large building. You may get inside a closed car or truck, but do not touch any metal. Electricity can pass through metal into you.

- Stay off bicycles, tractors, and other open vehicles.

- If you're outside, don't touch metal such as fishing poles or baseball bats.

- If you are out in the open and can't find shelter, stay low. Get into a ditch or low area if possible.

- Stay away from single trees or tall objects. Lightning usually hits the tallest object above ground. Stay lower than everything else. Do not stand on a beach, slope, hilltop or in an open field.

- If you are in a wooded area, get under some low bushes or under a group of trees that are all the same height.

- Stay away from water. Water conducts electricity.

Did you know?

Lightning strikes Earth about a hundred times each second. The temperature of a lightning flash can be more than 60,000 degrees Fahrenheit (33,000 degrees C). That's hotter than the surface of the sun!

LESSON CHECKUP

Check Your Facts

1. What are the two most important pieces of safety gear for skating sports?

2. CRITICAL THINKING Do you think a bike helmet law is a good thing? Why or why not?

3. List the clothing you would wear to keep warm and dry if you were going sledding.

4. Name five safety tips to remember during a thunderstorm.

Set Health Goals

5. Make a chart about how to stay safe while playing your favorite sport. List the safety gear needed to play it. Then draw pictures showing how to use the safety gear.

247

MAKE DECISIONS
About Staying Safe

Sometimes when you are all alone, you need to make a decision. Use the steps for decision making to help you stay safe.

Learn This Skill

Tom's mother is next door when his new friend, Ed, calls. Ed wants to come over, but Tom knows that having friends over when his parents aren't home is against the rules. He doesn't want to lose his new friend. What should he do?

1. Find out about the choices you could make.

Tom could
1. have Ed come over now and hope his parents don't find out.
2. tell Ed about his house rules.
3. invite Ed over another time when he has permission.

2. Imagine the possible result of each choice.

1. If Ed comes over, Tom might get in trouble.
2. If he tells Ed the rules, Ed might play with someone else.
3. If he invites Ed over later, Tom could have fun without breaking the rules.

3. Make what seems to be the best choice.

Tom decides to invite Ed over another time, when he has permission. Ed is excited, and they plan what they will do together.

4. Think about what happened as a result of your choice.

Tom does not get in trouble, and Ed is still his friend. Tom is looking forward to the time when Ed can come over.

Practice This Skill

Use the steps for making decisions to help you solve these problems.

Steps for Making Decisions

1. Find out about the choices you could make.

2. Imagine the possible result of each choice.

3. Make what seems to be the best choice.

4. Think about what happened as a result of your choice.

A. While looking under the kitchen sink, Doug notices several bottles of cleaning fluids. What decision should Doug make to protect his younger sisters from these poisons?

B. While going down to the basement, Sandra trips over some shoes on the stairs. What could she do to protect other family members from such falls?

Staying Safe on the Road

You have many choices when you want to travel from one place to another. You can walk, skate, skateboard, ride a bicycle, or ride in a car. No matter how you choose to go, you will probably be on the road.

What can you do to stay safe while on wheels?

Most bicycling, skateboarding, and skating injuries happen from falls. You need smooth ground for safe riding. Stay in an area that does not have holes, bumps, rocks, and other things on the ground. Know how to protect yourself if you think you are about to fall from skates and skateboards.

- If you start to lose your balance, crouch down so you won't have as far to fall.
- Try to roll rather than land on your hands.
- Relax your body—do not stiffen up.

Traffic is another danger. Do not skate or skateboard in the street. Never hold on to a car, bike, bus, or other vehicle. Don't wear headphones. Stop and look in all directions before crossing a street. Be especially careful around driveways.

Watch out for rocks, cracks, bumps, and holes in the sidewalk.

Skate on the sidewalk or designated paths—not in the street.

When bicycling, walk your bike across streets and intersections. Learn the proper hand signals for stops and turns, and follow the traffic signs and safety laws. You should also ride in a straight line near the right-hand side of the road. Watch out for doors opening from parked cars.

The chart below lists the safety gear that can help prevent injuries.

SAFETY EQUIPMENT

Bicycling	In-Line Skating	Skateboarding and Scooter Riding
Bicycle helmet: In many places the law says you must wear a helmet. Make sure your helmet fits snugly. Wear it level between your ears and low on your forehead.	**Helmet:** You need a helmet that protects the sides and lower back of your head as well as your forehead.	**Helmet:** Choose one that protects your entire head.
Bright- or light-colored clothing: Make yourself easy to see. If you must ride after dark, wear a reflective vest or clothing. Also, use a light.	**Wrist guards:** Wrist injuries are the most common injuries in skating sports.	**Closed, nonslip shoes**
	Padding: Always wear knee and elbow pads. You can add hip pads, padded pants, a padded jacket, and skating gloves.	**Padding:** Use knee and elbow pads. Hip pads and a padded jacket also help.
Backpacks: Avoid wearing a heavy backpack—use a basket or saddle bags instead.	**Mouth guard**	**Skating gloves:** They protect your hands in a fall.
		Mouth guard
		Wrist guards: Don't use wrist guards on scooters— they can make steering more difficult.

Slow down around people on foot. Sound a horn or bell to help others hear you coming. Pass on the left.

Ride in the backseat. It's the safest spot for passengers.

Do not play with sharp objects. In a sudden stop, you could get hurt. Do not drink from a bottle, can, or cup while the vehicle is moving.

Do not distract the driver, because he or she must give full attention to driving safely. Always speak softly to other passengers. Do not play with the windows or seats.

Did you know?

When you operate a machine that moves, such as a bicycle, you are considered a driver. And just like car and bus drivers, you must obey certain traffic signs and safety laws.

What can you do to stay safe in a motor vehicle?

Safety belts save lives. The safest thing you can do in a car is to always buckle your safety belt. Fasten the lap belt snugly across your hips, not across your stomach. Keep the shoulder harness across your chest. If it crosses your face or neck, you can sit on a pillow so the shoulder harness fits correctly. Don't share a safety belt with another person.

The children in the picture are wearing safety belts and following other safety measures that help prevent injuries.

School Bus Safety If you ride a bus to school, you need to follow some special safety rules. Always stand at least 10 feet from the bus while you are waiting to get on. Wait until the bus stops before you go near. Enter and leave the bus in a single-file line and hold the handrail to climb up and down the steps safely. Stay in your seat, and don't distract the driver. When you leave the bus, watch out for traffic.

Air Bag Safety An **air bag** is a safety device in a car that *inflates,* or blows up like a balloon, to protect a person from injury. Air bags inflate quickly during a collision. The force of the air bag inflating can injure a child riding in the front seat, so experts are working on ways to make air bags safer. One idea is to have the air bag system sense the weight of the passenger. The air bag would inflate with less force or not at all if the passenger were light in weight. Another idea is to let the driver turn off the air bag system for the passenger seat. Children are safer if they ride in the backseat.

LESSON CHECKUP

Check Your Facts

1. Name six safety practices for bicycling.
2. List the safety gear to wear while skateboarding.
3. CRITICAL THINKING Why is it important to learn how to fall if you skate?

4. CRITICAL THINKING Some people do not wear safety belts. What could persuade them to wear their safety belts?

Use Life Skills

5. REFUSE Suppose you were riding your bike and a friend wanted to ride on your handlebars. What would you say?

Staying Safe Near Water

Marc wants to go to the pool next summer with his friends, but he doesn't know how to swim. Marc knows that when people are around water, drowning is a danger. He decides to take swimming lessons this winter to learn how to be safe around water.

What can you do to stay safe while swimming?

The most important thing you can do to be safe around water is to learn how to swim. Most communities have classes in which people of all ages can learn to swim. Once you have learned to swim, you can continue taking swimming lessons to improve your skills. The following are some rules for safe swimming.

- It is unsafe to swim alone, so always swim with a partner. If one of you has a problem, the other can get help.

- Swim only when and where an adult such as a lifeguard is present. A **lifeguard** is a person who keeps people safe while they are swimming and while they are near the water.

- Follow the written rules at the pool or beach.

- Don't run or push. Wet decks are slippery and hard. Falls around pools can cause serious injuries.

- Many swimmers get injured by diving into water that is too shallow. "No Diving" signs tell you that the water is unsafe for entering headfirst. The water needs to be at least 9 feet deep for diving. If you cannot see the bottom or do not know how deep the water is, do not dive.

- Don't eat or chew gum while in the water. You could choke.

- Be aware of weather and surf hazards. If you see or hear a thunderstorm, get out of the water immediately. If you are in or near the water while there is lightning, you could get electrocuted. Read and obey all signs and flags warning about dangerous conditions.

- Remember the dangerous *too*s. If you feel too cold, too hot, too tired, too hungry or thirsty, too far from safety or if you think you are getting too much sun, STOP and do something about it.

Sunlight contains harmful rays that can cause sunburn and lead to skin diseases. Whenever you are outdoors, wear sunscreen to protect your skin. The higher the SPF number, the more protection the sunscreen gives. Apply sunscreen before you go outdoors and again each time you get out of the water.

Career
Lifeguard

What They Do

A lifeguard watches over swimmers; enforces rules of the pool or beach area; rescues swimmers, divers, and surfers; gives medical aid; and teaches swimming.

You will find lifeguards at your community pool or beach. You must follow the rules of the pool and the directions the lifeguard gives you. Lifeguards have to watch over the safety of all swimmers, so do not distract them while they are on duty.

Education and Training

Lifeguards must take a lifeguard training course such as the one offered by the American Red Cross. They also must know CPR (a way to help someone start breathing again), first aid, and lifesaving and rescue techniques. Lifeguards who want to work on beaches must take advanced training for open water safety and rescues.

What can you do when someone in the water needs help?

- **Yell for help.** Find an adult or send someone to get help.

- **Do not get into the water.** You could be in danger, too.

- **Reach.** Hold something long and strong out toward the person. While you do, hold on to something secure, such as a dock pole or a sturdy branch.

- **Throw.** If the person is too far away for you to reach, you can throw him or her something that floats. Attach the float to a rope, and tie the other end of the rope to something secure on the dock or pool deck.

Water Rescue

REACH

THROW

What can you do to stay safe while boating?

Knowing how to swim is always the best safety measure around water. On boats you should also

- wear a life jacket. If you fall in the water, you might need to stay afloat for some time before you are rescued. A proper life jacket will keep you afloat.

- stay still. Small boats can easily tip over if you stand up. If your boat tips and you fall in the water, hold on to the boat. It can help you stay afloat.

- make sure someone on shore knows where you are going and when you will return.

- never boat by yourself.

Always wear a life jacket when boating.

Stay still in a small boat. Don't make sudden movements or stand up.

LESSON CHECKUP

Check Your Facts

1. What is the most important thing you can do to be safe around water?

2. CRITICAL THINKING Think of several things that can happen if water safety rules aren't followed.

3. How can you help rescue a person who is in danger of drowning in a swimming pool? In a lake?

4. List three tips for boating safety.

Set Health Goals

5. List the swimming skills you now have. Write a plan for improving your skills.

MAIN IDEA
You can take steps to avoid getting harmed by fights, bullies, and weapons. You can learn skills for solving disagreements peacefully.

WHY LEARN THIS? Knowing how to stay out of fights can help keep you safe from injury.

VOCABULARY
- bully
- weapon

Staying Safe in a Conflict

What can you do to play safely with others?

All games and sports have rules. Rules help you understand how to play a game and help keep you safe from injury. When people play by the rules, everyone has a better chance of enjoying the game and not getting hurt.

In sports and games, sometimes you win and sometimes you lose. You may feel angry if someone plays unfairly, if you think you will lose, or if you do lose. However, you can learn to control your anger so the game stays fun. During games

- accept wins and losses as part of the game.
- keep cool.
- disagree without fighting.
- be polite and respectful, even when you disagree or want to win.

What can you do to avoid or resolve conflict?

Conflict is disagreement. A conflict becomes dangerous when it turns into a fight. The people fighting can get injured. Sometimes bystanders get injured too. Here are some things you can do to work out conflicts peacefully.

- Use respectful words such as "I'm sorry," "Excuse me," "Please," and "Thank you."
- Practice seeing things the way others might see them. Tell them you understand how they feel.

- Look for ways each person can give a little so that everyone can live with the choice.

- Keep your voice even, quiet, and calm. If you shout, others are likely to shout even louder. If it looks as if someone isn't following the rules, calmly say how you feel about that. You can also say that you don't want to fight.

- Get help from an adult if it looks as if a fight might happen.

A **bully** is a person who hurts or frightens others, especially those who are smaller or weaker than the bully. Bullies usually pick on people who are alone or different in some way. To be safe, stay with a group that avoids bullies. There is strength in numbers. If a bully threatens you, here are some tips for staying safe.

- Don't react. The bully is trying to control you and get you to react. You don't have to say anything. Keep your cool.

- If a bully pressures you to do something, simply say *no*.
  - Just walk away.
  - If a bully follows you, get help from an adult.

Avoiding Conflicts
- Avoid being alone. Stay with others.
- Stay away from people who fight.
- Ignore insults.
- Be quick to offer a way out of a fight.
- Use polite words.
- Get help from an adult.

Activity **Playing Peacefully** Look at the picture. What would you say and do to keep the game safe and fun if you were the person holding the ball?

259

▲ If you see a fight, walk away, and get an adult to help. How could these boys have avoided fighting?

What can you do when you see a fight?

Fights are dangerous. People in fights can move easily from using words to using fists or weapons. If you are near a fight, you can get injured even if you are not part of the fight. The safest thing to do if there is a fight is to walk away quickly and find an adult to help. Do not try to stop a fight.

Here are some things you can do if someone tries to get you to fight.

- Back off, and give the other person more space. A person is more likely to hit if he or she feels cornered or crowded. Give the person room to walk away.

- Work to avoid fighting. Don't return insults. Don't try to make the person look wrong. Say you are willing to talk about it later. You don't have to settle the disagreement now.

- Keep things light. Try laughing at yourself. Point out that the problem isn't worth fighting about.

- Don't feel like you have to "prove" yourself.

What can you do to stay safe around weapons?

A **weapon** (WEH•puhn) is something used to injure or threaten someone. Two examples are knives and guns. Weapons can also be used for self-defense. Some adults keep weapons in their homes to defend themselves from intruders. Other adults use guns or knives in sports such as hunting and target shooting.

Adults have a responsibility to keep children safe from deadly weapons. Guns are especially dangerous. Guns should be locked up and kept where children cannot find them. Playing with a gun can lead to injury or death.

If you find a gun, what should you do?

- Don't touch the gun. It can fire easily, even when you don't want it to.

- If you are with your friends and they want to touch the gun, say "Don't touch it. Guns are dangerous. They can kill you. Let's leave it alone. Let's go now!"

- Walk away as quickly as possible.

- Tell an adult about the weapon. An adult should make sure it is not in a place where others can find it or pick it up.

Weapon Safety Poster

With a Group On poster boards, write down important weapon-safety tips. Draw pictures that go along with your tips. Display your posters in hallways or on bulletin boards where other students will see them.

LESSON CHECKUP

Check Your Facts

1 CRITICAL THINKING **How has following the rules helped keep you safe during games?**

2 **List five ways to resolve a conflict peacefully.**

3 **What should you do if a bully insults you?**

4 CRITICAL THINKING **Describe what you would do if you saw a fight where someone had a weapon.**

Use Life Skills

5 COMMUNICATE **Suppose someone insulted you and tried to get you to fight. Write what you would say to keep from fighting.**

RESOLVE CONFLICTS
with Friends

Everyone has trouble getting along with others at times. When this happens, it is important to know what to do to stay safe. Use the conflict resolution steps to help you handle conflicts.

Learn This Skill

Nan is playing soccer. She kicks the ball and misses the goal. Her teammate Aki throws the ball at Nan, knocking her to the ground. The girls are about to fight. What should they do?

1. **Agree that you disagree.**

Nan tells Aki they need to talk about the problem.

2. **Listen to each other.**

Nan says Aki hurt her when she threw the ball at her. Aki says she is angry with Nan for not sharing the ball so other players can have chances to make goals.

3. Negotiate.

Nan says they could try to pass the ball more or try not to throw the ball at each other. Aki says maybe they should play on different teams.

4. Compromise on a solution.

Nan and Aki agree that the best solution is to pass the ball more. Players in scoring positions will have chances to make goals, and the team will do better.

Practice This Skill

Use the conflict resolution steps to help you solve these problems.

Steps for Resolving Conflicts

1. Agree that you disagree.
2. Listen to each other.
3. Negotiate.
4. Compromise on a solution.

A. Julie and Nathan are playing in the pool. Nathan keeps splashing Julie even after she tells him to stop. Use the conflict resolution steps to help Julie feel safe.

B. Eric is riding home from school with Lamar. Lamar buckles his safety belt. Eric refuses to wear his safety belt. Use the conflict resolution steps to help Eric stay safe.

USE VOCABULARY

air bag (p. 253) hazards (p. 238) lightning (p. 247) weapon (p. 261)
bully (p. 259) injury prevention safety gear (p. 244) wound (p. 236)
emergency (p. 234) (p. 238) safety measures
first aid (p. 236) lifeguard (p. 254) (p. 238)

Use the terms above to complete the sentences. Page numbers in ( ) tell you where to look in the chapter if you need help.

1. An electrical flash in the sky is called ____.

2. Things you can do to keep safe are called ____.

3. A person who hurts or frightens someone smaller or weaker is called a ____.

4. A safety device in a car that inflates in a crash is an ____.

5. A ____ is a cut or break in the skin.

6. Something used to injure someone is a ____.

7. Immediate treatment of an injury is called ____.

8. People wear ____ to prevent injuries.

9. ____ are conditions that can lead to injuries or emergencies.

10. A person who keeps people safe while they swim is a ____.

11. A situation in which help is needed right away is an ____.

12. ____ means keeping injuries from happening.

CHECK YOUR FACTS

Page numbers in ( ) tell you where to look in the chapter if you need help.

13. List four things you should keep in a first-aid kit. (pp. 236–237)

14. What three things should you do if your clothes catch on fire? (p. 240)

15. Name six of the dangerous *too*s. (pp. 246, 255)

16. What safety gear should you wear while skateboarding? (p. 251)

17. How deep should water be for you to dive safely? (p. 254)

18. What four things should you do if you find a gun? (p. 261)

THINK CRITICALLY

19. You are at home alone when a delivery truck comes to your house. A person carrying a box comes to the door and rings the bell. What should you do?

20. You and your friend are going sledding on a cold winter day. What will you wear?

APPLY LIFE SKILLS

21. **Make Decisions** You are at the beach when someone comes up to you. He kicks sand on you and tells you to move. What should you do?

22. **Resolve Conflicts** You and your brother want to watch different programs on TV. The programs are on at the same time, and you have only one TV. How could you solve the problem?

Promote Health Home and Community

1. Have a family fire drill. Each person should start in a different room in your home and use one of the room's escape routes. The whole family should meet at the chosen place outdoors.

2. Make posters urging people to wear their safety belts. With the owners' permission, hang the posters in stores and meeting places in your community.

Activities

First-Aid Kit

On Your Own • A few supplies for a first-aid kit are shown on pages 236–237. Do some research to find out other supplies that are often included in first-aid kits. Make a poster showing what you learned. On the poster, draw a picture of each thing you would include. Label each item, and explain how it is used.

Smoke and Fire

With a Partner • Research different kinds of smoke alarms and fire extinguishers to find out how they work. Decide which kind of smoke alarm and fire extinguisher would be best for a home.

Bandage Drill

With a Team • Look through first-aid books to find out how to bandage injuries to the head, arm, elbow, knee, hand, ankle, and foot. Also find information on how to make an arm sling. Using gauze and adhesive tape or rolled bandages and triangular cloth, practice bandaging each other.

Poison Hunt

At Home • Look up the phone number of the poison control center for your area. Write the number, along with a symbol that warns of poison, on some bright-colored stickers. With the help of an adult, go on a poison hunt. In each room, identify all the substances that could be poisonous. Put a sticker on each one.

Multiple Choice

Choose the letter of the correct answer.

1. You should put ____ on a burn.
   a. butter   b. ointment
   c. cold water   d. cream

2. The most common causes of home injuries are ____.
   a. fires   b. falls
   c. poisons   d. electric shocks

3. A helmet, wrist guards, and knee and elbow pads should be worn while ____.
   a. skating   b. walking
   c. swimming   d. running

4. *Reach* and *Throw* are things to do to rescue a ____.
   a. biker   b. skier
   c. skater   d. swimmer

5. Whenever you are outdoors, you should wear ____.
   a. a coat   b. sunscreen
   c. safety gear   d. a helmet

Modified True or False

Write *true* or *false*. If a sentence is false, replace the underlined term to make the sentence true.

6. The first thing to do in an emergency is to <u>call for help</u>.

7. You should <u>pop</u> a blister.

8. In a fire you should <u>stay low</u>.

9. If you are at home alone, you should keep the doors <u>unlocked</u>.

10. You should keep a house key <u>where everyone can see it all the time</u>.

11. When you are camping, you should use <u>insect repellent</u>.

12. It is <u>safe</u> to swim alone.

13. In cold weather, wear <u>layers of clothing</u>.

14. To stay safe, <u>ride</u> your bike across a street.

15. Weapons should be <u>left in the open</u>.

Short Answer

Write a complete sentence to answer each question.

16. Tell what you would do to treat a mild burn.

17. What is first aid for a small cut or scrape?

18. Why should you have a first-aid kit?

19. Describe a safe campfire.

20. Why are mouth guards worn in some sports?

21. Why should you wear a hat in cold weather?

22. Why should you stay away from water during a thunderstorm?

23. What safety device should you always wear when riding in a car?

Writing in Health

Write paragraphs to answer each item.

24. Steve wakes up one night and smells smoke. What should he do?

25. You are playing basketball and the other team is winning. You think one of the players is not following the rules. What should you do?

CHAPTER 9

Living in a Healthful Community

MAKE A COMMUNITY NEWS-CLIPPING BOOK

As you work through this chapter, think about the people who help make your community clean and safe. Cut out pictures of these community workers from newspapers or magazines. Glue the pictures on paper to make a news-clipping book. Write one or two sentences to go along with each picture.

For other activities, visit the Harcourt Learning Site.
www.harcourtschool.com

MAIN IDEA A clean environment is important to your health.

WHY LEARN THIS? You can use what you learn to enjoy your community in healthful ways.

VOCABULARY
• environment
• polluted
• recreation

Enjoying a Healthful Environment

What is a healthful environment?

Look at the picture on these two pages. It shows a type of environment in which you might like to play and have fun. Your **environment** (in•vy•ruhn•muhnt) is all the living and nonliving things that surround you—things such as plants, animals, air, water, and soil.

Think of some ways that you could have fun in this environment. You could breathe the clean air deeply while walking in a field. You could swim, fish, or paddle a canoe in the clean water of the lake. Or you could spread a blanket on the shoreline and eat a picnic lunch.

Suppose that the air in the picture filled with smoke. How would it feel to breathe in dirty air? Suppose that slimy green algae choked the water. How would it feel

to go for a swim? What if cans, plastic bags, and garbage littered the ground? No one would want to come here.

In an unhealthful environment the air, the water, the land, or all three are **polluted** (puh•LOO•tid), or dirty. In a healthful environment the air, the water, and the land are clean. A clean environment is important to human health.

People need oxygen from the air to stay alive. To take in oxygen, you use your lungs. You need clean air for healthy lungs. Dirty air harms your lungs.

People need clean water, too—and quite a lot of it. You should drink six to eight glasses of fresh, clean water every day. Drinking dirty water may satisfy your thirst. But it can also make you ill. Clean water depends on clean land. Most drinking water—more than 90 percent of the world's supply—comes from water deep in the ground.

People also need clean land to grow healthful food. Plants soak up materials that are in soil. If soil is polluted, the unhealthful materials can be passed on to the people who eat the plants grown in the soil. People can use and enjoy the clean air, water, and land in a healthful environment.

▼ **A healthful environment can also help your mental health. Explain why.**

What are healthful ways to enjoy your community?

These pictures show various forms of **recreation** (reh•kree•AY•shuhn)—things you do to have fun. The adults and children in the pictures enjoy healthful kinds of recreation, such as bike riding and soccer. What healthful kinds of recreation do you enjoy?

Most people don't have to go far for recreation. In cities and rural areas, communities offer ways to have fun outdoors. An elementary school may have a playground and a softball or kickball field. A middle school or high school may have basketball courts and tennis courts.

For people who live near a river, a lake, or a pond, recreation means water sports such as swimming and fishing. Ponds can also be used as skating and hockey rinks if the water freezes in winter.

Sports are not the only form of recreation. Many people enjoy growing flowers and vegetables in community gardens. Clean land is especially important to gardeners.

This family is having fun on a bicycle outing. What type of environment do they need to enjoy this form of recreation?

▲ These boys and girls need clean land, clean water, and clean air for their favorite sport. How do you suppose they use each one?

There are many ways of adding recreation areas to a community. For example, in some places abandoned railroad tracks have been recycled into networks of recreation trails called *rail trails*. The old railroad tracks are no longer needed because cars, trucks, and airplanes have replaced the trains.

What you can see from a rail trail varies greatly, depending on which trail you take. The Minuteman Trail outside Boston takes cyclists, hikers, wheelchair users, and in-line skaters along a route that soldiers followed during the Revolutionary War. In winter the Sugar River Trail in Wisconsin leads cross-country skiers through small towns and farms.

LESSON CHECKUP

Check Your Facts

1. Name five things in your environment.
2. Why are clean air, water, and land important to human health?
3. CRITICAL THINKING Describe two recreation areas in your community. What makes these areas healthful or unhealthful?
4. CRITICAL THINKING Describe the type of environment you need to enjoy your favorite forms of recreation.

Set Health Goals

5. Think back over the past week. What forms of recreation did you take part in? Identify the one you enjoyed the most. How can you increase the time you spend on it?

Keeping the Community Clean and Safe

Think about the room that you sleep in. Is it clean and neat? Clean and messy? Dirty and neat? A messy bedroom can bother a parent. A dirty bedroom can harm human health. Remember that pathogens can grow on and be spread by objects. Keeping your room clean helps keep pathogens from spreading.

Who keeps the community clean?

Like a bedroom, a community must be clean to protect human health. A community has outside areas, such as parks, and inside areas, such as schoolrooms. If parks are filled with trash, pathogens can spread. Pathogens can also spread if desks, books, doorknobs, and restrooms aren't kept clean.

Groundskeepers pick up litter in parking lots and picnic areas. They keep parks free of trash and **graffiti** (gruh•FEE•tee)—writings or drawings on public buildings and structures. Groundskeepers rake leaves, sweep walkways, and remove snow from sidewalks.

► The person who drives this beach-sweeping machine helps keep the beach clean and free of litter. This makes the beach a more healthful place to visit.

This janitor is cleaning the floor of a school cafeteria. Why is keeping floors clean important to health?

ART CONNECTION

Draw a Picture

On Your Own Think of a worker you have seen who helps keep the community clean and safe. Make a drawing that shows the worker doing his or her job. Write a sentence that explains why this job is important to health.

● ● ●

Some areas of a community are too big to be cleaned by hand. Imagine what downtown streets would look like if no one came to sweep away the dirt and trash. And what would happen if no one picked up the trash you and your family put out each week?

Janitors and cleaners help keep the inside areas of the community clean. You may have seen a janitor at your school emptying trash cans or sweeping a floor. Janitors and cleaners also work in office buildings and hotels.

In hospitals cleaners wash beds and mattresses. They keep rooms, equipment, and supplies free from pathogens. How are their jobs important to community health?

Communicate

Read the information about the dispatcher on the next page. Then imagine that you have an emergency and must call a dispatcher for help. Make a list of the information you will need to tell the dispatcher in order to get help.

• • •

Who keeps the community safe?

A healthful community is not only clean but also safe. People need streets and parks that are safe for outdoor exercise. People need to know that community workers will help them in medical emergencies or fires.

In many people's minds the badge of a police officer stands for safety. A police officer helps keep the community safe in a number of ways. In just one day a police officer may give first aid to a hurt bicyclist, direct traffic at the scene of a fire, and chase a robbery suspect. Police officers also give tickets to speeding drivers. How does this police action help keep people safe?

Firefighters like the one here face flames, smoke, explosive gases, and poisonous chemicals on the job. Firefighters work long hours. Day or night they must respond quickly to an alarm.

You don't need to have a fire to see a firefighter hard at work. Firefighters work with police officers, Red Cross volunteers, and others to keep the community safe during earthquakes, tornadoes, hurricanes, floods, and other emergencies. Some firefighters are teachers, too. Perhaps a firefighter has visited your school to talk about how to prevent fires and what to do in case of a fire.

◀ Teamwork is key to a firefighter's job. During a fire some team members connect hose lines to fire hydrants. Others operate pumps or set up ladders. What do you think the firefighter in this picture has done?

You may never have seen an emergency medical technician (EMT) face to face. But you have probably seen the ambulances that EMTs drive. **Emergency medical technicians** (ih•MER•juhnt•see MEH•dih•kuhl tek•NIH•shuhnz) are men and women trained to handle serious illnesses and injuries. They respond to calls from **dispatchers** (dih•SPA•cherz), who tell them where the emergencies are. EMTs give first aid at the scene of an emergency and take care of the patients on the way to the hospital.

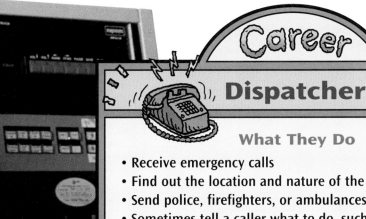

Career

Dispatcher

What They Do

- Receive emergency calls
- Find out the location and nature of the emergency
- Send police, firefighters, or ambulances to the scene
- Sometimes tell a caller what to do, such as ways to give first aid, until help arrives
- Keep a record of calls received and actions taken

Education and Training

Dispatchers need at least a high school education. They usually receive on-the-job training, but they also need to have good communication and computer skills.

LESSON CHECKUP

Check Your Facts

1. Name three workers who help keep a community clean.

2. Name four workers who help keep a community safe.

3. CRITICAL THINKING Why is cleanliness in a school lunchroom important to community health?

4. CRITICAL THINKING Describe how your community would be different without EMTs.

Set Health Goals

5. Make a list of school rules that students can follow to help the groundskeeper or janitor keep the school environment clean.

MAIN IDEA
People use natural resources for energy, for food, and to make things.

WHY LEARN THIS? You can use what you learn to understand where the resources you use come from.

VOCABULARY
• natural resources
• fossil fuels

Our Natural Resources

What are natural resources?

Look at the pictures on these two pages. These things are all **natural resources** (NA•chuh•ruhl REE•sohr•suhz), materials from nature that people use to meet their needs. As the pictures show, nature provides us with many types of resources. Our natural resources include materials such as minerals, and energy sources such as fossil fuels.

Plants and animals are natural resources, too. You can find plant resources by looking outdoors. You know we use plants for food. Trees also provide wood for building and pulp for making paper. Plants also give off oxygen into the air.

People use animal resources for food, clothing, and other materials. Animals as well as people need water resources, such as streams, lakes, and oceans. For example, a cow needs to drink four gallons of water to make one gallon of milk. If you look closely at a fish, you can see its gills. The gills take in oxygen from the water. Animals and plants need the clean air and clean water that a healthful environment provides.

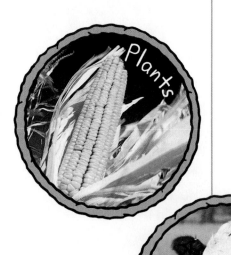

The pictures on these pages show seven kinds of natural resources that people depend on to meet their needs. What other things are made from the natural resources shown here?

Land resources are among the most important resources on Earth. To understand why, think about growing plants. Many kinds of plants will grow in good soil. Few plants will grow where soil has been washed away. Corn is one plant that grows well only in good soil.

When you think of mineral resources, gems like the diamonds shown on page 278 may come to mind. But if you have ever had juice in an aluminum can, you have had firsthand experience with another kind of mineral resource. Aluminum, iron, copper, nickel, and zinc come from mineral resources.

Although you may not have heard the term *fossil fuels*, you use at least one of these energy resources every day if you ride in a car or on the school bus. A fuel is a resource used to make energy. **Fossil fuels** are formed deep underground from the remains of plants and animals that lived long ago. Coal, oil, and natural gas are types of fossil fuels.

Kinds of Natural Resources

Plants
Animals
Minerals
Air
Fossil Fuels
Water
Land

Communicate

Make a list of all the natural resources that you and your class-mates use both at home and at school. Then tell how you use each of these natural resources. Use the steps for communi-cation shown on page *xii*.

• • •

How do people use natural resources?

The electrical energy that runs your television set comes from natural resources. So does the food energy that helps you move and grow. Making electricity and growing food are just two of the many ways that people use natural resources. What other ways can you think of?

People can use moving water, sunlight, wind, or energy from fossil fuels to spin machines that make electricity. At the energy plant shown on this page, a fossil fuel is burned to make electricity. People burn fossil fuels to heat and cool homes and businesses, too. Fossil fuels also run cars, trucks, buses, trains, and airplanes.

People use water resources for drinking, for growing crops, for washing clothes and dishes, and for taking showers. Water is also used to make steel, paper, paints, plastics, and many other products people use every day.

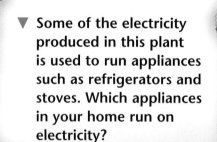

▼ Some of the electricity produced in this plant is used to run appliances such as refrigerators and stoves. Which appliances in your home run on electricity?

Many resources are being used to build this house. Mineral resources were used to make the metal window frames, the glass window panes, and the nails that hold the house together. Mineral resources are also used for pipes and gutters. Fossil fuels in the form of plastics will be used for carpets and drain pipes. What type of resource does the wood siding come from?

If you live on a farm, you know one way that people use land—for growing food. Ranchers use grasslands to graze cattle and sheep. Farmers use the rich topsoil that covers the land to grow food crops, such as wheat, rice, sugar cane, oranges, potatoes, and soybeans. People also use land to raise nonfood crops, such as cotton, flowers, and trees. Products made from trees include wood, paper, rubber, and medicines.

People also use land for the mineral resources and fossil fuels in the ground. They dig mines to get metals such as iron, aluminum, tin, zinc, silver, and gold. People also dig mines to get coal. They drill wells on land and on the ocean floor to get oil and natural gas.

LESSON CHECKUP

Check Your Facts

1. Name seven types of natural resources.

2. Give one example of how people use each resource that you named in Question 1.

3. CRITICAL THINKING Which of the seven resources is most important in your life? Explain your answer.

4. CRITICAL THINKING People use water resources at work as well as at home. Give one example of how people might use water in a restaurant, a fruit-canning plant, or a shopping mall.

Set Health Goals

5. Plant resources help humans in many ways. Think of one place at school or at home where you might be able to grow a plant. Make a plan for choosing and getting a plant. Ask a teacher or a family member to help you.

281

MAIN IDEA
People can protect natural resources by reducing pollution.

WHY LEARN THIS?
You can use what you learn to help protect our air, water, and land and keep the environment healthful.

VOCABULARY
• pollution
• solid waste
• scrubbers
• landfill

Preventing Air, Water, and Land Pollution

What can be done about air pollution?

Imagine you are traveling along the road in the picture below. The road will take you on a pollution tour. **Pollution** (puh•LOO•shuhn) is harmful material in the air, water, or land.

You can use the pictures on these pages to discover some possible causes of air pollution and ways in which air can be kept cleaner. Cars are a big part of the problem. Burning fossil fuels gives cars and trucks energy to move. It also sends polluting gases into the air. People have come up with many ways to reduce air pollution from cars. Devices on cars help clean the gases formed as fossil fuels are burned.

▼ Before the air was cleaned up, people couldn't use the bike path without getting ill.

Smokestacks on some factories release a lot of polluting gases, smoke, and dust. Energy plants that burn fossil fuels to make electricity also release gases that pollute the air.

You might also travel past a plant where trash is burned. Burning trash gets rid of **solid waste**, or garbage and litter. However, it could release harmful gases and chemicals into the air.

People need clean air to stay healthy. Breathing polluted air hurts the lungs. In cities where the air is polluted, heart disease and breathing disorders such as asthma get worse. People also become ill more often with colds and flu if the air is polluted. Eyes and throats feel itchy when people breathe polluted air. Noses feel stopped up.

Industry, government, and individuals are working together to solve the air pollution problem. For example, factories and plants that burn trash or fossil fuels use **scrubbers**, devices attached to smokestacks, to remove some pollutants. By forming carpools and using buses, streetcars, or subways, people are finding ways to reduce their use of cars. Instead of burning fossil fuels, some people make short trips by walking or riding a bike.

Myth: Air pollution affects only living things.

Fact: Some materials in air pollution can even eat away at the outside surfaces of buildings. Buildings made out of limestone are especially likely to suffer damage from air pollution.

▶ The factory shown has scrubbers on its smokestacks. How do these devices help reduce air pollution?

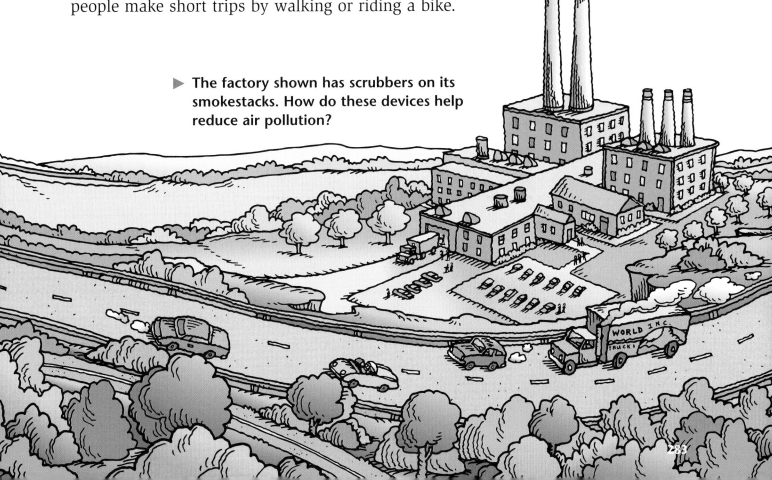

What can be done about water pollution?

The second stop on the pollution tour shows possible sources of water pollution. If people drank untreated water from this river, they would became very ill. Even swimming in the river would be risky. But the river is a lot cleaner than it used to be.

You can use the pictures to identify activities that could pollute a river. Notice the pipes that come out of the factory. Harmful chemicals flow through those pipes, straight into the water. A few miles downstream, a sewage treatment plant sends only partly treated human wastes into the water. Look at the ship on the next page. It is leaking oil into the water. Oil could pollute this river again.

Notice the farm field. Some farmers use chemical products to make the soil rich and to kill insects on the crops. When it rains, the chemicals wash off the field and into the river, polluting the water. Many farmers are finding ways to use fewer chemicals.

In what ways do water pollutants harm human health? Some chemical wastes from factories can cause diseases

HUMAN BODY CONNECTION

Water Pollution and Your Body

Water pollution harms both the environment and human health. Turn to pages 1–15. Identify the body systems affected by water pollution.

• • •

284

of the liver, kidneys, or brain. Human wastes carry pathogens into the water. Swallowing these germs can cause illness and possibly death. Chemicals that are used to make crops grow better or to kill insects can poison fish. Eating these fish can make people ill.

But don't give up drinking water! The U.S. government began to do something about polluted water long before you were born. The Safe Drinking Water Act of 1974 set limits on pollutants that can be released into public water supplies. The Act has been amended several times to expand its control. The Clean Water Act of 1977 aimed to make all lakes, rivers, and streams safe for swimming and fishing. Almost all big cities have improved sewage treatment to obey the Clean Water Act. And each state must report on its water quality every two years.

▲ The woman above is changing the motor oil in her car. Why should she dispose of the used oil properly?

The Environmental Protection Agency (EPA) watches factories to make sure they are not illegally dumping chemicals into water. Factories must get permits before dumping anything into the water.

What can be done about land pollution?

Notice that people on the pollution road are throwing trash out the car window. Littering harms the environment by making it ugly and unhealthful.

Litter can harm human health, too, when it is left in uncovered dumps. Dumps breed flies, mosquitoes, and rats, which carry disease. Broken glass and sharp pieces of metal can injure people. Chemical wastes placed carelessly in dumps can cause cancer.

Because they pollute the environment, dumps such as the one on page 287 are being replaced by sanitary land-fills. In a **landfill** layers of trash and soil are buried in a large pit that has a waterproof lining of plastic or clay.

You have read that spilled oil pollutes water. Oil washed off parking lots and driveways by rain pollutes land, too. In 1989 an oil tanker named the *Exxon Valdez* spilled 11 million gallons (about $41\frac{1}{2}$ million L) of oil off the coast of Alaska. The oil washed onto beaches, polluting them and killing hundreds of seabirds and mammals. Each year people in the United States pollute the environment with 20 times that much oil. Some of that pollution occurs when people don't properly dispose of materials such as motor oil. These materials can seep into the groundwater,

▲ Salt makes icy roads safer to drive on. But if salt gets into soil or water, it harms or kills plants and animals. Many communities now use sand to make icy roads less slippery.

▼ The tractor is spreading organic fertilizer onto the field. This type of fertilizer is made from plant or animal products instead of chemicals. It will help the crops grow better without harming the groundwater.

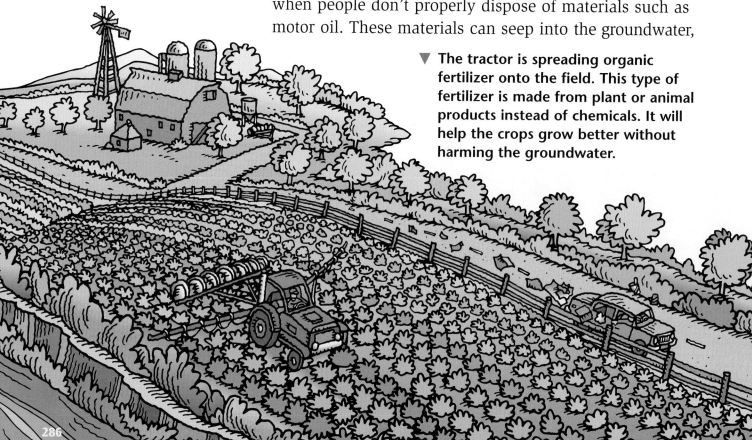

Activity **Protect Earth's Resources** Study the picture at left. Describe how the air, water, and the land could be harmed by what you see in the picture. Then tell what could be done to protect each of these resources.

the source of drinking water for many people, if they are washed down the drain or dumped into the ground. Oil from roads and parking lots is another souce of pollution.

People can help reduce land pollution by not dumping trash or garbage. They can also help protect the land by planting trees. Trees help hold one of our most valuable resources—soil—in place.

Another way to reduce land pollution is by recycling, or reusing, different kinds of trash. Metal cans, for example, can be melted down and used to make new cans. Glass and newspapers can be recycled, too.

LESSON CHECKUP

Check Your Facts

❶ How can air pollution be reduced?

❷ Name two laws that have helped reduce water pollution in the United States.

❸ CRITICAL THINKING Explain how people's actions in one part of the environment affect other parts.

❹ List three things people can do to help reduce land pollution.

Use Life Skills

❺ COMMUNICATE Think about how your school can use some of the suggestions in this lesson to reduce pollution. Make a list to share with your classmates.

MAIN IDEA
Conserving resources such as water, air, and land is important to people's health.

WHY LEARN THIS? You can use what you learn to practice conservation.

VOCABULARY
• conservation

Myth and fact

Myth:
Recycling aluminum saves only aluminum.

Fact:
Recycling aluminum saves energy, too. The energy saved by recycling one aluminum can could run a television set for three hours.

• • • • • • •

Ways to Practice Conservation

Clean water, air, and land link the three forms of recreation that you see in these pictures. People can enjoy walking on sandy beaches, fishing, and hiking in parks—as long as they use these resources wisely.

Why is conservation important?

Conservation (kahn•ser•VAY•shuhn) is the careful use of resources. Everyone needs clean air, land, and water to stay healthy. Conservation makes clean resources last longer. Clean resources are needed for a healthful environment.

Recall the natural resources shown on pages 278 and 279. You can divide these resources into two groups. Some resources, such as plants and land, can be replaced over time. Other resources, such as fossil fuels and minerals, are limited. Once they are used up, these resources cannot be replaced, or they can be replaced only after a very long time.

The first group of resources will last and last, as long as people conserve them. Think about plant resources such as forests. As long as old trees are not cut down faster than new trees can grow, we will always have forest resources.

In the same way, if land resources such as soil are conserved, people many years from now will have plenty of rich soil in which to grow food. Conserving soil involves using certain plants to keep soil from blowing or washing away. It involves rotating crops from field to field each year. Planting the same crop in the same field year after year damages the soil.

The environment has a limited supply of resources such as fossil fuels. If people use up Earth's supply, these resources will be gone for a very long time.

Think back to Lesson 1, where you read about the parts of a healthful environment. Suppose that people polluted or wasted this clean water. What difference would it make to the people walking on the beach, fishing, or feeding the birds in the park?

How can people practice conservation?

Conserving resources requires the efforts of everyone— older people, children, business owners, and farmers. People in homes could save about 20,000 gallons (about 75,760 L) of water each year by not letting water run when they are not using it. People should turn off the faucet while they brush their teeth. When running water for baths, people should plug the tub before turning on the water. Better yet, they should take showers. A shower generally uses about one-third as much water as does a bath.

People can also install low-flow showerheads in their bathrooms. One type of low-flow showerhead adds air to the water. It can cut the amount of water used when showering by one-half. Low-flow aerators can also be installed on all the faucets in a home. They mix air with water, too. The flow of water is reduced, but the air makes the flow feel stronger.

Remember that fossil fuels are often used to make electricity. People can help conserve fossil fuels by putting on sweaters instead of turning up the heat. People can also turn off the lights when they leave rooms. And people can hang clothes on lines to dry, instead of running clothes dryers. What are some other ways to conserve fossil fuels?

Do your part to conserve!

◄ **This girl is replacing a regular (incandescent) light bulb with a fluorescent bulb. The new light bulb uses 75 percent less energy. That's a lot of energy saved over time. The fluorescent bulb also lasts up to 12 times longer than the regular bulb does.**

Activity **Conserve Water** Estimate how much water a family of four uses each day for the activities listed here. Which activity uses the most water? What other things does the family use water for?

Think of some ways that this family can practice water conservation. Share your ideas with your classmates.

WATER USE

Flush toilet (not low-flow):
5–7 gallons (19–26.5 L)

Flush toilet (low-flow):
1–2 gallons (3.7–7.6 L)

Take shower:
5–10 gallons (19–38 L)
per minute

Brush teeth with water running:
1–2 gallons (3.8–7.6 L)

Shave with water running:
10–15 gallons (38–57 L)

Wash dishes by hand:
20 gallons (76 L)

Use dishwasher:
10–25 gallons (38–95 L)

Let faucet drip:
2–3 gallons (7.6–11.3 L)
per day

CONSUMER FOCUS

Access Valid Health Information

Is bottled water better for you and the environment than tap water? Use library resources to find an answer. Use the steps for accessing valid health information on page *xvi* in the front of this book.

• • •

LESSON CHECKUP

Check Your Facts

❶ Why is conservation important to health?

❷ Give two examples of limited resources.

❸ CRITICAL THINKING You can conserve water and money with a low-flow shower-head. How is this possible, when you have to spend money to buy the showerhead?

❹ Name five ways to conserve resources.

Set Health Goals

❺ List ways people use electricity or water. Identify three ways people could change their use to conserve resources.

SET GOALS to Conserve Resources

We use resources every day. Have you ever thought of ways to reduce the amount of resources you use? You and your family can use goal-setting steps to make a plan to save resources.

Learn This Skill

Colleen knows that water is an important resource. She sees many examples of water being wasted in her own home. She and her parents want to do something about it, but what?

1. Set a goal.

Colleen and her parents decide that their goal will be to reduce the amount of water wasted in their home.

2. List steps to reach the goal.

The family discusses ways to save water.

3. Check progress toward the goal.

Colleen and her mom check the water bill each month to see how much water the family is using. Colleen makes a chart to show how much water is being saved.

4. Evaluate the goal.

Colleen's family can save many gallons of water each month. After a few weeks, her family finds that conserving water is simple, and they feel happy to have met their goal.

Practice This Skill

Use this summary to set goals.

Steps for Setting Goals

1. Set a goal.
2. List steps to reach the goal.
3. Check progress toward the goal.
4. Evaluate the goal.

A. Mr. Cavelli knows how important it is to save resources. Use the goal-setting steps to help Mr. Cavelli use less electricity at his office.

B. Katrina has noticed that the air in her town is polluted. How could Katrina and her parents use the goal-setting steps to help their town reduce air pollution?

USE VOCABULARY

conservation (p. 288)
dispatchers (p. 277)
emergency medical
  technicians (p. 277)

environment (p. 270)
fossil fuels (p. 279)
graffiti (p. 274)
landfill (p. 286)

natural resources
  (p. 278)
polluted (p. 271)
pollution (p. 282)

recreation (p. 272)
scrubbers (p. 283)
solid waste (p. 283)

Use the terms above to complete the sentences. Page numbers in ( ) tell you where to look in the chapter if you need help.

1. Your _____ includes all the living and nonliving things around you.

2. Bike riding, swimming, fishing, and soccer are all kinds of _____.

3. People who give emergency treatment and drive patients to hospitals are _____.

4. _____ take information over the phone about emergencies and send for help.

5. _____ are materials from the environment that people use to meet their needs.

6. Coal, oil, and natural gas are all _____.

7. _____ is harmful materials in the air, water, or land.

8. Devices that remove harmful materials from factory smokestacks are _____.

9. _____ is the careful use of resources.

10. _____ is something written or drawn on public buildings and structures.

11. Garbage and litter are examples of _____.

12. A _____ is a place with a waterproof lining where layers of trash and soil are buried.

13. Dirty, or _____, air, water, and land harm the environment.

CHECK YOUR FACTS

Page numbers in ( ) tell you where to look in the chapter if you need help.

14. Describe what a healthful environment is, and tell three ways you can enjoy one. (pp. 270–271)

15. Name the workers shown, and tell what they do to help keep the community safe. (pp. 276–277)

16. Tell where fossil fuels come from, and explain how people use them. (pp. 279–280)

17. Tell two ways that water pollution can harm health. (pp. 284–285)

18. Why is it important to conserve fossil fuels and minerals? (pp. 288–289)

THINK CRITICALLY

19. Farmers and other people who live in the country often get water from their own wells. Many of these people take samples of their well water to their local health departments to be tested. Why do you think they do this?

20. Think about all the signs in your community reminding people to follow health and safety rules. Make your own sign reminding students to follow school health and safety rules.

APPLY LIFE SKILLS

21. **Communicate** Keisha and two of her friends had a picnic lunch in the park. When Keisha stayed to clean up, her friends just walked away. What could Keisha have said to her friends about why it is important to clean up their trash?

22. **Set Goals** Think about a resource that people use every day. How could people use the goal-setting steps to encourage others to conserve?

Promote Health **Home and Community**

1. Ask several of your classmates to help you make a "Pollution Prevention" chart. Make three columns on the chart, labeled *Air, Water,* and *Land.* Discuss with your classmates how you can prevent each of these kinds of pollution. Write down the ideas you agree on. Display your chart where other students can see it.

2. You, your friends, and adults can help the environment by adopting a stream or lake in your area. Get a group together to patrol and clean up the stream bank. Be sure to have adults with you. Take heavy leather gloves and trash bags. Collect all the trash you find. Take the trash home to throw away or recycle. Your group might want to plant trees along the bank of the stream or lake. Trees will keep soil from washing into the stream or lake when it rains or snows.

Activities

Use It Again and Again

With a Partner • Recall that some resources can be replaced, while supplies of others are limited. Make lists of things you use at school and at home that are made from each of these two kinds of resources. Hint: Plastic products are made from oil, a fossil fuel. Make a plan for reusing some of them to conserve resources.

Playing Around

With a Team • Find out what people do for recreation in your community. Make a pamphlet to present what you find. Use words and pictures. Invite others in your school to use the pamphlet to get ideas for recreation.

Home Cleanup

At Home • Ask your parents about setting aside a weekend morning for a family cleanup project. Decide together on an area to clean inside or outside your home. Reward yourselves after the cleanup by playing a favorite game or preparing a special meal.

Lighten Up

On Your Own • Find out what resource an energy plant near you uses to make electricity. For example, it could be uranium, water, or a fossil fuel. Find out how electricity is made with this resource. Make a poster showing what you learned.

Multiple Choice

Choose the letter of the correct answer.

1. A worker who helps keep the community clean is a(n)
   a. police officer   b. EMT
   c. groundskeeper   d. firefighter

2. Doing things to have fun is called
   a. recreation   b. environment
   c. resources   d. conservation

3. Animal resources include
   a. fish and deer   b. coal and oil
   c. nickel and zinc   d. air and land

4. People help reduce land pollution by
   a. dumping trash   b. recycling
   c. spilling oil   d. taking baths

5. Which of the following natural resources is a fossil fuel?
   a. oil   b. minerals
   c. forests   d. corn

Modified True or False

Write *true* or *false*. If a sentence is false, replace the underlined term to make the sentence true.

6. All the living and nonliving things that surround you are your <u>environment</u>.

7. A worker who helps keep the community safe is a <u>police officer</u>.

8. At energy plants fossil fuels can be burned to make <u>water</u>.

9. <u>Scrubbers</u> are devices attached to smokestacks to remove pollutants.

10. Harmful materials in the air, water, or land are <u>conservation</u>.

11. Breathing polluted air can harm a person's <u>lungs</u>.

12. One way that people use water resources is to <u>grow crops</u>.

13. The <u>Safe Drinking Water Act</u> helps make lakes safe for swimming.

14. Wind can blow <u>soil</u> from fields where no plants are growing.

15. Materials from the environment that people use to meet their needs are called <u>natural resources</u>.

Short Answer

Write a complete sentence to answer each question.

16. Give two examples of recreation.

17. Tell one way that people use land resources.

18. Tell one way you could help reduce air pollution from cars.

19. How can farm chemicals sprayed on the land pollute water?

20. What is one way you could conserve water?

21. How does the Environmental Protection Agency (EPA) protect water?

22. What is one way you could conserve fossil fuels?

23. How could land pollution cause food shortages?

Writing in Health

Write paragraphs to answer each item.

24. Why do people need clean air, water, and land to be healthy?

25. Suppose you were walking in the woods and got thirsty. Should you drink water from a stream? Explain.

Energy!

Good Nutrition

The Food Guide Pyramid 300
Estimating Serving Sizes 301
More Food Guide Pyramids 302
Dietary Guidelines for Americans 304

Preparing Foods Safely

Fight Bacteria.....................................306
Food Safety Tips 307

Being Physically Active

Planning Your Weekly Activities 308
Guidelines for a Good Workout........309
Warm-Up and Cool-Down Stretches....310
Building a Strong Heart and Lungs....312
The President's Challenge.................314

Being Safe

Good Posture at the Computer 316
Safety on the Internet.......................317
Evaluating Health Websites 318
Backpack Safety.................................319
When Home Alone 320
Bike Safety Check 322
Your Bike Helmet 323
Safety While Riding..........................323
Fire Safety 324
Storm Safety 325
Earthquake Safety 325
Make a Family Emergency Plan 326

First Aid

Universal Precautions 328
For Choking 329
For Burns 330
For Nosebleeds 330
For Insect Bites and Stings 331
For Skin Rashes from Plants 331

Alcohol, Tobacco, and Other Drugs

What to Do When Others Use Drugs 332
A Drug-Free School 333

The Food Guide Pyramid

No one food or food group supplies everything your body needs for good health. That's why it's important to eat foods from all the food groups. The Food Guide Pyramid can help you choose healthful foods in the right amounts. By choosing more foods from the groups at the bottom of the pyramid and fewer foods from the group at the top, you will eat the foods that provide your body with energy to grow and develop.

Fats, oils, and sweets
Eat sparingly.

Meat, poultry, fish, dry beans, eggs, and nuts 2–3 servings

Milk, yogurt, and cheese
2–3 servings

Fruit
2–4 servings

Vegetables
3–5 servings

Breads, cereals, rice, and pasta 6–11 servings

Estimating Serving Sizes

Choosing a variety of foods is only half the story. You also need to choose the right amounts. The table below can help you estimate the number of servings you are eating of your favorite foods.

Food Group	Amount of Food in One Serving	Some Easy Ways to Estimate Serving Size
Bread, Cereal, Rice, and Pasta Group	1 ounce ready-to-eat (dry) cereal	large handful of plain cereal or a small handful of cereal with raisins and nuts
	1 slice bread, $\frac{1}{2}$ bagel	
	$\frac{1}{2}$ cup cooked pasta, rice, or cereal	ice cream scoop
Vegetable Group	1 cup of raw, leafy vegetables	about the size of a fist
	$\frac{1}{2}$ cup other vegetables, cooked or raw, chopped	
	$\frac{3}{4}$ cup vegetable juice	
	$\frac{1}{2}$ cup tomato sauce	ice cream scoop
Fruit Group	medium apple, pear, or orange	a baseball
	$\frac{1}{2}$ large banana or one medium banana	
	$\frac{1}{2}$ cup chopped or cooked fruit	
	$\frac{3}{4}$ cup of fruit juice	
Milk, Yogurt, and Cheese Group	$1\frac{1}{2}$ ounces of natural cheese	two dominoes
	2 ounces of processed cheese	$1\frac{1}{2}$ slices of packaged cheese
	1 cup of milk or yogurt	
Meat, Poultry, Fish, Dry Beans, Eggs, and Nuts Group	3 ounces of lean meat, chicken, or fish	about the size of your palm
	2 tablespoons peanut butter	
	$\frac{1}{2}$ cup of cooked dry beans	
Fats, Oils, and Sweets Group	1 teaspoon of margarine or butter	about the size of the tip of your thumb

More Food Guide Pyramids

The Food Guide Pyramid from the U.S. Department of Agriculture, or USDA (page 300), shows common foods from the United States. Foods from different cultures and lifestyles also can make up a healthful diet. These other pyramids can help you add new foods to your diet. Use the serving guide on page 301 with all four pyramids.

Vegetarian

Vegetarians (vej•uh•TEHR•ee•uhns) are people who choose not to eat any meat, poultry, or fish. A balanced vegetarian diet is just as healthful as a balanced diet that includes meats.

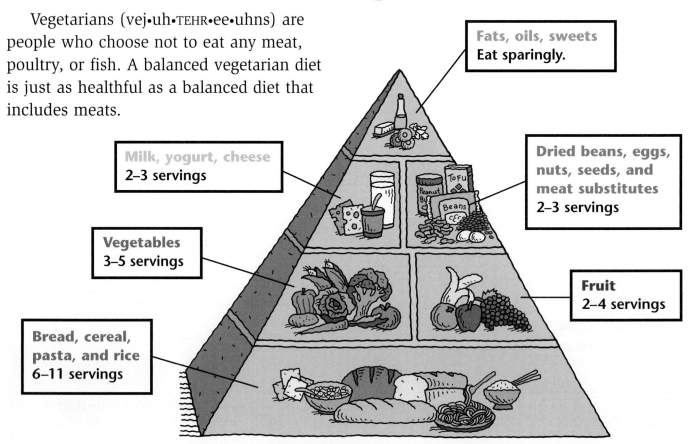

Fats, oils, sweets
Eat sparingly.

Dried beans, eggs, nuts, seeds, and meat substitutes
2–3 servings

Milk, yogurt, cheese
2–3 servings

Fruit
2–4 servings

Vegetables
3–5 servings

Bread, cereal, pasta, and rice
6–11 servings

The tops of these two pyramids differ from the one on page 300. They suggest eating seafood, poultry, eggs, and meat each week or month rather than each day. Moderate daily use of vegetable oils is also recommended. What other differences do you notice?

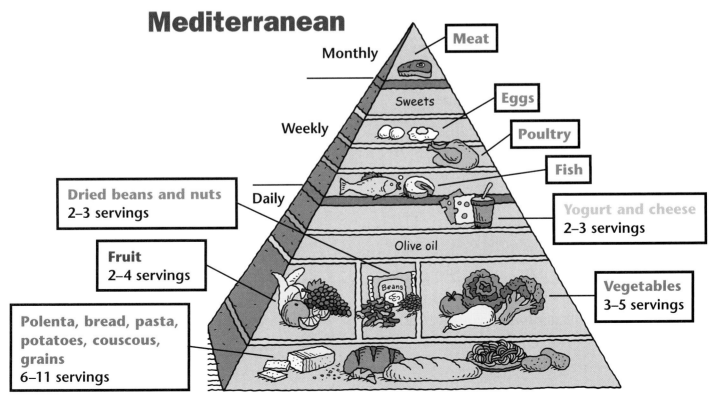

Asian

Monthly — **Meat**

Weekly — **Sweets, eggs, poultry**

Fish, shellfish, dairy

Daily

Vegetable oils

Dried beans, nuts, seeds, meat substitutes
2–3 servings

Fruit
2–4 servings

Vegetables
3–5 servings

Noodles, bread, rice, millets, and other grains
6–11 servings

Mediterranean

Monthly — **Meat**

Sweets

Eggs

Weekly — **Poultry**

Fish

Daily

Olive oil

Yogurt and cheese
2–3 servings

Dried beans and nuts
2–3 servings

Fruit
2–4 servings

Vegetables
3–5 servings

Polenta, bread, pasta, potatoes, couscous, grains
6–11 servings

Dietary Guidelines for Americans

These dietary guidelines come from the USDA. Following them will help you make good choices about nutrition and health. Making the right choices will help you feel your best.

Aim for Fitness

- Aim for a healthy weight. Find out your healthy weight range from a health professional. If you need to, set goals to reach a healthier weight.

- Be physically active each day. (Use the Activity Pyramid on page 308 to help you plan each week's activities.)

Build a Healthy Base

- Use the Food Guide Pyramid to guide your food choices.

- Each day choose a variety of grains such as wheat, oats, rice, and corn. Choose whole grains when you can.

- Each day choose a variety of fruits and vegetables.

- Keep food safe to eat. (Follow the tips on pages 306–307 for safe preparation and storage of food.)

Choose Sensibly

- Choose a diet that is moderate in total fat and low in saturated fat and cholesterol.

- Choose foods and drinks that are low in sugar. Lower the amount of sugars you eat.

- Choose foods that are low in salt. When you prepare foods, use very little salt.

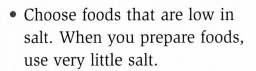

Fight Bacteria

You probably already know to throw away food that smells bad or looks moldy. But food doesn't have to look or smell bad to make you ill. To keep your food safe and yourself from becoming ill, follow the steps outlined in the picture below. And remember—when in doubt, throw it out!

FIGHT BAC!

CLEAN
Wash hands and surfaces often.

SEPARATE
Don't cross-contaminate.

CHILL
Refrigerate promptly.

COOK
Cook to proper temperatures.

Keep Food Safe From Bacteria

TM

Food Safety Tips

Tips for Preparing Food

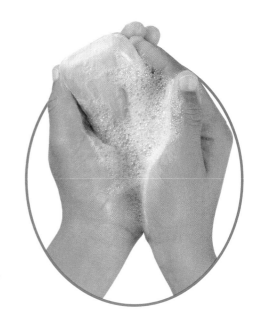

- Wash hands in warm, soapy water before preparing food. It's also a good idea to wash hands after preparing each dish.

- Defrost meat in the microwave or the refrigerator.

- Keep raw meat, poultry, fish, and their juices away from other food.

- Wash cutting boards, knives, and countertops immediately after cutting up meat, poultry, or fish. Never use the same cutting board for meats and vegetables without washing the board first.

Tips for Cooking Food

- Cook all food completely, especially meat. Complete cooking kills the bacteria that can make you ill.

- Red meats should be cooked to a temperature of 160°F. Poultry should be cooked to 180°F. When done, fish flakes easily with a fork.

- Never eat food that contains raw eggs or raw egg yolks, including cookie dough.

Tips for Cleaning Up the Kitchen

- Wash all dishes, utensils, and countertops with hot, soapy water. Use a soap that kills bacteria, if possible.

- Store leftovers in small containers that will cool quickly in the refrigerator. Don't leave leftovers on the counter to cool.

Planning Your Weekly Activities

Being active every day is important for your overall health. Physical activity helps you manage stress, maintain a healthful weight, and strengthen your body systems. The Activity Pyramid, like the Food Guide Pyramid, can help you choose a variety of activities in the right amounts to keep your body strong and healthy.

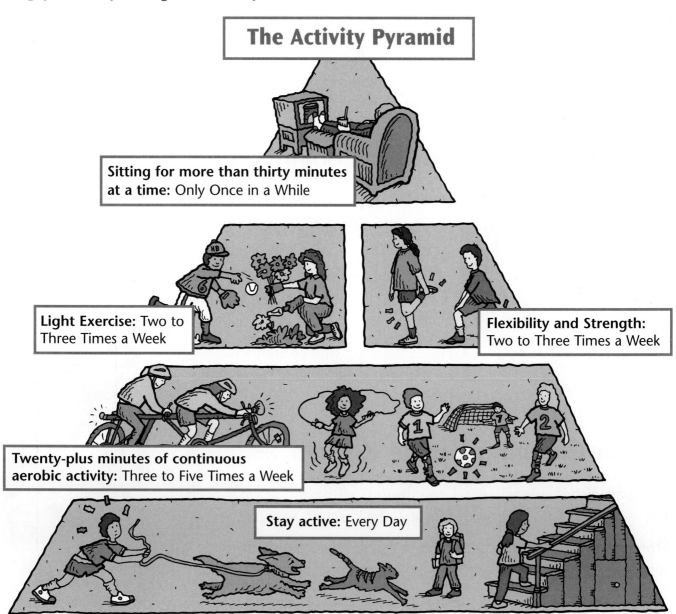

The Activity Pyramid

Sitting for more than thirty minutes at a time: Only Once in a While

Light Exercise: Two to Three Times a Week

Flexibility and Strength: Two to Three Times a Week

Twenty-plus minutes of continuous aerobic activity: Three to Five Times a Week

Stay active: Every Day

Guidelines for a Good Workout

There are three things you should do every time you are going to exercise—warm up, work out, and cool down.

Warm-Up: When you warm up, your heart rate, breathing rate, and body temperature increase and more blood flows to your muscles. As your body warms up, you can move more easily. People who warm up are less stiff after exercising, and are less likely to have exercise-related injuries. Your warm-up should include five minutes of stretching, and five minutes of low-level exercise. Some simple stretches are shown on pages 310–311.

Workout: The main part of your exercise routine should be an aerobic exercise that lasts 20 to 30 minutes. Aerobic exercises make your heart, lungs, and circulatory system stronger.

Some common aerobic exercises are shown on pages 312–313. You may want to mix up the types of activities you do. This helps you work different muscles, and provides a better workout over time.

Cool-Down: When you finish your aerobic exercise, you need to give your body time to cool down. Start your cool-down with three to five minutes of low-level activity. End with stretching exercises to prevent soreness and stiffness.

Warm-Up and Cool-Down Stretches

Before you exercise, you should warm up your muscles. The warm-up exercises shown here should be held for at least fifteen to twenty seconds and repeated at least three times. At the end of your workout, spend about two minutes repeating some of these stretches.

▶ **Sit-and-Reach Stretch**
HINT—Remember to bend at the waist. Keep your eyes on your toes!

◀ **Hurdler's Stretch**
HINT—Keep the toes of your extended leg pointed up.

▶ **Upper Back and Shoulder Stretch** HINT—Try to stretch your hand down so that it rests flat against your back.

▼ **Thigh Stretch** HINT— Keep both hands flat on the ground. Lean as far forward as you can.

▶ **Calf Stretch** HINT—Keep both feet on the floor during this stretch. Try changing the distance between your feet. Is the stretch better for you when your legs are closer together or farther apart?

▼ **Shoulder and Chest Stretch** HINT—Pulling your hands slowly toward the floor gives a better stretch. Keep your elbows straight, but not locked!

Tips for Stretching

- Never bounce when stretching.
- Hold each stretch for fifteen to twenty seconds.
- Breathe normally. This helps your body get the oxygen it needs.
- Do NOT stretch until it hurts. Stretch only until you feel a slight pull.

Building a Strong Heart and Lungs

Aerobic activities cause deep breathing and a fast heart rate for at least twenty minutes. These activities help both your heart and your lungs. Because your heart is a muscle, it gets stronger with exercise. A strong heart doesn't have to work as hard to pump blood to the rest of your body. Exercise also allows your lungs to hold more air. With a strong heart and lungs, your cells get oxygen faster and your body works more efficiently.

▲ **Swimming** Swimming is great for your endurance and flexibility. Even if you're not a great swimmer, you can use a kickboard and have a great time and a great workout just kicking around the pool. Be sure to swim only when a lifeguard is present.

◀ **In-line Skating** Remember to always wear a helmet when skating. Always wear protective pads on your elbows and knees, and guards on your wrists, too. Learning how to skate, stop, and fall correctly will make you a safer skater.

▼ **Walking** A fast-paced walk is a terrific way to build your endurance. The only equipment you need is supportive shoes. Walking with a friend can make this exercise a lot of fun.

▲ **Jumping Rope** Jumping rope is one of the best ways to increase your endurance. Remember to always jump on an even surface and always wear supportive shoes.

▼ **Bicycling** Bicycling provides good aerobic activity *and* a great way to see the outdoors. Be sure to learn and follow bicycle safety rules. And *always* remember to wear your helmet!

The President's Challenge

The President's Challenge is a physical fitness program designed for students ages 6 to 17. It's made up of five activities that promote physical fitness. Each participant receives an emblem patch and a certificate signed by the President.

The five awards:

 Presidential Physical Fitness Award—presented to students scoring in the top 15 percent in all events.

 National Physical Fitness Award—presented to students scoring in the top 50 percent in all events.

Health Fitness Award—awarded to all other participants.

 Participant Physical Fitness Award—presented to students who complete all items but score below the top 50 percent in one or more events.

 Active Lifestyle Award—recognizes students who participate in daily physical activity of any type for five days per week, 60 minutes a day, or 11,000 pedometer steps for six weeks.

The Five Activities

1. **Curl-Ups or Sit-Ups** measure abdominal muscle strength.

   - Lie on the floor with your arms across your chest and your legs bent. Have a partner hold your feet.

   - Lift your upper body off the ground, then lower it until it just touches the floor.

   - Repeat as many times as you can in one minute.

2. **Shuttle Run** measures leg strength and endurance.

   - Run to the blocks and pick one up.

   - Bring it back to the starting line.

   - Repeat for the other block.

3. **One Mile Run or Walk** measures leg muscle strength and heart and lung endurance.

- Run or walk a mile as fast as you can.

4. **Pull-ups** measure the strength and endurance of arm and shoulder muscles.

- Hang by your hands from a bar.
- Pull your body up until your chin is over the bar. Lower your body again without touching the floor.
- Repeat as many times as you can.

5. **V-Sit Reach** measures the flexibility of your legs and back.

- Sit on the floor with your feet behind the line. Your feet should be shoulder-width apart.
- Reach forward as far as you can.

Good Posture at the Computer

Good posture is important when using the computer. To help prevent eyestrain, stress, and injuries, follow the posture tips shown below. Also remember to grasp the mouse lightly and take frequent breaks for stretching.

top of screen at or just below eye level

shoulders in line with ears and hips

neck and shoulders relaxed

arms at sides, bent as shown

wrists straight

feet flat on floor

Safety on the Internet

You can use the Internet for fun, education, research, and more. But like anything else, you should use the Internet with caution. Some people compare the Internet to a real city—not all the people there are people you want to meet and not all the places you can go are places you want to be. Just like in a real city, you have to use common sense and follow safety rules to protect yourself. Below are some easy rules to follow to help you stay safe on-line.

Rules for On-line Safety

- Talk with an adult family member to set up rules for going on-line. Decide what time of day you can go on-line, how long you can be on-line, and appropriate places you can visit. Do not access other areas or break the rules you establish.

- Don't give out information like your address, telephone number, your picture, or the name or location of your school.

- If you find any information on-line that makes you uncomfortable, or if you receive a message that is mean or makes you feel uncomfortable, tell an adult family member right away.

- Never agree to meet anyone in person. If you want to get together with someone you meet on-line, check with an adult family member first. If a meeting is approved, arrange to meet in a public place and take an adult with you.

Evaluating Health Websites

Many people find health facts on the Web. However, it's important to remember that almost anyone can put information on the Web. Here are some questions to think about when you are looking at health websites.

Who controls the website?

Look for sources that you know about. Sites run by universities and the government are usually more reliable (their addresses usually end with .edu or .gov).

Who is saying it?

Information from health professionals is usually reliable. Look for the initials of a college degree, such as M.D., R.N., or Ph.D., after the writer's name.

Does the site look good?

Bad design and poor spelling or grammar are signs of a less-than-reliable site.

Are they selling something?

Websites that sell products or services may tell you only what makes their items sound good.

Double-check your facts!

What is the evidence?

Personal stories may sound convincing, but they're not the same as proof. Look for sites that show evidence from science research.

Does everyone agree?

Always check the information in more than one source. If several sites agree, the information is probably reliable.

Backpack Safety

Carrying a backpack that is too heavy can injure your back. Carrying one incorrectly also can hurt you.

A Safe Weight

Most doctors recommend that a full backpack weigh between 5 and 10 percent of your body weight. To find 10 percent, divide your body weight by 10. Here are some examples:

Your Weight (lbs)	Maximum Backpack Weight (lbs)
60	6
65	$6\frac{1}{2}$
70	7

▲ **This is the right way to wear a backpack.**

▲ **This is the wrong way to wear a backpack.**

Safe Use

- Always use both shoulder straps to carry the pack.

- Use a pack with wide shoulder straps and a padded back.

- Place any heavy items in the pack so that they will be next to your back.

- Store extra books in your locker instead of in your backpack. Visit your locker often to switch books.

- When riding a bicycle, avoid wearing a heavy pack. The weight makes it harder to stay balanced. Use a basket or saddlebags instead.

When Home Alone

Everyone stays home alone sometimes. When you stay home alone, it's important to know how to take care of yourself. Here are some easy rules to follow that will help keep you safe when you are at home by yourself.

Do These Things

- Lock all the doors and windows. Be sure you know how to lock and unlock all the locks.

  - If someone calls who is nasty or mean, hang up. Your parents may not want you to answer the phone at all.

    - If you have an emergency, call 911 or 0 (zero) for the operator. Describe the problem, give your full name, address, and telephone number. Follow all instructions given to you.

      - If you see anyone hanging around outside, tell an adult or call the police.

      - If you see or smell smoke, go outside right away. If you live in an apartment, do not take the elevator. Go to a neighbor's home and call 911 or the fire department immediately.

- Entertain yourself. Time will pass more quickly if you are not bored. Try not to spend your time watching television. Instead, work on a hobby, read a book or magazine, do your homework, or clean your room. Before you know it, an adult will be home.

Do NOT Do These Things

- Do NOT use the stove, microwave, or oven unless an adult family member has given you permission, and you are sure about how to use these appliances.

- Do NOT open the door for anyone you don't know or for anyone who is not supposed to be in your home.

  - If someone rings the bell and asks to use the telephone, tell the person to go to a phone booth.

  - If someone tries to deliver a package, do NOT open the door. The delivery person will leave the package or come back later.

  - If someone is selling something, do NOT open the door. Just say, "We're not interested," and nothing more.

- Do NOT talk to strangers on the telephone. Do not tell anyone that you are home alone. If the call is for an adult family member, say that they can't come to the phone right now and take a message. Ask for the caller's name and phone number and deliver the message when an adult family member comes home.

- Do NOT have friends over unless you have gotten permission from your parents or other adult family members.

▼ A telephone with a caller ID display can help you decide whether to answer the telephone.

Bike Safety Check

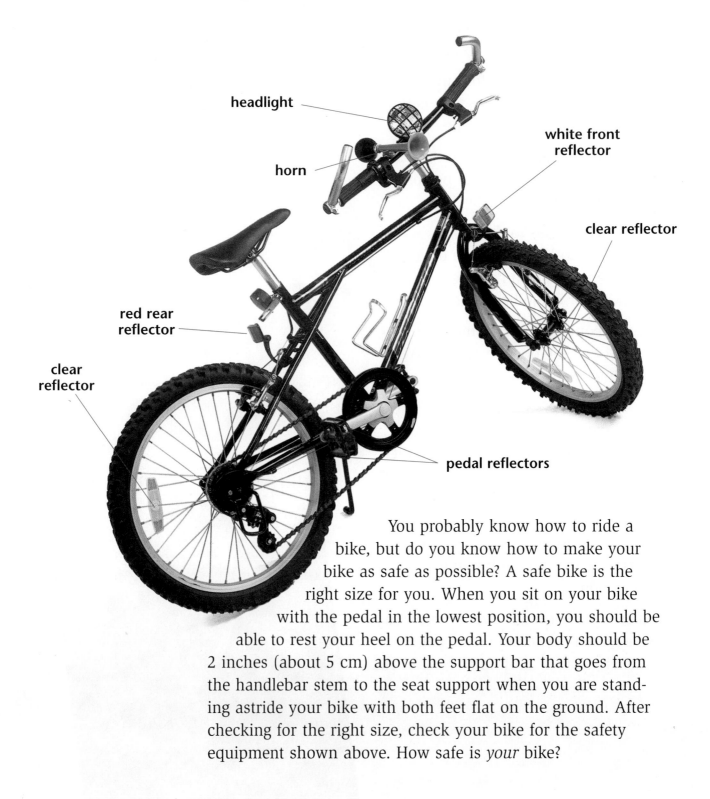

headlight

white front reflector

horn

clear reflector

red rear reflector

clear reflector

pedal reflectors

You probably know how to ride a bike, but do you know how to make your bike as safe as possible? A safe bike is the right size for you. When you sit on your bike with the pedal in the lowest position, you should be able to rest your heel on the pedal. Your body should be 2 inches (about 5 cm) above the support bar that goes from the handlebar stem to the seat support when you are standing astride your bike with both feet flat on the ground. After checking for the right size, check your bike for the safety equipment shown above. How safe is *your* bike?

Your Bike Helmet

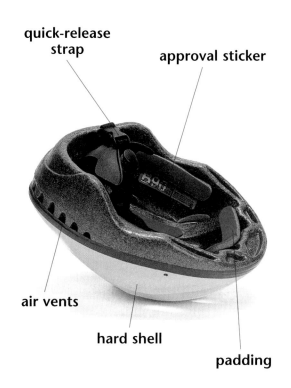

quick-release strap

approval sticker

air vents

hard shell

padding

About 400,000 children are involved in bike-related crashes every year. That's why it's important to *always* wear your bike helmet. Wear your helmet flat on your head. Be sure it is strapped snugly so that the helmet will stay in place if you fall. If you do fall and strike your helmet on the ground, replace it, even if it doesn't look damaged. The hard foam inside the helmet may be crushed, which reduces the ability of the helmet to protect your head in the event of another fall. Look for the features shown here when purchasing a helmet.

Safety While Riding

Here are some tips for safe bicycle riding.

- Check your bike every time you ride it. Is it in safe working condition?

- Ride in single file in the same direction as traffic. Never weave in and out of parked cars.

- Before you enter a street, **STOP. Look** left, then right, then left again. **Listen** for any traffic. **Think** before you go.

- Walk your bike across an intersection. **Look** left, then right, then left again. Wait for traffic to pass.

- Obey all traffic signs and signals.

- Do not ride your bike at night without an adult. Be sure to wear light-colored clothing and use reflectors and front and rear lights for night riding.

Fire Safety

1. STOP

Fires cause more deaths than any other type of disaster. But a fire doesn't have to be deadly if you prepare your home and follow some basic safety rules.

- Install smoke detectors outside sleeping areas and on every other floor of your home. Test the detectors once a month and change the batteries twice a year.

- Keep a fire extinguisher on each floor of your home. Check them monthly to make sure they are properly charged.

- Make a family emergency plan. See pages 326–327 for help. Ideally, there should be two routes out of each room. Sleeping areas are most important, as most fires happen at night. Plan to use stairs only, as elevators can be dangerous in a fire.

- Pick a place outside for everyone to meet. Choose one person to go to a neighbor's home to call 911 or the fire department.

- Practice crawling low to avoid smoke.

- If your clothes catch fire, follow the three steps shown here.

2. DROP

3. ROLL

Storm Safety

- **In a Tornado** Take cover in a sheltered area away from doors and windows. An interior hallway or basement is best. Stay in the shelter until the danger has passed.

- **In a Hurricane** Prepare for high winds by securing objects outside or bringing them indoors. Cover windows and glass with plywood. Listen to weather bulletins for instructions. If asked to evacuate, proceed to emergency shelters.

- **In a Winter Storm or Blizzard** Stock up on food that does not have to be cooked. Dress in thin layers that help trap the body's heat. Pay special attention to the head and neck. If you are caught in a vehicle, turn on the dome light to make the vehicle visible to search crews.

Earthquake Safety

An earthquake is a strong shaking or sliding of the ground. The tips below can help you and your family stay safe in an earthquake.

Before an Earthquake	During an Earthquake	After an Earthquake
• Attach tall, heavy furniture, such as bookcases, to the wall. Store the heaviest items on the lowest shelves. • Check for fire risks. Bolt down gas appliances, and use flexible hosing and connections for both gas and water lines. • Strengthen and anchor overhead light fixtures to help keep them from falling.	• If you are outdoors, stay outdoors and move away from buildings and utility wires. • If you are indoors, take cover under a heavy desk or table, or in a doorway. Stay away from glass doors and windows and from heavy objects that might fall. • If you are in a car, drive to an open area away from buildings and overpasses.	• Keep watching for falling objects as aftershocks shake the area. • Check for hidden structural problems. • Check for broken gas, electric, and water lines. If you smell gas, shut off the gas main. Leave the area. Report the leak.

Make a Family Emergency Plan

By having a plan, your family can protect itself during an emergency. To make an emergency plan, your family needs to gather information, make some choices, and practice parts of the plan.

Know What Could Happen

Learn the possible emergencies in your area, such as fires, storms, earthquakes, or floods. List the possible emergencies.

Have Two Meeting Places

Pick two places to meet. One place should be within a block of your home. The second place should be farther away, such as the main door of your school building.

Know Your Family Contact

Choose someone who lives far away to be a contact person. Each family member should memorize the full name, address, and telephone number of the person.

Out-of-State Contact
Ms. Jane Doe
43212 Janeway Blvd.
Big City, IL 12345
(123) 555-1234

Practice Evacuating

During a fire, you need to evacuate, or get out of, your home right away. Use your list of emergencies to plan how to evacuate. Practice evacuating at least twice a year.

▼ This woman is showing her daughter how to turn off the main water valve at their home.

Learn How to Turn Off Utilities

Water, electricity, and gas are *utilities*. Some emergencies may damage utilities or make them dangerous. With an adult's help, learn when and how to turn off utilities. **CAUTION:** If you turn off the gas, a professional must turn it back on.

◄ Outdoor water shut-off valve

Make an Emergency Supply Kit

After an emergency, your family may need first aid supplies or food. Your family can use a checklist from the American Red Cross or another disaster group to make an emergency supply kit.

Universal Precautions

You can get some diseases from another person's blood. Universal precautions are steps to protect you from that. Because there is no easy way to tell if someone's blood will make you ill, you should avoid touching anyone's blood. To treat a wound, follow the steps below.

If someone else is bleeding . . .

Wash your hands with soap, if possible.

Put on protective gloves, if available.

Wash small wounds with soap and water. Do *not* wash serious wounds.

Place a clean gauze pad or cloth over the wound. Press firmly for ten minutes. Don't lift the gauze during this time.

If you don't have gloves, have the injured person hold the cloth in place with his or her own hand.

If after ten minutes the bleeding has stopped, bandage the wound. If the bleeding has not stopped, continue pressing on the wound and get help.

If you are bleeding . . .

Follow the steps shown above. You don't need gloves to touch your own blood. Tell an adult about your injury.

For Choking

If someone else is choking . . .

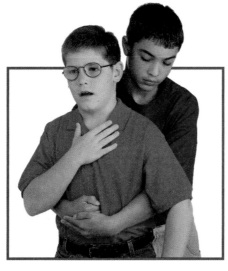

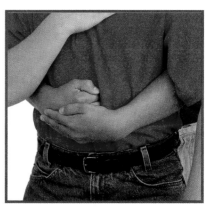

1. Recognize the Universal Choking Sign—grasping the throat with both hands. This sign means a person is choking and needs help.

2. Put your arms around his or her waist. Make a fist and put it above the person's navel. Grab your fist with your other hand.

3. Pull your hands toward yourself and give five quick, hard, upward thrusts on the choker's belly.

If you are choking when alone . . .

1. Make a fist and place it above your navel. Grab your fist with your other hand. Pull your hands up with a quick, hard thrust.

2. Or, keep your hands on your belly, lean your body over the back of a chair or over a counter, and shove your fist in and up.

For Burns

Minor burns are called first-degree burns and involve only the top layer of skin. The skin is red and dry and the burn is painful. More serious burns are called second- or third-degree burns. These burns involve the top and lower layers of skin. Second-degree burns cause blisters, redness, swelling, and pain. Third-degree burns are the most serious. The skin is gray or white and looks burned. All burns need immediate first aid.

Minor Burns

- Run cool water over the burn or soak it in cool water for at least five minutes.

- Cover the burn with a clean, dry bandage.

- Do *not* put lotion or ointment on the burn.

More Serious Burns

- Cover the burn with a cool, wet bandage or cloth. Do *not* break any blisters.

- Do *not* put lotion or ointment on the burn.

- Get help from an adult right away.

For Nosebleeds

- Sit down, and tilt your head forward. Pinch your nostrils together for at least ten minutes.

- You can also put an ice pack on the bridge of your nose.

- If your nose continues to bleed, get help from an adult.

For Insect Bites and Stings

- Always tell an adult about bites and stings.

- Scrape out the stinger with your fingernail.

- Wash the area with soap and water.

- Ice cubes will usually take away the pain from insect bites. A paste made from baking soda and water also helps.

- If the bite or sting is more serious and is on the arm or leg, keep the leg or arm dangling down. Apply a cold, wet cloth. Get help immediately!

- If you find a tick on your skin, remove it. Crush it between two rocks. Wash your hands right away.

- If a tick has already bitten you, do not pull it off. Cover it with oil and wait for it to let go, then remove it with tweezers. Wash the area and your hands.

▲ **Deer ticks may carry diseases.**

For Skin Rashes from Plants

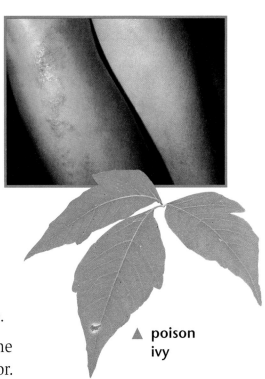

Many poisonous plants have three leaves. Remember, "Leaves of three, let them be." If you touch a poisonous plant, wash the area. Put on clean clothes and throw the dirty ones in the washer. If a rash develops, follow these tips.

- Apply calamine lotion or a baking soda and water paste. Try not to scratch. Tell an adult.

- If you get blisters, do *not* pop them. If they burst, keep the area clean and dry. Cover with a bandage.

- If your rash does not go away in two weeks or if the rash is on your face or in your eyes, see your doctor.

▲ **poison ivy**

What to Do When Others Use Drugs

You should make a personal commitment to not use alcohol, tobacco, or other drugs. But you may be around other students or adults who make unhealthful choices about drugs. Here is what you can do.

Know the Signs

Someone who has a problem with drugs may be sad or angry all the time, skip school or work, or forget events often.

Talk to a Trusted Adult

Do not keep someone's drug use a secret. Ask a trusted adult for help. You can also get support from adults to help you resist pressure to use drugs.

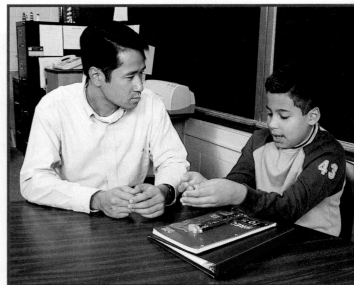

Be Supportive

If a person decides to stop using drugs, help them quit. Suggest healthful activities you can do together. Tell them you are happy that they have quit.

Stay Healthy

Do not stay anywhere that drugs are being used. If you cannot leave, politely ask others not to use drugs while you are there.

Where to Get Help

- Hospitals
- Alateen
- Alcoholics Anonymous
- Narcotics Anonymous
- Al-Anon
- Drug treatment centers

A Drug-Free School

Many schools make rules and sponsor activities to encourage people to say *no* to drugs. This makes the schools a more healthful environment for everyone.

School Rules

Many schools decide to be drug free. They often have strict penalties for anyone found with drugs. For example, a person found with drugs may be expelled or suspended from school.

DRUG FREE SCHOOL ZONE

MINIMUM 3 YEARS IN PRISON TO SELL, PURCHASE, MANUFACTURE, DELIVER OR POSSESS WITH INTENT TO SELL AN ILLEGAL DRUG WITHIN 1,000 FEET OF A SCHOOL
STATE STATUTE 893

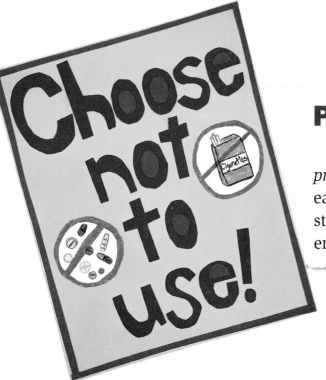

Choose not to use!

Positive Peer Pressure

Peer pressure can be bad or good. *Positive peer pressure* is when people the same age encourage each other to make healthful choices. For example, students may make posters or hold rallies to encourage others to choose not to use drugs.

Glossary

Numbers in parentheses indicate the pages
on which the words are defined in context.

PRONUNCIATION RESPELLING KEY

Sound	As in	Phonetic Respelling	Sound	As in	Phonetic Respelling
a	b<u>a</u>t	(BAT)	oh	<u>o</u>ver	(OH•ver)
ah	l<u>o</u>ck	(LAHK)	oo	p<u>oo</u>l	(POOL)
air	r<u>a</u>re	(RAIR)	ow	<u>ou</u>t	(OWT)
ar	<u>ar</u>gue	(AR•gyoo)	oy	f<u>oi</u>l	(FOYL)
aw	l<u>aw</u>	(LAW)	s	<u>c</u>ell	(SEL)
ay	f<u>a</u>ce	(FAYS)		<u>s</u>it	(SIT)
ch	<u>ch</u>apel	(CHAP•uhl)	sh	<u>sh</u>eep	(SHEEP)
e	t<u>e</u>st	(TEST)	th	<u>th</u>at	(THAT)
	m<u>e</u>tric	(MEH•trik)	th	<u>th</u>in	(THIN)
ee	<u>ea</u>t	(EET)	u	p<u>u</u>ll	(PUL)
	f<u>ee</u>t	(FEET)	uh	med<u>a</u>l	(MED•uhl)
	sk<u>i</u>	(SKEE)		t<u>a</u>lent	(TAL•uhnt)
er	pap<u>er</u>	(PAY•per)		penc<u>i</u>l	(PEN•suhl)
	f<u>er</u>n	(FERN)		<u>o</u>nion	(UHN•yuhn)
eye	<u>i</u>dea	(eye•DEE•uh)		playf<u>u</u>l	(PLAY•fuhl)
i	b<u>i</u>t	(BIT)		d<u>u</u>ll	(DUHL)
ing	go<u>ing</u>	(GOH•ing)	y	<u>y</u>es	(YES)
k	<u>c</u>ard	(KARD)		r<u>i</u>pe	(RYP)
	<u>k</u>ite	(KYT)	z	bag<u>s</u>	(BAGZ)
ngk	ba<u>nk</u>	(BANGK)	zh	trea<u>s</u>ure	(TREZH•er)

abdominal muscles (ab•DAH•muh•nuhl MUH•suhlz): body muscles located in the area of the stomach (6)

abstinence (AB•stuh•nuhnts): avoiding a behavior that will harm your health (165)

acquired traits (uh•KWYRD TRAYTS): things about you that did not come from either your mother or your father (65)

acute (uh•KYOOT): lasting only a short time (143)

addiction (uh•DIK•shuhn): the constant need or craving that makes a person use a drug even when he or she knows it is harmful (180)

aerobic exercise (air•OH•bik EK•ser•syz): hard exercise that speeds up your heart and breathing rates (100)

air bag (AIR BAG): a safety device in a car that inflates to protect a person from injury (253)

alcohol (AL•kuh•hawl): a drug found in drinks such as beer, wine, and liquor (212)

alcoholic (AL•kuh•HAW•lik): a person who suffers from the disease of alcoholism (217)

alcoholism (AL•kuh•haw•lih•zuhm): a disease in which a person is addicted to alcohol and cannot stop drinking without help (217)

allergy (A•ler•jee): a noninfectious disease in which a person has a reaction to a certain thing (158)

antibodies (AN•tih•bah•deez): chemicals made by the body to help fight disease (151)

arteries (AR•tuh•reez): blood vessels that carry blood away from the heart (10)

arthritis (ar•THRY•tuhs): a noninfectious disease in which the body's joints become swollen and painful (159)

asthma (AZ•muh): a noninfectious disease that sometimes causes difficulty in breathing (161)

attitude (A•tuh•tood): the way you look at things (19)

bacteria (bak•TIR•ee•uh): one-celled living things that can cause disease (147)

balanced diet (BA•luhntst DY•uht): a diet made up of a healthful amount of foods from each of the food groups (121)

basic needs (BAY•sik NEEDZ): the physical, mental, emotional, and social needs that we all share (22)

biceps (BY•seps): front upper arm muscles (6)

blended family (BLEN•did FAM•lee): a family that forms when two single parents marry and the children of both parents become part of the new family (51)

blood alcohol level (BAL) (BLUHD AL•kuh•hawl LEH•vuhl): the amount of alcohol in a person's blood (212)

blood vessels (BLUHD VEH•suhlz): arteries, veins, and capillaries that carry blood throughout the body (10)

body language (BAH•dee LANG•gwij): body movements that go with your words, like a nod (27)

body systems (BAH•dee SIS•tuhmz): groups of organs that work together (67)

brain (BRAYN): main organ of the body's nervous system (14)

brain stem (BRAYN STEM): part of the brain that connects the cerebrum to the spinal cord (71)

bully (BU•lee): a person who hurts or frightens others, especially those who are smaller or weaker than the bully (259)

caffeine (ka•FEEN): a drug found in coffee, tea, chocolate, and some soft drinks that speeds up the heart and makes most people feel more awake (182)

cancer (KAN•ser): a noninfectious disease that happens when one kind of cell grows out of control (157)

carbohydrates (kar•boh•HY•drayts): your body's main source of energy (112)

cardiovascular system (kar•dee•oh•VAS•kyuh•ler SIS•tuhm): circulatory system; includes your heart and your blood vessels (101)

cavities (KA•vuh•teez): holes in the outer surface of your teeth (84)

cell (SEL): the smallest working part of your body (64)

cell membrane (SEL MEM•brayn): a special structure that holds the cell together and lets only needed materials into the cell (66)

cerebellum (sair•uh•BEH•luhm): part of the brain located in back of the cerebrum; controls your movements (71)

cerebrum (suh•REE•bruhm): the biggest part of the brain where all the thinking takes place (71)

chronic (KRAH•nik): lasting a long time (143)

cilia (SIH•lee•uh): small hairs that line the body's air passages and trap pathogens and push them out of the body (151)

cirrhosis (suh•ROH•suhs): a liver disease that results from drinking too much alcohol (215)

clavicle (KLA•vih•kuhl): collarbone (4)

cocaine (koh•KAYN): a powerful drug made from the leaves of the coca plant (187)

compassion (kuhm•PA•shuhn): sensitivity to the needs and feelings of others (40)

compromise (KAHM•pruh•myz): a solution that considers everyone's feelings and ideas (35)

conflict (KAHN•flikt): a disagreement that occurs when people have different needs or wishes (34, 258)

conflict resolution (KAHN•flikt reh•zuh•LOO•shuhn): the solving of problems you and your friends may have (34)

conservation (kahn•serv•VAY•shuhn): the careful use of resources (288)

contaminated water (kuhn•TA•muh•nay•tid WAW•ter): water that has dangerous pathogens (149)

cooperate (koh•AH•puh•rayt): work together and get along with other people (56)

cytoplasm (SY•tuh•pla•zuhm): jellylike fluid inside a cell (66)

decay (dih•KAY): rot (84)

deltoid (DEL•toyd): shoulder muscle (6)

dermis (DER•muhs): the thick bottom layer of skin containing blood vessels and nerve endings (80)

diabetes (dy•uh•BEE•teez): a noninfectious disease in which the body cannot properly use sugar (160)

diaphragm (dy•uh•FRAM): partition that separates the chest and abdomen (12)

digestive juices (dy•JES•tiv JOO•suhz): substances that break down large nutrients (116)

disability (dih•suh•BIH•luh•tee): a physical or mental impairment (40)

disease (dih•ZEEZ): an illness (142)

dispatchers (dih•SPA•cherz): people who receive emergency calls and send fire, police, and ambulance crews to the scene (277)

dose (DOHS): the correct amount of the medicine that you should take every time you use it (177)

drug (DRUHG): a substance other than food that changes the way the body works (174)

drug dependence (DRUHG dih•PEN•duhnts): the need to take a drug just to feel normal (187)

drug user (DRUHG YOO•zer): someone who uses illegal drugs (184)

ear canal (IR kuh•NAL): connects outer ear to middle ear (2)

eardrum (IR•druhm): thin membrane in the ear that vibrates when hit by sound waves (2)

emergency (ih•MER•juhnt•see): a situation in which help is needed right away (234)

emergency medical technicians (ih•MER•juhnt•see MEH•dih•kuhl tek•NIH•shuhnz): men and women trained to handle serious illnesses and injuries (277)

endurance (in•DUR•uhnts): the ability to work hard for a long time (98)

environment (in•VY•ruhn•muhnt): where you live and all the living and nonliving things that surround you, such as plants, animals, air, water, and soil (20, 270)

environmental tobacco smoke (ETS) (in•vy•ruhn•MEN•tuhl tuh•BA•koh SMOHK): the smoke in the air surrounding burning cigarettes, pipes, or cigars and the smoke that is breathed out by smokers (211)

epidermis (eh•puh•DER•muhs): the tough, waterproof top layer of the skin that holds moisture in your body and keeps germs out (80)

esophagus (ih•SAH•fuh•guhs): food tube (8)

expiration date (ek•spuh•RAY•shuhn DAYT): the last date it is safe to take a medicine (181)

extended family (ik•STEN•did FAM•lee): a family that includes parents, children, and grandparents or other close relatives (54)

farsighted (FAR•sy•tuhd): a visual impairment in which the eye focuses images behind the retina, causing people to have a hard time seeing things that are close to them (91)

fats (FATS): nutrients that give your body more energy than any other kind of nutrients (112)

femur (FEE•mer): upper leg bone (4)

fiber (FY•ber): the woody substance in plants that helps move food and wastes through your digestive system (117)

fibula (FIH•byuh•luh): the outer of the two bones between the knee and the ankle (4)

first aid (FERST AYD): the immediate treatment of an injury (236)

flexibility (flek•suh•BIH•luh•tee): the ability to bend and twist comfortably (98)

flexors (FLEK•suhrz): muscles that help bend body parts such as limbs (6)

fluoride (FLAWR•yd): a mineral that helps prevent cavities (86)

Food Guide Pyramid (FOOD GYD PIR•uh•mid): a tool that can help you have a healthful diet (121)

food poisoning (FOOD POYZ•ning): an illness caused by eating food that contains germs (133)

fossil fuels (FAH•suhl FYOO•uhlz): resources that are found deep underground from the remains of plants and animals that lived long ago and that are used to make energy including coal, oil, and natural gas (279)

generations (jeh•nuh•RAY•shuhnz): family members who came before you (your parents, grandparents, and great-grandparents) and who come after you (your children) (56)

goal (GOHL): something you are willing to work for (21)

graffiti (gruh•FEE•tee): writings or drawings on public buildings and structures (274)

habit (HA•buht): something you do so often that you don't even think about it (122)

hazards (HA•zerdz): conditions that are not safe (238)

hearing loss (HIR•ing LAWS): the inability to hear sounds that you were once able to hear (92)

heart (HART): organ in the chest that pumps blood throughout the body; part of the circulatory system (10)

humerus (HYOO•muh•ruhs): upper arm bone (4)

hypothalamus (hy•poh•THA•luh•muhs): located in the brain stem; controls growth (71)

illegal drug (ih•LEE•guhl DRUHG): a drug that is not a medicine and that is against the law to sell, buy, have, or use (184)

immune system (ih•MYOON SIS•tuhm): the body system that fights disease (150)

immunity (ih•MYOO•nuh•tee): the body's ability to defend itself against certain kinds of pathogens (151)

infection (in•FEK•shuhn): the growth of pathogens somewhere in the body (147)

infectious disease (in•FEK•shuhs dih•ZEEZ): an illness that can be spread from person to person (142)

ingredients (in•GREE•dee•uhnts): all the things used to make a food (129)

inhalants (in•HAY•luhnts): substances that give off fumes that some people sniff deeply to get high (182)

inherited traits (in•HAIR•uh•tid TRAYTS): characteristics that were passed on to you from your parents (64)

injury prevention (INJ•ree prih•VENT•shuhn): keeping injuries from happening (238)

intoxicated (in•TAHK•suh•kay•tuhd): strongly affected by alcohol (216)

iris (EYE•ruhs): colored part of the eye that changes size to adjust the amount of light coming through the pupil (2)

landfill (LAND•fil): layers of trash and soil buried in a large pit that has a waterproof lining of plastic or clay (286)

large intestine (LARJ in•TES•tuhn): the lower part of the digestive system where water is absorbed (8, 9)

lens (LENZ): clear, curved structure of the eye that bends light to form an image on the back part of the eye (2, 90)

lifeguard (LYF•gard): a person who keeps people safe while they are swimming and while they are near the water (254)

lightning (LYT•ning): an electrical flash in the sky (247)

lungs (LUHNGZ): organs for breathing located in the chest; part of the respiratory system (12)

marijuana (mair•uh•WAH•nuh): an illegal drug made from the hemp plant (184)

medicine (MEH•duh•suhn): a drug used to treat or cure a health problem (174)

minerals (MIN•ruhlz): nutrients that help your body grow and work but do not give your body energy (115)

motor nerves (MO•ter NERVZ): nerves that carry signals from the brain to the muscles (14)

mouth (MAUTH): opening through which food passes into the body (8, 12)

mucus (MYOO•kuhs): a sticky liquid that coats the body's passageways and traps and destroys pathogens (151)

muscle strength (MUH•suhl STRENGKTH): the ability of muscles to apply a lot of force (98)

nasal cavity (NAY•zuhl KA•vuh•tee): main opening inside the nose (3)

natural resources (NA•chuh•ruhl REE•sohr•suhz): plants, animals, minerals, air, fossil fuels, water, and land; materials from nature that people use to meet their needs (278)

nearsighted (NIR•sy•tuhd): a visual impairment in which the eye focuses images in front of the retina, causing people to have a hard time seeing objects that are far away (91)

negotiate (nih•GOH•shee•ayt): work together to resolve a conflict (35)

nervous system (NER•vuhs SIS•tuhm): a communication network made up of your brain and your nerve cells that coordinates all your body's activities (70)

neurons (NOO•rahnz): nerve cells used by the nervous system to carry messages (72)

nicotine (NIH•kuh•teen): a highly addictive drug contained in all forms of tobacco that speeds up the nervous system (207)

noninfectious disease (nahn•in•FEK•shuhs dih•ZEEZ): an illness not caused by pathogens and that cannot be spread from person to person (142)

nose (NOZ): the part of the face between the mouth and eyes that has two openings for breathing and smelling (3)

nostrils (NAHS•truhlz): openings to the nose (3)

nuclear family (NOO•klee•er FAM•lee): a family made up of mother, father, and children (50)

nucleus (NOO•klee•uhs): the control center of a cell containing your body's inherited plan (66)

nutritious (nu•TRIH•shuhs): having a high nutritional value (128)

oil glands (OYUHL GLANDZ): glands, located in the dermis, that produce oil that helps soften your skin (81)

olfactory bulb (ahl•FAK•tuh•ree BUHLB): contains nerves that carry information about odors (3)

olfactory tract (ahl•FAK•tuh•ree TRAKT): part of the nose that carries information from the olfactory bulb to the brain (3)

optic nerve (AHP•tik NERV): part of the eye that transmits nerve signals to the brain (2)

organs (AWR•guhnz): groups of tissues joined together in structures, including heart, stomach, and lungs (67)

over-the-counter medicines (OTC) (OH•ver THUH KOWN•ter MEH•duh•suhnz): medicines adults can buy without prescriptions (177)

pathogen (PA•thuh•juhn): an organism or virus that causes disease (146)

peer pressure (PEER PREH•sher): the influence of others on an individual's choices, decisions (190, 219)

pelvis (PEL•vuhs): hipbone (4)

pharmacists (FAR•muh•sists): people trained to prepare medicines (175)

pituitary gland (puh•TOO•uh•tair•ee GLAND): gland, located at the base of the brain, that releases chemicals that make cells multiply quickly, causing you to grow (71)

plaque (PLAK): a sticky natural material, partially made up of bacteria, that sticks to your teeth (84)

polluted (puh•LOO•tid): dirty or containing unhealthful matter (271)

pollution (puh•LOO•shuhn): harmful material in the air, water, or land (282)

pores (PORZ): openings in the skin through which sweat reaches the skin's surface (81)

posture (PAHS•cher): the way you hold your body (94)

prescription (prih•SKRIP•shuhn): a doctor's order for a medicine (176)

prescription medicines (prih•SKRIP•shuhn MEH•duh•suhnz): medicines that an adult can buy only with a doctor's order (176)

privacy (PRY•vuh•see): time by yourself (24)

proteins (PROH•teenz): nutrients that give you energy and help build and repair your cells (113)

pupil (PYOO•puhl): the hole through which light enters the eye (2, 90)

quadriceps (KWAH•druh•seps): front thigh muscles (6)

radius (RAY•dee•uhs): the bone on the thumb side of the forearm (4)

recovery (rih•KUH•vuh•ree): the process a drug user goes through to stop taking drugs (199)

recreation (reh•kree•AY•shuhn): things you do to have fun (272)

resistance (rih•ZIS•tuhnts): the ability of the body to fight pathogens by itself (163)

retina (REH•tuhn•uh): the back part of the eye (2, 90)

rib cage (RIB KAJ): the bones that protect the chest, including the ribs and the bones that connect them (4)

role model (ROHL MAH•duhl): someone who sets a good example (43)

S

safety gear (SAYF•tee GIR): clothing or equipment worn to prevent injury (244)

safety measures (SAYF•tee MEH•zherz): actions you can take to stay safe (238)

scrubbers (SKRUH•berz): devices attached to smokestacks; used to remove some pollutants from factories and plants that burn trash or fossil fuels (283)

self-concept (SELF KAHN•sept): the general picture you have of yourself (18)

self-control (SELF kuhn•TROHL): the ability to restrain your emotions or desires (28)

self-respect (SELF rih•SPEKT): the satisfied, confident feeling you have about yourself when you like yourself and are proud of what you do (18, 191)

sensory nerves (SENS•ree NERVZ): nerves that carry signals to the brain from the sense organs (14)

serving (SER•ving): the measured amount of a food you would probably eat during one meal or as a snack (121)

side effects (SYD ih•FEKTS): unwanted changes in the body caused by a medicine (175)

single-parent family (SING•guhl PAIR•uhnt FAM•lee): a family made up of one parent and children (50)

skull (SKUHL): the bones that protect the brain (4)

small intestine (SMAWL in•TES•tuhn): the part of the digestive system between the stomach and the large intestine through which the body absorbs nutrients (8, 9)

solid wastes (SAH•luhd WAYSTS): garbage and litter (283)

spinal cord (SPY•nuhl KAWRD): bundle of nerves that relays messages between the brain and the rest of the nerves in the body (14)

spine (SPYN): backbone (4)

stomach (STUH•muhk): organ of the digestive system located between the esophagus and the small intestine (7, 8, 9)

stress (STRES): tension in your body and your mind (27)

sunscreen (SUHN•skreen): a lotion or cream that protects your skin from the sun's harmful rays (83)

sweat glands (SWET GLANDZ): glands that produce sweat (81)

symptoms (SIMP•tuhmz): signs and feelings of a disease (150)

talent (TA•luhnt): natural ability (19)

tar (TAR): a dark, sticky material that coats the lungs and air passages of smokers (207)

taste buds (TAYST BUHDZ): tiny nerve cells on the tongue that pick out tastes and send signals to the brain (3)

tibia (TIH•bee•uh): the inner and larger of the two bones between the knee and the ankle (4)

tissue (TIH•shoo): a group of cells that work together to do a job in the body (67)

tobacco (tuh•BA•koh): the shredded brown material inside a cigarette made from the dried leaves of the tobacco plant (206)

trachea (TRAY•kee•uh): tube that lets air go from the nose and mouth into the chest; also called windpipe (12)

traditions (truh•DIH•shuhnz): customs you do over and over (54)

traits (TRAYTS): special qualities that make up a large part of who you are (18)

triceps (TRY•seps): back upper arm muscles (6)

ulna (UHL•nuh): the bone on the little-finger side of the forearm (4)

vaccines (vak•SEENZ): substances made to prevent certain diseases (154)

values (VAL•yooz): strong beliefs about how people should live (56)

veins (VAYNZ): blood vessels that carry blood to the heart (10)

viruses (VY•ruh•suhz): the smallest pathogens (146)

vitamins (VY•tuh•muhnz): nutrients that help your body perform specific functions but do not give your body energy (114)

water (WAW•ter): a nutrient that helps break down foods, carries digested nutrients to your cells, and carries away wastes (117)

weapon (WEH•puhn): something used to injure or threaten someone (261)

white blood cells (HWYT BLUHD SELZ): blood cells that kill pathogens; part of the immune system (150)

wound (WOOND): a cut or break in the skin (236)

Index

Boldfaced numbers refer to illustrations.

Abdominal muscles, 6
Abdominal thrust, for choking, 329, **329**
Abstinence
   defined, 165
   from alcohol, 162, 218–221
   from drugs, 162, 180, 190–193, 201
   from tobacco, 218–221
   from unnecessary medicines, 194–195, **194–195**
Acquired traits, 65
Activity Pyramid, 308, **308**
Acute disease, 143
Addiction, 180
   resources for help with, 199, 332
Advertising Messages, Analyzing, xv, 43, 124, 181, 220
Advertisements
   alcohol, 205, 220–221
   medicine, 202
   tobacco, 205, 220–221, **220**
Aerobic exercise, 100–101
Air bag, 253
Air pollution, 282–283, **282–283**
   myth and fact about, 283
Al-Anon, 226
Alcohol
   abstinence from, 162, 218–221
   advertisements for, 220–221
   defined, 212
   driving and, 214, 216
   effects of, on body, 212–217
   effects of, on other people, 216–217
   help for users of, 224–227
   myth and fact about, 214
   refusing, 218–221, 222–223, **222–223,** 229
   researching history of, 213
Alcohol treatment counselor, 227
Alcoholics, 217
   help for, 224–227
   sources of help for, 226–227

Alcoholics Anonymous, 226
Alcoholism, 217
Allergies, 158
American Cancer Society, 226
American Dental Association, 88
Anger, controlling, 28–29
Antibodies, 151
Arteries, 10
Arthritis, 159
Asthma
   defined, 161
   myth and fact about, 160
Attention, gaining, 34
Attitude, 19

Bacteria
   defined, 147
   in food, 134, 306–307, **306**
   in plaque, 84–85, **85**
   researching good, 147
Balanced diet, 121
Balanced meals, planning, 111
Bandage injuries, learning how to, 266
Biceps, 6–7
Bicycle safety, 322–323, **322–323**
Bleeding, first aid for, 328, **328**
Blended family, 51
Blood alcohol level (BAL), 212
Blood cells
   red, 11
   white, 11, 150
Blood safety, 11, 236
Blood vessels, 10
   exercise and, 101, **101**
Boating safety, 257, **257**
Body image, 127, 181
Body language, 27
Body systems, 2–15, 66
   circulatory system, 10–11. See also Circulatory system.
   defined, 67
   digestive system, 8–9. See also Digestive system.

effects of air pollution on, 283
effects of alcohol on, 212–217
effects of caffeine on, 182
effects of drugs on, 173–179
effects of tobacco on, 206–211
effects of water pollution on, 284–285
immune system, 67, 150–151, 187. See also Immune system.
muscular system, 6–7. See also Muscular system.
nervous system, 14–15. See also Nervous system.
respiratory system, 12–13. See also Respiratory system.
sense organs, 2–3. See also Sense organs.
skeletal system, 4–5. See also Skeletal system.
Bones, 4–5
   fixing broken, 76
   growth of, 69
   See also Skeletal system.
Brain, 14
   actions of, 70–73
   effects of alcohol on, 214–215, **215**
   effects of inhalants on, 183, **183**
   effects of marijuana on, 185–186, **186**
   effects of tobacco on, 210, **210**
   life choices that affect, 73
   parts of, 70–71, **70–71**
Brain stem, 70–71, **70–71**
Bread, cereal, rice, and pasta food group, 118, 120
Breakfast
   importance of, 113
   making decisions about, 126–127, **126–127**
   planning time for, chart, 25
Breathing, 13
Bronchi, 13
Bully, 259
Burns
   first aid for, 330
   myth and fact about, 237

Buying Decisions, Making, xiv, 88, 130

Caffeine
defined, 182
effects of, on body, 182
in foods, 182
in soft drinks, 182
Calcium, 115
to help bones grow, 5
Camping safety, 243
Cancer
defined, 157
lung, 210, **210**
marijuana as cause of, 185
mouth, 210
skin, 83
smoking as cause of, 207
tobacco use as cause of, 164
Carbohydrates, 112
Cardiovascular system, 101. See
also Circulatory system.
Cavities, 84–85, **85**
Cell membrane, 66, **66**
Cells
defined, 64
parts of, 66–67, **66–67**
Central nervous system, 70
Cerebellum, 70–71, **70–71**
Cerebrum, 70–72, **70–72**
Chewing tobacco, 206
Chicken pox, 146–147, **147**
Choking, first aid for, 329, **329**
Chronic disease, 143
Cilia, disease fighting role of,
150–151, **150–151**
Circulatory system, 10–11, **10–11**
brain as control center for, 71,
71
building strong, 312–315
caring for, 11
diabetes, 160
effects of air pollution on, 283
effects of alcohol on, 212,
214–215, **215**, 230
effects of caffeine on, 182
effects of cocaine on, 187–189
effects of inhalants on, 183, **183**
effects of marijuana on, 186,
186

effects of tobacco on, 210–211,
210, 230
effects of water pollution on, 284
exercise and, 100–101
exercise for preventing diseases
of, 162
heart diseases, 156
identifying organs in, 66
Cirrhosis, 215
Clavicle, 4
Clean Water Act, 285
Cocaine, 174, 180
defined, 187
effects of, 187–189, **187–189**
Cold weather safety, 246, **246**
Communication, 75
family, 62–63, **62–63**
of feelings, 57
with friends, 35
as life skill, xii
practicing, 62–63, **62–63**
using sign language, 41
Community
healthful ways to enjoy, 272–273
keeping a clean and safe,
274–277
making a difference in your,
42–46
Community health project, 269
Compassion, 40
Compromise, 35
Computer, posture at, 96–97, **96**
Computer safety, 316–317, **316**
Conflict
avoiding, 258–259, 265
defined, 34
staying safe during, 258–261
Conflict resolution, 75, 258–259
chart, 39
defined, 34
family, 59, 75, 265
with friends, 262–263, **262–263**
as life skill, xiii
practicing, 37–39 **38–39**, 45–46,
59
skit about, 17
Connective tissue, 67, **67**
Conservation
defined, 288
setting goals for, 292–293,
292–293
water, 291
ways to practice, 288–291

Consumer awareness, xiv–xvi, 43,
69, 88, 113, 124, 130, 159, 181,
220, 254, 290
Contact lenses, 91
Contaminated water, 149
Cool-down, 310–311, **310–311**
Cooperation
defined, 56
family, 58–59
Cornea, 2
Crack, 187, **187**
Crown, of tooth, 85, **85**
Cytoplasm, 66, **66**

Decay, 84
Decision making
about dental products, 88
as life skill, ix
practicing, 127
steps for, chart, 122
Deltoid muscles, 6
Dental care products, choosing,
88–89, **88**, 108
Dental floss, 86–87, **86**
Dental hygienist, 89
Dentin, 85, **85**
Dermis, 3
defined, 80–81, **81**
Diabetes, 160
Diaphragm, **12**
Diet
balanced, 121
heart disease and, 156
Differences among people, 40–43
Digestive juices
defined, 116
disease fighting role of,
150–151, **150–151**
Digestive system, 8–9, **8–9**, 67
caring for, 9
diet and, 9
disease fighting role of,
150–151, **150–151**
effects of water pollution on, 284
how food moves through,
116–117, **116**
identifying organs in, 66
nutrients and, 112–117
Disability, 40

Diseases
acute, 143
avoiding, 152–153
body's defense against, 150–151, **151**
chronic, 143
defined, 142
exercise as prevention against, 141
heart, 156
infectious, 142, 150–155
noninfectious, 143, 156–161
types of, 142–143
Disinfectant, 153
Dispatchers, 277
Distress, 27
Dose, 177
Drug addiction, resources for help, 199, 332
Drug counseling, 193, 332
Drug dependence, 187
Drug user, 184
Drugs
abstinence from, 162, 180
defined, 174
effects of, on body, 173–179
help for users of, 196–199, **199**, 202
refusing, 189–193
reporting to adults, 198, 332
warning signs of use of, 196–197, **196–197**

E

Ear, 2, **2**
caring for, 2
making model of, 108
inner, 2, 92, **92**
middle, 2, 92, **92**
outer, 2, 92, **92**
parts of, 92, **92**
problems with, 92
protecting, 93
Ear canal, 2, 92, **92**
Eardrum, 2, 92, **92**
Earthquake safety, chart, 321
Eating habits, healthful, 122–123
EKG, 156, **156**
Electric shock, preventing, 238
Electricity, researching resources used to make, 296

Emergencies
defined, 234
responding to, 234–237
safety in, 324–327, **324–327**
Emergency medical technicians (EMTs), 277
Emergency phone numbers, 234–235
Emergency plan, family, 326–327
Emotional needs, 23
Emotions, brain as control center for, 73
Enamel, of tooth, 85, **85**
Endurance, 98
Environment
defined, 270
healthful, 270–273
personal, 20
Environmental Protection Agency (EPA), 285
Environmental tobacco smoke (ETS), 211
Epidemics, researching, 170
Epidermis, 3
defined, 80–81, **81**
Epithelial tissue, 67, **67**
Esophagus, 8, **116**
Eustress, 27
Exercise
aerobic, 100–101
as aid in preventing heart disease, 162
as disease prevention, 141
effects of, on body, 101, **101**
for heart and lungs, 312–315
muscles and, 98–99
older people and, 55
planning, 308
President's Challenge, 314–315, **314–315**
Exercise program, planning, 102, **102**
Expiration date, on medicine, 181
Extended family, 54–55
Exxon Valdez disaster, 286
Eyelid, 7
Eyes, **2**, 2
caring for, 2
colored part of, 90, **90**
making model of, 108
protecting, 93

F

Falls, preventing, 239
Family
activities with, 76
blended, 51
conflict resolution within, 59, 75, 265
cooperation within, 58–59
extended, 54–55
learning from, 56–57
nuclear, 50
planning activities for, 59
respect within, 75
roles in, 52–53
rules in, 60–61
single-parent, 50
types of, 49–51
your contributions to, 52
Family counselor, 61
Family emergency plan, 326–327
Farsighted vision, 91, **91**
Fats, 112
Fats, oils, and sweets food group, 119–120
Feelings, 26–27
expressing, 28–29
identifying, 26–27, **26–27**
Femur, 4–5
Fiber
defined, 117, **117**
digestive system and, 9
Fibula, 4
Fights, avoiding, 260
Filtering, 13
Fire safety, 324, **324**
researching, 266
Firefighter, 276
Fires
preventing, 239
staying safe in, 240
First aid, 234–237
for bleeding, 328, **328**
for burns, 330, **330**
chart, 236
for choking, 329, **329**
defined, 236
for insect bites and stings, 331, **331**
for nosebleeds, 330, **330**

First-aid kit, 237, **237**
   researching supplies for, 266
Fish inspector, 135
Fitness
   physical, 98–105
   setting goals for, 104–105,
     104–105, 108
Flexibility
   defined, 98
   stretching to build, 99, **99**
Flexors, 6
Flu, 146–147, **147**
Fluoride, 86
Flu shots, 154–155
Follicles, 81
Food
   making healthful choices,
     122–125
   safe preparation of, 132–135,
     149, 306–307
Food groups
   bread, cereal, rice, and pasta,
     118, 120
   fats, oils, and sweets, 119–120
   fruit, 118, 121
   meat, poultry, fish, dry beans,
     eggs, and nuts, 119–120
   milk, yogurt, and cheese,
     119–120
   nutrients in, 118–121
   vegetable, 119–120
Food Guide Pyramid, 118, 120,
   120, 300–303, **300, 302–303**
   defined, 121
   making your own, 138
   using, 122–125
Food inspector, 134
Food labels, understanding,
   128–131, **129**
Food poisoning, 133
Food preparation, safe, 132–135,
   133
Food safety, while camping, 243
Fossil fuels, 279
Friends
   communicating with, 35
   solving problems with, 34–36
Friendship
   challenges of, 32–37
   help with problems in, 35–36
   value of, 33
Friendship rules, chart, 34
Fruit food group, 118, 121

Gastrocnemius muscles, 7
Generations, 56
Glasses, 91
Goal setting
   as life skill, viii
   planning time for breakfast,
     chart, 25
   practice in, 25
Goals
   defined, 21
   fitness, 104–105, **104–105**, 108
Graffiti, 274
Groups, your roles in, 21
Growth, 68–69, **68**
   brain as control center for,
     70–73
Growth spurt, 68
Gums, 85, **85**
   caring for, 84–87

Habit, 122
Hamstring muscles, 7
Hand washing, 82, 153, 163
Hashish, 184
Hazards
   defined, 238
   recognizing, 238–239, **238–239**
Health Information, Accessing
   Valid, xvi, 69, 113, 159, 254,
   291
Hearing
   problems with, 92
   protecting, 93
Hearing loss, 92
Heart, 7, 10
   brain as control center for,
     71, **71**
   building strong, 312–315
   effects of alcohol on, 215, **215**
   effects of cocaine on, 187–189
   effects of marijuana on,
     186, **186**
   effects of tobacco on, 210–211,
     210
   exercise and, 100–101

   job of, 67
Heart diseases
   exercise as aid in preventing,
     162
   tobacco use as cause of, 164
   types of, 156
Heart rate, effects of caffeine on,
   182
Helmet, bicycle, 323, **323**
Hemp, research uses of, 185
Heroin, 180
Home alone, safety while, 242, **242**
Home safety, 238–242, 320–321
Humerus, 4
Hypothalamus, 71

Illegal drug, 184
Immune system, 67
   defined, 150
   effects of marijuana on, 187
Immunity, 151
Infection, 147
Infectious diseases, 146–149
   defined, 142
   fighting, 150–155
Ingredients
   analyzing, 129, **129**
   defined, 129
Inhalants
   defined, 182
   reading labels on, 202
Inherited traits, 64–65
Injuries
   helping someone with, 236–237
   preventing, 238–239, **238–239**
Inner ear, 2, 92, **92**
Insect bites and stings, first aid for,
   331, **331**
Insulin, 160
Internet safety, 317–318
Intoxicated, 216
Involuntary muscles, 7
Iris, 2
Iron, 115

Janitor, 275, **275**

Labels
checking for caffeine on soft drink, 182
food, 128–131, **129**
on inhalants, 202
medicine, 177
warning, on tobacco products, 165, 207, **207**
Land pollution, 286–287
Landfill, 286
Large intestine, 8–9, **116**
Lens, 2
defined, 90, **90**
Leukemia, 157
Life skills
communicate, xii, 35, about alcohol, 226, about allergies, 158, about illness, 145, compassion and respect, 43, feelings, 57, response to emergencies, 235, values, 57, with a dispatcher, 276, with family, 62–63, **62–63,** with friends, 95,
make decisions, ix, 88, about breakfast, 126–127, **126–127,** about how to stay safe, 248–249, **248–249,** about illness, 144, 155, about medicines, 175, 199, 201, choosing healthful snacks, 123–125, 137. making good food choices, 117, 126–127, **126–127,** 131, 137. See also Decision making.
manage stress, x, 30–31, **30–31,** 45, 107, at doctor's office, 166–167, **166–167**
refuse, xi, refusing alcohol, 218–223, **222–223**, 229, refusing drugs, 190–193, refusing tobacco, 218–223, **222–223**, 229, refusing unhealthful snacks, 89, refusing unnecessary medicines, 194–195, **194–195**
resolve conflicts, xiii, 37–39, **38–39**, 45, 59, 75, controlling anger, 28–29. See also

Conflict resolution.
set goals, viii, fitness, 104–105, **104–105,** conserving resources, 281, 292–293, **292–293** See also Goal setting.
Lifeguard, 254–255, **255**
Lifestyle, healthful, 162–163, **162–163**
Lightning, 247
Liver, effects of alcohol on, 215, **215**
Lung cancer, tobacco use as cause of, 210, **210**
Lungs, 12, 13
building strong, 312–315
effects of cocaine on, 187–189
effects of marijuana on, 186–187, **186**
effects of tobacco use on, 206–207, 210–211, **210**
exercise and, 100–101

Malnutrition, alcohol as cause of, 215
Marijuana, 174
defined, 184–185, **184–185**
effects of, 185–187, **186**
Measles, 146–147, **147**
Meat, poultry, fish, dry beans, eggs, and nuts food group, 119–120
Media Messages, Analyzing, xv, 43, 124, 181, 220
Medical assistant, 145
Medicine
alternative, 177
defined, 174–175
expiration date on, 181
myth and fact about, 178
over-the-counter, 177
over-the-counter, misuse of, 181
over-the-counter, refusing unnecessary, 194–195, **194–195**
prescription, 176–177, **177**
researching, 202
safe use of, 178–179, **179**
safety seal on, 181
Medicine labels, 177
Medicine safety checklist, 178

Mental needs, 23
Menu, planning, 121
Middle ear, 2, 92, **92**
Milk, yogurt, and cheese food group, 119–120
Minerals, 115
Motor nerves, 14
Motor vehicle safety, 252–253, **252–253**
Mouth, 8, 12, **116**
Mouth cancer, tobacco use as cause of, 210
Mucus, 3, 13
disease fighting role of, 150–151, **150–151**
Muscle strength, 98
Muscle tissue, 67, **67**
Muscles
exercising to help, 98–99, **99**
involuntary, 7
voluntary, 7
Muscular system, **6–7**, 6–7
effects of alcohol on, 214, 230
exercise and, 98–99, **99**
identifying organs in, 66
nervous system and, 14–15
posture and, 94, **94**
tissue of, 67, **67**
working together, 98

Nasal cavity, 3
Natural resources, 278–281, **278–279**
conserving, 288–291
defined, 278
protecting, 287
reusing, 296
Nearsighted vision, 91, **91**
Needs
basic, 22
emotional, 23
identifying, 23, **23**
meeting your, 23–25
mental, 23
physical, 22
social, 24
Negotiate, 35
Nerve, optic, 2
Nerve tissue, 67, **67**

Nervous system, 14–15, **14–15,**
  67, 73,
  caring for, 15
  central, 70
  defined, 70–71, **70–71**
  diet and, 15
  effects of alcohol on, 214–215,
    215, 230
  effects of cocaine on, 187–189
  effects of inhalants on, 183, **183**
  effects of marijuana on,
    185–186, **186**
  effects of tobacco on, 207, 210,
    210, 230
  effects of water pollution on, 284
  identifying parts of, 66, 72, **72**
  life choices that affect, 73
  peripheral, 70
  safety gear as protection for, 15
  tissue of, 67, **67**
Neurons, 72, **72**
Nicotine
  defined, 207
  effects of, on body, 210, **210**
Noninfectious diseases, 142–143,
  156–161
Nose, 3, **3,** 12
  caring for, 3
Nosebleeds, first aid for, 330, **330**
Nostrils, 3
Nuclear family, 50
Nucleus, 66, **66**
Nutrients
  digestive system and, 112–117
  energy, 112–113
  in food groups, 118–121
  getting the amount you need,
    121
Nutrition
  for children with diabetes, 160
  estimating serving sizes, chart,
    301
  Food Guide Pyramid,
    300–303, **300, 302–303**
  researching, 138
  safe food preparation, 149,
    306–307
Nutritious, 128

Oil glands, 80–81, **81**

Olfactory bulb, 3
Olfactory tract, 3
Optic nerve, 2
Organs, 67
Outdoor safety, 244–247
Outer ear, 2, 92, **92**
Over-the-counter medicines
  defined, 177
  misuse of, 181
  refusing unnecessary, 194–195,
    194–195

Pancreas, effects of alcohol on,
  215, **215**
Pathogens
  defined, 146, **146**
  killing, 153
  reducing spread of, 149, 170
  spread of, 148, **148**
Peer pressure
  defined, 190
  positive, 333
  to use alcohol and tobacco, 219
Pelvis, 4–5
Peripheral nervous system, 70
Pharmacists, 175–176
Pharmacy technician, 176
Phosphorus, 115
Physical fitness, 98–105
  setting goals for, 104–105,
    104–105
Physical needs, 22
Pinkeye, 152, **152**
Pituitary gland, 71
Plants, poisonous, rashes from,
  331, **331**
Plaque, 84–85, **84–85**
Plasma, 10
Platelet cells, 11
Poison control center, 235, 266
Poisoning
  food, 133
  preventing, 241
Poisonous household products,
  chart, 241
Poisonous plants, 243, **243**
  rashes from, 331, **331**
Poisonous substances, identifying,
  266
Police officer, 276

Polluted, 271
Pollution
  air, 282–283
  defined, 282
  land, 286–287
  preventing, 295
  water, 284–285, **284–285**
Pores, 80–81, **81**
Posture
  at computer, 96–97, **96,**
    314, **314**
  defined, 94, **94**
  practicing good, 95, **95**
Potassium, 115
Prescription, 176
Prescription medicines,
  176–177, **177**
President's Challenge, 314–315,
  314–315
Privacy, 24
Proteins, 113
Pulp, of tooth, 85, **85**
Pupil, 2
  defined, 90, **90**

Quadriceps, 6

Radius, 4
Rail trails, 273
Rational Recovery, 226
Recovery, from drugs, 199
Recreation
  defined, 272
  in your community, 296
Rectum, **116**
Recycling, myth and fact about, 288
Red blood cells, 11
Red Cross, 233
Red Cross first-aid manual, 233
Refusing
  alcohol, 218–223, **222–223,** 229
  drugs, 189–193, 201
  as life skill, xi
  steps for, 195
  tobacco, 218–223, **222–223,** 229
Resistance, 163

Resources, natural, 278–281, **278–279**
  conserving, 288–291
  protecting, 287
  reusing, 296
  setting goals for conserving, 292–293, **292–293**
Respect, in family, 52
Respiratory system, 12–13, **12–13**, 67
  allergies affecting, 158
  asthma, 160–161
  brain as control center for, 71, **71**
  building strong, 310–313
  cancer within, 157
  caring for, 13
  catching diseases through, 152–153
  disease fighting role of, 150–151, **150–151**
  effects of air pollution on, 283
  effects of cocaine on, 187–189
  effects of inhalants on, 183, **183**
  effects of marijuana on, 186–187, **186**
  effects of pollution on, 13
  effects of tobacco on, 206–211, **210**, 230
  exercise and, 13, 100–101
  identifying organs in, 66
  smoking and, 164–165
Rest, need for, 103
Retina, 2
  defined, 90, **90**
Rib cage, 4
Road safety, 250–253
Role model, 43
Root, of tooth, 85, **85**
Rules, family, 60–61

Safe Drinking Water Act, 285
Safety
  around water, 254–257
  bicycle, 322–323, **322–323**
  blood, 236
  boating, 257, **257**
  camping, 243
  cold weather, 246, **246**
  computer, 316–318, **316**

  during conflict, 258–261
  earthquake, chart, 325
  emergency plan, family, 326–327
  in emergencies, 324–327, **324–327**
  fire, 324, **324**
  home, 238–242, 320–321
  Internet, 317–318
  making decisions about, 248–249, **248–249**
  motor vehicle, 252–253, **252–253**
  outdoor, 244–247
  while playing with others, 258
  road, 250–253
  severe storm, 325
  swimming, 254–255
  thunderstorm, 247
  water, 254–257
  around weapons, 261
  on wheels, 250–251, **250–251**
Safety gear
  defined, 244–245, **244–245**
  for bicycling, skating, and skateboarding, 251
Safety measures, 238
Safety seal, on medicine, 181
Saliva, disease fighting role of, 150–151, **150–151**
School counselor, 37
Scrubbers, 283
Self-concept, 18
Self-control, 28–29
Self-respect, 18, 191
Sense organs, **2–3**, 2–3
  brain as control center for, 71, **71**
  ears, 92–93, **92**, 108
  effects of alcohol on, 230
  effects of marijuana on, 187
  eyes, 90–91, **90**, 108
  hearing or speech impairment, 41
  identifying, 66
  nervous system and, 14–15
  of peripheral nervous system, 70
Sensory nerves, 14
Serving, 121
Serving sizes, estimating, chart, 301
Shock, electric, preventing, 238
Side effects, 175
Sign language, 41
Single-parent family, 50

Skeletal system, 4–5, **4–5**
  arthritis in joints of, 159
  building blocks of, 67, **67**
  caring for, 5
  connective tissue of, 67, **67**
  fixing broken bones, 76
  growth of bones in, 69
  identifying parts of, 66
  posture and, 94, **94**
Skills. See Life skills.
Skin, 3, **3**
  burns of, 330
  caring for, 3, 80–83, **81**
  catching diseases through cuts in, 153
  disease fighting role of, 150–151, **150–151**
  effects of inhalants on, 183, **183**
  epithelial tissue of, 67, **67**
  parts of, 80–81, **81**
  rashes on, 331, **331**
  Skin cancer, 83, 157
Skull, 4–5
Sleep, need for, 103
Small intestine, 8–9, 116
Smoking
  cost of, 165
  effects of, on lungs, 206, **206**
  See also Tobacco.
Snacks
  choosing healthful, 122–125
  healthful, 87, 138
Snuff, 206
Social needs, 24
Solid wastes, 283
Spinal cord, 4–5, 14, 70–71
Spine, 4–5
Sports safety gear, 244–245, **244–245**
Stomach, 7–8, **116**
  effects of alcohol on, 215, **215**
Storm safety, severe, 325
Strength, muscle, 98
Strep throat, 147, **147**
Stress
  defined, 27
  managing, 30–31, **30–31**, 45–46
  managing, as life skill, x
  managing, as part of healthful lifestyle, 162–163
  managing, at doctor's office, 166–167, **166–167**
  managing, chart, 31
  managing, steps for, 167
  myth and fact about, 27

Stretching, 310–311, **310–311**
  to build flexibility, 99, **99**
Sunscreen, 3, 83, 255
  as protection against skin
    cancer, 157
Sweat glands, 81
Sweat, purpose of, 80–81, **81**
Swimming safety, 254–255
Symptoms, 150

Talent, 19
Tar
  defined, 206–207, **206**
  effects of, on body, 210, **210**
Taste buds, 3
Teeth
  caring for, 84–89
  cleaning, 86–89, **86–88**
  effects of tobacco use on, 208,
    211, **211**
  parts of, 85, **85**
THC, 185
Thunderstorm safety, 247
Tibia, 4
Tissue, 67
Tobacco
  advertisements for, 220–221,
    220
  as cause of heart disease, 156
  as cause of respiratory
    diseases, 157
  chewing, 206
  defined, 206–207
  effects of, on body, 206–211
  help for users of, 224–227, 230
  reasons to abstain from,
    164–165
  refusing, 218–223, **222–223**,
    229
  sources of help for users of,
    226–227
  warning labels on, 165, 207,
    207
  See also Smoking.
Tongue, 3, **3**
Toothbrush, 86–87, **87**, 89
  history of, 86
Toothpaste
  choosing, 108
  kinds of, 88, **88**

Trachea, 12–13
Traditions, 76
  defined, 54
Traits
  acquired, 65
  defined, 18
  emotional, 18–19
  inherited, 64–65, 76
  mental, 18–19
  overcoming negative, 46
  physical, 18
  social, 18–19
  your special, 20
Triceps, 6–7
Tumors, 207
Twins, 65, **65**

Ulna, 4
Universal precautions, 328

Vaccines, 155, 162
  chart, 154
  defined, 154
Values
  defined, 56
  identifying, 56–57, **56–57**
Vegetable food group, 119–120
Veins, 10
Vertebrae, 5
Viruses, 146
Vision
  myth and fact about, 97, 114
  problems with, 90–91, **90–91**
  protecting, 93
Vitamins, 114, **114**
  to help prevent disease, 163
Voluntary muscles, 7
Volunteering in your community,
  42–43

Warm-up, 310–311, **310–311**
Water, 117
  contaminated, 149
Water pollution, 284–285, **284–285**
Water rescue, 256, **256**
Water safety, 254–257
Weapons
  defined, 261
  safety around, 261
Wellness, 162–165
White blood cells, 11
  defined, 150
Windpipe, 12–13
Workouts, guidelines for, 309
Wound, 236

Zinc, 115

CREDITS

Cover Design: MKR Design, Inc./Robert B. Allen.

Key: (bkgd) background, (tl) top left, (tc) top center, (tr) top right, (c) center, (bl) bottom left, (bc) bottom right, (br) bottom right.

PHOTOGRAPHS:

Cover: Michael Groen.

Your Health Skills: all photographs by Ken Kinzie.

Body Atlas: 1(bl), Ron Chapple/FPG; (bc), Mark Scott/FPG; (br), David Lissy/Index Stock.

Chapter 1: 16–17, Bill Losh/FPG International; 18(br), Digital Imaging Group; 19(bc), Todd Champlin; 20, Digital Imaging Group; 21, Myrleen Ferguson Cate/PhotoEdit; 24, Rob Gage/FPG International; 25, Digital Imaging Group; 26(bl), David Young-Wolff/PhotoEdit; (br), Pascal Crapet/Tony Stone Images; 27(bl), Michael Newman/PhotoEdit; (br), Martin Rogers/Tony Stone Images; 28, David Young-Wolff/PhotoEdit; 30(bl), Eric Camden Photography; (br), Eric Camden Photography; 31(tl), Eric Camden Photography; (tr), Eric Camden Photography; 32, Mary Kate Denny/Tony Stone Images; 33, Andy Sacks/Tony Stone Images; 34, Digital Imaging Group; 35, Michael Newman/PhotoEdit; 36, Uniphoto; 37, Jack Holtel; 38(bl), Eric Camden Photography; (br), Eric Camden Photography; 39(tl), Eric Camden Photography; (tr), Eric Camden Photography; 40, Myrleen Ferguson Cate/PhotoEdit; 41, Ed McDonald Photography; 42(tl), Uniphoto; (tc), Ed McDonald Photography; (tr), Mary Kate Denny/Tony Stone Images; (c), Don & Pat Valenti/Tony Stone Images; (bl), Digital Imaging Group; (bc), Eric Camden Photography; (br), Tom Tracy/Tony Stone Images; 45(tr), Digital Imaging Group; 46(bl), Brian Coats.

Chapter 2: 48–49, David Young-Wolff/PhotoEdit; 50(bl), Ariel Skelley/The Stock Market; (br), Arthur Tilley/FPG International; 51(tr), Index Stock; (br), SuperStock; 52, Rob Gage/FPG International; 53(tl), John Henley/The Stock Market; (br), David Young-Wolff/PhotoEdit; 54, George Disario/The Stock Market; 55(tl), Ed McDonald Photography; (bc), David Lissy/Index Stock; 57, Index Stock; 58(bl), Ronnie Kaufman/The Stock Market; (bc), Jon Riley/Tony Stone Images; (br), Ed McDonald Photography; 59, Paul Barton/The Stock Market; 60(tl), SuperStock; (bl), Maratea/International Stock; 61, Ed McDonald Photography; 62(bl), Ed McDonald Photography; (br), Ed McDonald Photography; 63(tl), Ed McDonald Photography; (tr), Ed McDonald Photography; 64, Paul Barton/The Stock Market; 65(tc), Kindra Clineff/Tony Stone Images; (br), SuperStock; 67(tl), Eric Grave/Phototake; (tc), Richard Wehr/Custom Medical Stock Photo; (tr), Dr. Mary Notter/Phototake; (c), Runk/Schoenberger/Grant Heilman Photography; 68, Ed McDonald Photography; 69(bl), Wright State University/Felf Research Institute; (bl), Wright State University/Felf Research Institute; (bc), Wright State University/Felf Research Institute; (br), Jim Cummins/FPG International; 73, Mike Magnuson/Frozen Images; 76, Laurie Bayer/International Stock.

Chapter 3: 78–79, Eric Camden Photography; 80, Eric Camden Photography; 82, Eric Camden Photography; 83, Eric Camden Photography; 84, Digital Imaging Group; 86(bl), Digital Imaging Group; (br), Eric Camden Photography; 87(bl), Eric Camden Photography; (br), Eric Camden Photography; 88(c), American Dental Association; (bc), Eric Camden Photography; 89, Tom Croke/Liaison International; 91(tr), Ed McDonald Photography; (br), Ed McDonald Photography; 93(bl), Bill Auth/Uniphoto; (br), David Young-Wolff/PhotoEdit; 94(bl), Eric Camden Photography; (br), Eric Camden Photography; 95(tl), Ken Kinzie; (tc), Ken Kinzie; (tr), Eric Camden Photography; (c), Eric Camden Photography; 99(tr), Digital Imaging Group; (bc), Eric Camden Photography; 101(tr), Runk/Schoenberger/Grant Heilman Photography; (br), M. Cubberly/Phototake; 102, Eric Camden Photography; 103, Eric Camden Photography; 104(bl), Eric Camden Photography; (br), Eric Camden Photography; 105(tl), Eric Camden Photography; (tr), Eric Camden Photography; 107(tl), Eric Camden Photography; (bl), Eric Camden Photography; 108, John Henley/The Stock Market.

Chapter 4: 110–111, Michael Newman/PhotoEdit; 112, Richard Hutchings/PhotoEdit; 113, Digital Imaging Group; 114, Digital Imaging Group; 115, Digital Imaging Group; 117, Jack Holtel; 118(c), Digital Imaging Group; (bl), Digital Imaging Group; 119(tr), Digital Imaging Group; (c), Digital Imaging Group; (c), Digital Imaging Group; (br), Digital Imaging Group; 120, Digital Imaging Group; 122–123(bc), Digital Imaging Group; 124, Digital Imaging Group; 125, Jack Holtel; 126(bl), Jack Holtel; (br), Jack Holtel; 127(tl), Jack Holtel; (tr), Jack Holtel; 128, Digital Imaging Group; 130, Digital Imaging Group; 131, Digital Imaging Group; 134, Digital Imaging Group; 135, Jeff Greenberg/PhotoEdit; 138(tr), Photodisc; (bl), Digital Imaging Group.

Chapter 5: 140–141, Digital Imaging Group; 142, Charles Gupton/The Stock Market; 143, F. Carrie/Liaison International; 144, Ed McDonald Photography; 145, Arthur Tilley/FPG International; 146(bc), David Young-Wolff/Tony Stone Images; (br), GJLP/CNRI/Phototake; 147(tl), SuperStock; (tc), SuperStock; (tc), SuperStock; (tr), Howard Sochurek/The Stock Market; 148(tl), Ed McDonald Photography; (tr), Digital Imaging Group; 149(tr), Richard Megna/Fundamental Photographs; (br), M.I. Walker/Photo Researchers; 150, Institut Pasteur/CNRI/Phototake; 151, SuperStock; 152(c), Digital Imaging Group; (bl), Denise Hesse; 155, David Young-Wolff/PhotoEdit; 156, Uniphoto; 157, Digital Imaging Group; 158(bl), Digital Imaging Group; (br), Roy Morsch/The Stock Market; 159, Digital Imaging Group; 160, Digital Imaging Group; 161, Victoria Bowen Photography; 163, Digital Imaging Group; 164, Digital Imaging Group; 166(bl), Ed McDonald Photography; (br), Ed McDonald Photography; 167(tl), Ed McDonald Photography; (tr), Ed McDonald Photography; 170(bl), Michael Newman/PhotoEdit; (br), Rudi Von Briel.

Chapter 6: 172–173, Ed McDonald Photography; 174(bl), Digital Imaging Group; (br), Gary Conner/PhotoEdit; 175(bl), Ed McDonald Photography; (br), Bruce Ayers/Tony Stone Images; 176, Digital Imaging Group; 179(tl), Blair Seltz/Frozen Images; (tr), Digital Imaging Group; (bl), Digital Imaging Group; (br), Digital Imaging Group; 180(br), SuperStock; 181, Digital Imaging Group; 182, National Inhalant Prevention Coalition-800-269-4237; 184(tl), Phil Schermeister/Tony Stone Images; (tr), A. Ramey/PhotoEdit; 185(tl), Eric R. Berndt/Unicorn